The Glory of
Puttaparthi...

V. BALU

MOTILAL BANARSIDASS PUBLISHERS
PRIVATE LIMITED • DELHI

First Edition: 1980
Revised Edition: Delhi, 1990
Reprint: Delhi, 1993, 1994, 1995, 1996

ISBN: 81-208-0838-x (Cloth)
ISBN: 81-208-0839-8 (Paper)

Also available at:

MOTILAL BANARSIDASS
41 U.A. Bungalow Road, Jawahar Nagar, Delhi 110 007
120 Royapettah High Road, Mylapore, Madras 600 004
16 St. Mark's Road, Bangalore 560 001
8 Camac Street, Calcutta 700 017
Ashok Rajpath, Patna 800 004
Chowk, Varanasi 221 001

PRINTED IN INDIA
BY JAINENDRA PRAKASH JAIN AT SHRI JAINENDRA PRESS,
A-45 NARAINA, PHASE I, NEW DELHI 110 028
AND PUBLISHED BY NARENDRA PRAKASH JAIN FOR
MOTILAL BANARSIDASS PUBLISHERS PRIVATE LIMITED,
BUNGALOW ROAD, DELHI 110 007

To

Bhagawan

Sri Sathya Sai Baba

with

love and reverence

ACKNOWLEDGEMENTS

I would like to place on record my special gratitude to several devotees for use of material relating to their personal experiences of Bhagawan Sri Sathya Sai Baba. I would also like to thank the Manipal Power Press, Manipal, Mr. B. Krishnayya and the other dedicated staff of the Press, for their excellent co-operation in printing this book and bringing it out in time.

My thanks are due to Mr. V. K. Narasimhan for going through the manuscript. My thanks are also due to Mr. Mistry for the front cover picture, as well as black and white photographs. I am grateful to Mr. Dhiraj Chawda for the back cover photograph of my college painting of Sri Baba.

V. BALU

Please Note: The terms Sathya, Swami, Baba, Sri Baba and Sai Baba used in the text refer to Bhagawan Sri Sathya Sai Baba.

PAY YOUR TAX TO GOD !

"When you live in a house, you pay a House Tax to the Municipality or the Corporation, for the provision of various conveniences by the Municipality or the Corporation. When you use electricity in your home, you pay charges to the Electricity Board, for supply of electric power. When you use water, you pay for it, since the water is supplied at your house. If for such little efforts you are prepared to pay something regularly, is it not your duty to pay your tax to God, the Supreme Creator, for providing the air to breathe and for having created the orderly, systematic universe, with its magnificent solar system, the planet earth — its mountains, rivers, flora, fauna and beautiful scenic spots? The method of discharging your debt to the great creator is through prayers, or the thought of God atleast for a short while every day".

— SRI SATHYA SAI BABA

With Love
Sri Sathya Sai Baba

PREFACE

The glory of Puttaparthi is the glory of Bhagawan Sri Sathya Sai Baba--the phenomenon of the twentieth century, the ideal man, the super scientist of the consciousness, the miraculous man, the *avatar* (divine in human form) of the modern age, who though unfathomable, gives immense joy to millions round the globe. Puttaparthi, a remote village in the Anantapur District of Andhra Pradesh in S. India, is not only the sacred place of birth of Sri Baba but also the centre of his spiritual work. It is the Vatican of India, the Mecca of Sai devotees and the meeting point of the East and the West. Thus the Puttaparthi connection is not only the connection between Sri Baba and his devotees but also the only real link between man and man.

Although I have lived in Bangalore since 1964 (and in Mysore since 1961) it was only in 1976 that I first got the Whitefield connection leading to Puttaparthi; this, in spite of the fact that subconsciously, for several years I had been on the quest for Sri Sathya Sai Baba.

In this book, I have endeavoured to share with readers my discovery of several facets of Indian spirituality and religion, as expounded by Sri Baba; the myriad facets of Sri Baba's personality; Sri Baba's concern for youth; Sri Baba's views on several subjects and, most important, Bhagawan Sri Sathya Sai Baba as the ideal man and the divine man, engaged in the mission of uplifting humanity.

At a time the world is in sore need of a great moral transformation, it is of supreme significance that millions of people in India and several parts of the world are already experiencing a spiritual renaissance, inspired by the life and message of Bhagawan Sri Sathya Sai Baba.

V. BALU

ILLUSTRATIONS

PHOTOGRAPHS

CONTENTS

THE QUEST

"Our destination is Divinity......"

—SRI SATHYA SAI BABA

For quite a long time, subconsciously and even unconsciously, I had been on the quest for Sri* SATHYA SAI BABA. Once in Delhi. at the Vigyan Bhavan Hall, I heard him speak in Telugu, at a public meeting. The Telugu** language is a sweet language and also referred to as "the Italian of the East." Sri Sathya Sai Baba's talk filled me with admiration not only for his thoughts but also for the melody he introduced into a language already mellifluous. His reference to members of the audience as *Divya Atma Swaroopulaara* (or Divine souls in human form!) in his rich and resonant voice struck a chord in my heart.

I was lucky that day as I had a seat in the front row. Listening to Sri Baba, I secretly hoped he would notice me, but he didn't! I thought I might get a chance of being seen

* *Sri* (pronounced *Shree)* is a Sanskrit honorific, meaning auspicious or blessed.

** Spoken in the Andhra Pradesh State of South India.

by him, after the talk, as he walked towards the exit but alas! he never saw me! This left me a little unsatisfied and I could not brush aside the thought that Sri Baba did not direct his glance at me.

Some time later in Bangalore, I met Mr. Arthur Osborne, the guru who initiated me into the world of journalism and writing, as Editor of "The Indian Express". I was then a student of the Presidency College, Madras and Mr. Osborne asked me to write for their children's page. Every week, I used to do a special story for children and hand it over to Mr. Osborne personally. Initially, my stories were published without illustrations; but once, Mr. Osborne suggested that I should try illustrating my stories. I did so and soon discovered that I could indeed illustrate my stories. Later, when I also wrote for their Sunday Magazine a series of over a hundred articles on the *Wonders of Nature*, I did them as illustrated pieces. Many years later I learnt that Mr. Osborne had become a devotee of Bhagawan Ramana Maharshi and settled down at Tiruvannamalai in South India. I wrote to him and his reply led to a regular exchange of letters between us.

Once when Mr. Osborne happened to come down to Bangalore from Thiruvannamalai, I called on him. He looked excited and said he had just returned after visiting Sri Sathya Sai Baba. He recounted how some one had once suggested to him to publish the photograph of Sri Baba on the cover page of "The Mountain Path"- the magazine he edited from Thiruvannamalai. He had reacted to the suggestion most violently saying, "No, I will not have the photograph of that charlatan on the cover.!"

"But now!...after meeting Sri Sathya Sai Baba," confessed Mr. Osborne, "I know how wrong I have been in my estimation of such a scholarly personality, who is a mine of learning and philosophy of the most abstruse kind." Mr. Osborne also advised me to meet Baba and earn his grace. This gave further impetus to my quest and intensified my longing to meet Sri Baba.

Soon, an opportunity arose when a dignitary from Nepal wished to visit Puttaparthi in Andhra Pradesh to have the *darshan** of Sri Sathya Sai Baba. It was decided that I should accompany the dignitary and make all the arrangements. I went about the job quite excitedly. I learnt that Puttaparthi was only 185 kilometres from Bangalore and that the route by road was *via* Penukonda of Andhra Pradesh. I tried to find out the mean-

* Sight of holy person.

ing of *Puttaparthi* (the birth place of Sri Sathya Sai Baba) and learnt that 'Putta' referred to an ant-hill and 'Parthi' meant a spread. It would appear that, spread all over the place were ant hills and there was nothing there to attract any one till Sri Sathya Sai Baba decided to make it the centre of his activities. The place of Baba's abode in Puttaparthi is known as *Prasanti Nilayam* (or the house of Supreme Peace).

I also took a letter from a close devotee of Baba, and was all agog for the trip, but alas! at the last moment, a telegram arrived with the cryptic message that the dignitary from Nepal had cancelled his visit! One of my office colleagues, who happened to be with me at that time, mentioned that "It is difficult to meet Sri Sathya Sai Baba unless he calls us!" I had perforce to nod my head in agreement!

Some months' later I learnt that Sri Baba was in Whitefield,* Bangalore. So, I planned a trip to Whitefield in the company of a friend and members of my family.

We all went to Whitefield to the place called *Brindavan.* A large number of devotees had gathered at that time and were chanting *bhajans*† in the bhajan shed. Sri Baba was

---

* Whitefield is sixteen miles off Bangalore.

† Songs in praise of God.

seated on a chair, eyes closed. After a while, he opened his eyes, got up and walked towards the devotees. We had hoped that he would come near us and that we would be able to see him at close quarters. This was not to be, since he only went near a few devotees and received letters given by them. The *bhajans* came to a close and he walked away, after materialising *vibhuti* (or sacred ash) for a few persons here and there in the gathering.

A few months later, I learnt that Sri Baba would be presiding over a function at the Lalbagh gardens in Bangalore. It was a convocation function and I had received an invitation. So I went with my family; however, we reached Lalbagh gardens a little late only to find the place over-crowded. We could not even enter the hall and had to come away disappointed.

The D...Day dawned on Thursday, the 28th October 1976, when I went with an old devotee of Sri Sathya Sai Baba, Dr. R. S. Padmanabhan. I stood near the entrance at the gate of his Brindavan residence, under a tree.

Sri Sathya Sai Baba came out and for the first time looked at me. I was in the seventh heaven of delight and could not answer when he asked whether I wanted some *vibhuti* (sacred ash). Suddenly, I found the palm of his right hand moving in circles. White powder began to appear on his palm, which he caught with the fingers as it dropped down. He then handed it over to me. I asked Sri Sathya Sai Baba whether he would accept an invitation to address the meeting of a Society with which I was connected and I was happy when he said he would!

Three days later, I again went to Brindavan and stood under the same tree. Sri Sathya Sai Baba went for the *bhajans* and as he returned, he looked at me and said *Achcha!** The way he said it seemed to connote the thought, "Oh! you are here again!" Then I went near him and said that my wife and I would like to have an appointment to meet and talk to him. He promptly said "You come tomorrow at 4.30 p.m. with your wife."

The next day, we went a little before time and waited under the tree near the gate. I sat on one side and my wife sat on the other, since it is the practice, in Brindavan for the men and women to sit separately.

At the appointed time, we asked the volunteers at the gate to let us in. But they wouldn't, even though we told them that Sri Sathya Sai Baba himself had given us the appointment. So we waited helplessly for one hour, two hours and finally three hours!

---

* meaning Good!

At about seven in the evening, we thought that the interview had eluded us. I was deeply disappointed and my wife was greatly upset. Still, we thought we should tarry a little longer, particularly as we learnt that Sri Sathya Sai Baba was giving a lecture inside and that at the end of it he was likely to come out. At about 7.20 p.m. Sri Baba came out to the portico and noticed us, as well as a few others who had collected there by then. Immediately he sent word through one of the volunteers that we should all stay and that he would come and distribute *prasadam*. Shortly afterwards, he came out and distributed a savoury preparation *(Kara sevai)* to all of us.

As soon as he came near us, I burst out : "Baba! we have been waiting outside for more than three hours, in spite of your giving us an appointment!"

Instantly he uttered the words : "*Aiyyo! Paapam!*" meaning Oh! what a pity! In a bid to appease us, he asked us both to go over to a small room in his Brindavan residence. He produced *vibhuti* (sacred ash) from the palm of his hand, for both of us and handed over pieces of paper to pack it. He also gave an appointment for us to meet him with the children, the next day. The abundance of love he showered on us was immeasurable and I struggled in ecstasy in a sea of love. I felt utterly unable to express my feelings in words. At that moment, I was reminded of a story connected with a song that is often sung when old friends meet after a long period of separation. The song is titled *Auld Lang Syne* and runs :

> Lest old acquaintance be forgot
> And not brought to mind
> We'll drink a cup of kindness yet
> For the sake of
> *Auld Lang Syne.*

Once, in a ship somebody came running breathlessly to the ship's Captain. The Captain knew that the person had some important news to convey but found him unable to speak. As a student of psychology, the Captain knew that sometimes when a person is full of emotion and unable to speak, he might be able to express himself in song. So he asked him to sing, when the latter burst forth :

> Lest old acquaintance be forgot
> And not brought to mind
> The ship's cook has fallen overboard
> And is fifty miles behind!

Similarly, after experiencing the love showered by Sri Sathya Sai Baba I felt unable to express my feelings in prose. So I tried poetry and thus was born the free verse : "Ocean of Love."

OCEAN OF LOVE...

Several times I tried
To be seen
By HIM......
I wondered
How?...Why?...When?...
He would see me ...
I saw
Hair as wiry waves of halo
Build small but full of brio
Saffron *dhoti* and maxi on!
@Lips red with blood of *paan!**
Moving hands blessing
Materialising ash and many things
The moment he saw me
And smiled
I no longer saw his eyes.
I only saw a stream of love
A flood of feeling,
An ocean of *prema*
I swam,
Joyfully struggling
Breathlessly breathing
Floundering

@ At first, I had written, "Mouth full of blood of *paan!*" When I showed it to Sri Sathya Sai Baba a few days later, he observed, "This is not correct; but if you so wish you may retain it!" I thought about it and changed it to "Lips red with the blood of *paan!*"

* Betel leaf juice.

Suffocating
Zooming
Blooming
Heart drumming
BaaBub...BaBa...
Baa...Bub...Ba...Ba
Greedily I drank...
But alas!
Can you drink
More than
You can
From an ocean of love?
That moment
Every thing I forgot
A current of love
In my body glowed...
But, even a spark of love
A mickle of love
Becomes a muckle of love...
When that love is limitless.
I gasped
I swam in air
I ran inside water
I could have done anything
For I became part of the infinite.
I realised
How sweet love is!

I felt grateful after the interview to Dr. R. S. Padmanabhan for having given me the opportunity to meet Sri Sathya Sai Baba and to Mr. Arthur Osborne for providing fresh stimulus to my quest. It was then that I wondered how Mr. Osborne, who had been so much against Sri Baba, had changed his attitude and got truly transformed. I asked Dr. V. K. Gokak about it, since he was the one who had taken the Osbornes to Sri Sai Baba.

Early in 1968, Dr. Gokak* had halted at Ramana Ashram en route to Pondicherry. He knew the Osbornes lived there and felt they would be the kind of persons he would love to meet. He enjoyed talking to them and invited them to stay with him during their next sojourn in Bangalore. Accordingly, during the summer months of the same year, when the Osbornes visited Bangalore, they stayed with the Gokaks.

Dr. Gokak was a staunch devotee of Aurobindo, but after knowing Sri Sathya Sai Baba, he used to visit Sri Baba often in Whitefield. Sri Baba knew that Dr. Gokak followed Sri Aurobindo but still was exceedingly nice to him. During the stay of the Osbornes, the Gokaks visited Sri Sathya Sai Baba as usual. Initially the Osbornes did not show any inclination to meet Sri Baba, though they plied Gokak with questions as to what had

---

* Dr. Gokak was then Vice-chancellor of the Bangalore University and had seen the *Mountain Path edited by Mr. Osborne.*

happened and what Sri Baba had told him. They soon got deeply interested and once when Dr. Gokak, was preparing to go to Whitefield, they expressed a desire to accompany him.

Sri Sathya Sai Baba spoke to the Osbornes. They were struck by his simplicity and humility and experienced the love showered by him. Their attitude changed completely. They felt like meeting Sri Baba again and having discussions with him. In the mean-time, Dr. Gokak had to go to Delhi for a week and so went to take leave of Sri Sathya Sai Baba. When he mentioned that the Osbornes would be alone, Sri Baba suggested that they could stay at Whitefield for a week, if they so desired. The Osbornes were only too happy to do so.

An incident during their stay touched them greatly. One day, Sri Baba walked into their room. Being great devotees of Ramana Maharshi, they had a photograph of Bhagawan Ramana Maharshi in the room. Sri Baba who saw it, took a flower from a bowl nearby and placed it on the photograph, as any devotee of Ramana Maharshi would have done! This struck the Osbornes as a great and noble gesture and they admired his generosity of spirit and respected Sri Baba all the more for it. It showed them clearly that Sri Baba did not want them to give up their worship of Ramana Maharshi!

In the meantime, a *hatha* yogi had personally attacked Sri Baba using language that was indecorous and Dr. Gokak, even though an Aurobindonian, had felt greatly hurt. So he wrote a letter to the 'Deccan Herald' pointing out how ill informed the attack was and how Dr. Gokak had as much respect for Sri Sathya Sai Baba as he had for Aurobindo. To his surprise, he found Mrs. Osborne had also written a letter on the same lines, stating they were disciples of Bhagawan Ramana Maharshi but had full faith in Sri Baba and the causes for which Sri Baba has been working.

Later, the Osbornes attended the first World Sathya Sai Conference in May 1968 in Bombay. Mr. Osborne also addressed the conference, when he made it clear that he had no doubt at all about Sri Baba's divinity.

It was indeed most fortunate that in his life time, Mr. Osborne came into close contact with two lights - Bhagawan Ramana Maharshi and Bhagawan Sri Sathya Sai Baba. For, of the billions of people in the world, only a few are fortunate to be prompted to seek the divine. The majority get lost in the little joys and turmoils of the material world; so they fail to think of the immortal soul within and become blind to the main purpose of human life.

My first encounter with Sri Baba became memorable as the end of one quest and the beginning of a more magnificent one...

---

*"Man is not born to go in quest of food but to go in quest of the **atma**."*

—SRI SATHYA SAI BABA

SRI BABA ON YOUTH

"Youth is the golden age"

—SRI SATHYA SAI BABA

Sri Sathya Sai Baba graciously granted us a private interview, on the morning of November 2, 1977, which was truly fantastic. He sat on a chair and my wife, my sons (Ashok, Vivek and Ganesh) and I sat cross-legged on the floor of a small room, for over an hour.

At the outset, Baba surprised all of us by telling things about our past and present. For instance, he told my wife, "You do paintings on cloth (batik) but now you are doing more writing and you are keen about the publication of your books."

My wife had planned to write an article on Baba's views on youth and had wanted to ask him several questions on the subject. Although she never asked him the questions which she had noted down, he came out with all the answers!

A flood of love shone from his eyes and face as he spoke about the young people. The face of Sathya Sai Baba, framed by that distinctively dark Afro hair has a special charisma; his *prema* (love) and compassion give it a special halo.

Sri Sathya Sai Baba's mission in life is to lead man to God through the path of *satya* (truth), *dharma* (righteousness), *shanti* (peace) and *prema* (love). "Man is moving away from truth and love and that is why he has moved away from God", said Baba. "I love every one, but I love youth more... I will do everything possible for the betterment of the young, for youth is the golden age" he added, with intense feeling.

"It is the young who need guidance, for they should avoid the bad precedents set by elders and pursue the path of truth, honesty and hard work... The Sathya Sai Education Trust runs many colleges and I select the students." I thought that one could be sure of the *soul value* of the students, after being screened by Sri Baba! An accurate mind reader, Sri Baba is known to fathom at once the inner thoughts, the personality and the life pattern of every one he meets.

"I am a disciplinarian... I insist on good personal habits. Students should get up early in the morning, have bath, meditate, study, play games, do social work and retire to bed early." Baba sees to it that the boys handle the hostel canteen work by rotation, so that they are trained to run homes. "My students learn cooking, cleaning, marketing and even farming and dairy management."

Sri Baba disarms listeners with his simple and down-to-earth logic. He baffles them with erudite quotations not only from Sanskrit texts, but also western scholars! One's wonder and awe never cease not only when one is with him, but even afterwards, because of that indefinable something in his personality which he passes on to others as currents of comfort and joy through his compassion.

The abundance of love he pours out for the world becomes evident as he says:

Start the day with Love
Fill the day with Love
End the day with Love
For that is the way to God.

He always addresses those near him endearingly as "Bangaaru" (Telugu word for "gold") and says to those who bring him offerings, "Don't bring anything... not even flowers... I only want your *prema*, your love."

It is difficult to think of this embodiment of love as one coming from the small obscure village of Puttaparthi in Andhra Pradesh. Born of a Raju family of modest means, on November 23, 1926, as the fourth child and second son of Easwaramma and Pedda

Venkappa Raju, he was named Sathya Narayana.* His birth was heralded by strange signs - musical instruments hung on the wall produced music of their own accord, rather mysteriously, and a snake under the bed rocked the baby with its movements.

As a boy, he demonstrated extra-ordinary powers. He was so knowledgeable that he was nick-named *Brahmajnani*†. He loved animals and was a model of sweetness and helpfulness to all. He preferred vegetarian food and often did the cooking himself.

Several episodes of his school days show Sri Baba as a boy of principles. Thus, he refused a bus ride from his scout camp, because he did not have money to pay the fare! His strict principles would not allow him to accept a free lift!

It is said that in those days Sri Baba earned pocket money through composing songs. He was sought after by a shop to compose *commercial* ditties for the shop's new products! The procedure was for him to compose the songs and organise a group to go round the streets singing them. Sai Baba loved the assignments! Even now, he retains his

---

* The name was shortened by his relatives and friends to Sathya.

† One with knowledge of *Brahman* or God.

penchant for rhyming words and uses popular slogans to emphasise his points of view.

Sri Baba's first slogan for youth in regard to studies is: START EARLY... DRIVE SLOWLY AND REACH SAFELY. He smiled as he described the usual student practice of mugging up lessons during the last few days before the examinations, pouring out the crammed stuff on to the answer papers and then coming out of the hall, with completely empty heads!

"Is this the purpose of education?... As it is, the Universities give a pass at 35%, allowing a student a gap of 65%! Do you know what happens, when this 35% (student) goes to work? Very shortly he forgets the mugged up 35% of knowledge and the result is leaking bridges, squeaking roads and bad decisions!"

"Education should be given on the lines of the old gurukula system, where the *guru* (teacher) will not let a *shishya* (student) out of the hermitage till he absorbs 100% *Vidya* (knowledge). A student should record permanently in his mind what is taught so that throughout life he can take out prints, whenever needed... that is the purpose of learning", he added.

It was interesting the way Baba switched on to English, whenever he had recourse to slogans or puns, from his customary Telugu conversation. He said modern youth are getting to be harsh in their talk; they are angry, they shout and yell needlessly!... Baba was pained that from childhood, the habit of sweet talk or *madhura swara* is not inculcated. It is good to remember that "You can't always oblige a person, but you can always talk to a person obligingly."

"Youth have slided into the path of laziness of many forms... idle gossip, wayside chatter, seeing useless films and reading bad books. They should shake themselves out of this stupor; then only will they be happy and find real values."

Ashok, my teenage son, looked up at Sri Baba. He instantly turned towards him, "I know what you are thinking... How is it possible to give up these, when you are so used to them? If you are told that you are holding a cobra in your hand, would you release it, inch by inch or bit by bit? Wouldn't you instantly fling it away? These habits are like a cobra in your hand. You have to decide and throw it off instantly and not gradually... For, once bitten, it may be too late to save yourself!"

"I am always fond of telling my students in the colleges about the Four Fs they should follow", explained Sri Baba, continuing his slogans for youth.

Follow the Master*
Face the Devil
Fight to the end
Finish the game**

"In life it is very important to learn to play the game properly and truthfully", he added.

Sri Baba discussed at length the question of discipline and the role of parents in guiding children, at every stage, with gentleness, sweetness and love. This was like training a snake-gourd to grow straight by tying a stone to its tail-end. When the snake gourd is tender, a small stone is tied. Later, bigger and still bigger stones are used, as the length and size of the gourd increase. Finally one gets a long and straight snake-gourd.

"If you fail to tie the stone at the tender stage of the snake-gourd, you can never straighten it later... you will only break it, if you use force! A young boy is like the snake-gourd... Give him discipline, in short doses, from childhood and increase it gradually, till he thinks straight and judges for himself. Then he can come to no harm and will become an asset to society."

---

* Master stands for the *Atma* or the light within.

** Means Finish at the goal of liberation from delusion and ignorance.

"MONEY COMES AND GOES, BUT MORALITY COMES AND GROWS", said Sri Baba, talking about the craze for money and possessions. He asked, "Haven't you seen in railway compartments the slogan: LESS LUGGAGE, MORE COMFORT! Why do you want to add to possessions? Life is like a train journey. Anger, hatred, envy, jealousy - these are heavy luggage you should avoid taking with you on your journey."

"*Prema* and *Shanti* are two things our youth should cultivate. For if you are happy, you think the world is happy. If you are restless, the whole world appears hopeless. Only disgruntled people find fault with the world. It is such people who see the world with coloured eyes. Only such people, who have no peace in their hearts, are responsible for causing disturbances in the world at large. Young people should understand this very carefully."

"The heart should be filled with love and not with ego. People often say that "I did this", or "I am this." This is not right and one should forget this I. Once people forget the I, the ego gets crucified!... Yes!... Strike off the I and lo! it becomes a cross (+). Man *minus* ego is God!"

As Sri Sathya Sai Baba spoke, the words came out effortlessly, fluently and with a honeyed cadence. His gentle manners, love and the magnetic appeal of his words fascinated us.

Suddenly Sri Sathya Sai Baba asked, "Do you wish to have anything?" I did not feel like asking for any thing and so kept silent. I soon saw his right hand move in circles. His palm was open and turned downwards and the fingers stretched out as he moved his hand and lo! a silver ring appeared with a finely embossed portrait of Sri Baba on it.

Sri Baba was quite casual and totally unaffected by what he did, but I felt excited. I had read that even as a school boy, Sri Baba used to materialise sweets from his satchel for *good* children! For a moment, my (uncrucified) ego made me feel that I too had perhaps been considered a good child!

Again Sri Baba waved his right hand in a few quick, small circles. All of us watched carefully the movements, as *vibhuti* (ash) appeared close to the palm and started falling. He caught the *vibhuti* with his fingers and distributed it to all of us. There was the right amount of *vibhuti* for the five of us! He also handed over to us 5 pieces of paper to package the *vibhuti*.

'*Vidya** and *Vaidya***' are Sri Baba's two main service projects and Sai Educational Institutions and Hospitals are fast coming up

*Vidya – education. **Vaidya = medication.

in different parts of the country. For training children, Sri Baba's Samithis run Bal Vikas Centres, under his guidance. Says Sri Baba "Parents sadly neglect prayers and spiritual education for children." The Bal Vikas centres provide *bhajans* and *slokas** for children besides stories with good morals.

Sri Baba firmly believes in catching people young, for inculcating the age-old spiritual values of the country. He asked, "Do you know that since time immemorial, Bharat is known as *punya-bhoomi* (sacred land) and *dharma-bhoomi* (land of *dharma)*, why should man try to degrade it to mere *bhoga bhoomi* (or land of enjoyment)?"

Pleasures and physical enjoyment are not for Bharat, which stands for quite another kind of happiness - the attainment of Supreme Bliss!

Stressing the role of *prema*, Baba said, "*Prema* or love is what the individual and the nation must cultivate now for progress... *Prema* must transform all relationships, social, economic, educational, professional, family, religious, legal and others... The sense of equality that every one is the repository of Divine Essence must transmute social and individual behaviour."

Sri Baba has several plans for spreading his gospel of love. For, to him, *the only reli-*

***slokas = devotional verses in Sanskrit.**

gion in the world is the religion of love. Sri Baba surprised every one in the recent past by materialising a map, which showed the shape of things to come during the next over four decades. Yes! over four decades!... because Baba says he will live up to ninety six years in the present body...

Not only that! Sri Baba says he was *Sai Baba of Shirdi* in his past birth. He is Sathya Sai Baba now, and as he knows the future, he says he will be born as *Prema Sai* in the Gunaparthi village of the Mandya District of the Karnataka State!

Thus, in the Sai plan of things, Sri Baba will be there to guide and take the youth and the world on the spiritual path. Imagine what is in store when Sri Sathya Sai, who is already the embodiment of love, appears with love *plus* as *Prema Sai!*

Sri Baba talked a little more of philosophy explaining the divinity in man. When man breathes, his breath says, "So... hum" (inhaling... exhaling) which means *I* and *He*. When he sleeps (his eyes twinkled as he said with a smile, "Check on a snoring man next time and you will agree with me!") this dual image of I and HE merges and the sound is only "*O...M*" or "*OM!*" Thus man knows he is divine in his unconscious state. He has only to realise his divinity in the conscious state too!

Sri Baba's communication is simple, straight-forward and direct. Even the highest of philosopy expounded by him is understood by the oldest member as well as the youngest of children in an audience. Hence, all of us in our family found the interview equally illuminating.

Sri Baba asked whether we had any more doubts and questions... We realised we had already taken over 75 minutes of his valuable time and so took leave.

The interview was an unforgettable experience and wafted us to great heights of ecstasy. Besides Sri Baba's message, the power and grace of his benign personality produced a strange exhilaration in us.

* * * * *

Our interest fully kindled, we discussed with other devotees and went through books on Sri Baba. We learnt that though his early schooling was at Puttaparthi and Bukkapatnam, Sri Baba went to Uravakonda for his high school education, since his brother Seshama Raju worked as a Telugu teacher there. However, on the 23rd of May 1940, he threw away his school satchel and announced to every one : "I am Sai Baba!"

At that stage, he met with stiff opposition from the members of his family, who believed that the young lad must be either insane or possessed by the devil! They took him to village doctors, who tortured and tormented Sathya in a variety of ways to "drive out" the spirit in him. Finding normal methods in-effective they tried extremely ferocious treatments. The head was shaved off, deep cuts in the shape of crosses were inflicted on the scalp and the juice of limes and other acid fruits poured over the wounds!... The severity of the treatment was enhanced till the head and eyes got swollen! He never protested and gave no external signs of his suffering.

Thus, the young Sai Baba bore excruciating pain and suffering in the morning of his life, just as Jesus Christ of Nazareth suffered immense bodily pain on the cross, in the evening of his life. Both Sai and Jesus thus demonstrated to the world the *sahanam* (fortitude), or the tranquillity of spirit, with which bodily pain should be borne. Finally, the young Sai cured himself of his cross-shaped wounds on the scalp and his mightily swollen eyes, with the mere application of a juice from a herb, even as Jesus resurrected himself, after the crucifixion.

In October 1940, Sathya left his brother's house at Uravakonda saying "I am no longer your Sathya! I am Sai... My devotees are calling me." He moved over to a garden and sang the famed song "*Manasa Bhajare Guru-charanam*" (Meditate on the feet of the Guru... Oh!... Mind.)

He came back to Puttaparthi and devotees started flocking to him. A kind lady by name, Subbamma, wife of the village accountant, persuaded him to stay in her house, as it had facilities for meetings and *bhajans*. The young Sai Baba performed a large number of miracles, gave visions and a wealth of evidence to show that his human form notwithstanding, his was the infinite power of the Lord.

"If the youth of today must become exemplary citizens of tomorrow, they must frame their lives on moral principles like sathya (truth), dharma (righteousness), shanti (peace), prema (love) and ahimsa (non-violence)."

—SRI SATHYA SAI BABA

PUTTAPARTHI AND PRASANTI NILAYAM

"Instead of transforming his home, his village, his state and his country, and thereby the world into a Prasanti Nilayam (Abode of higher peace), man has made them arenas for wild passions like anger, greed, hatred and violence... Oh! the pity of it!"

—SRI SATHYA SAI BABA

As Sri Sathya Sai Baba's name and fame began to spread, visitors to the remote village increased by the hundreds. Some devotees, who had become regular visitors, erected a temple in 1944, which is today referred to as the old *Mandir* (temple). The place has been converted into a *Kalyana Mantap* (marriage hall) named after Sri Baba's father, Pedda Venkappa Raju.

The arduous nature of the journey* to Puttaparthi as well as the hot climate of the place in no way deterred the flow of an ever-

* People had to travel by bus up to a point, then by bullock carts and finally wade across the Chitravathi river. They had also to do some walking over difficult, rocky terrain.

increasing number of devotees. As a result, a bungalow and some rooms for visitors were put up. The bungalow was later given several decorative touches and a *gopuram* was built converting it into a *mandir* (temple).

This main building or *Prasanti Mandir* at "Prasanti Nilayam" (Abode of Supreme Peace), is both a temple and the home of Sri Sathya Sai Baba, who resides here for the maximum period during a year. It is the very spiritual core and nerve centre of the township. From this main building starts the *Omkar* (chanting of *Om,* the first sound of the Supreme, pronounced A-U-M), *suprabhatam* (early morning song to awaken the Lord), *bhajans* and daily meditation of the devotees.

The Prasanti Nilayam was inaugurated on November 23, 1950 by Sri Baba on his twentyfifth birthday. Several modern flats sprang up around the Mandir in 1966 after the place was separated from the Puttaparthi village and constituted into an administrative unit, called the Prasanti Nilayam Township.

I first visited Prasanti Nilayam* during August 1977 and found the serenity of the

---

* I went by car from Bangalore, the distance being 185 k.m. There are direct buses from Bangalore to Puttaparthi. The Ashram can also be reached by train up to Dharmavaram or Penukonda (both railway stations on the Secunderabad - Bangalore line). The rest of the journey which is only 50 kilometres can be done by road.

place soothing. The place is also faintly reminiscent of Tirupathi-Tirumalai, with its *gopuram*, hillocks and even multitudinous stalls selling trinkets and mementoes.

Prasanti Nilayam is organised on the lines of an ashram and provides simple, clean accommodation and hygienic, vegetarian food. There are many permanent ashram residents, who look after the ashram duties as *seva* or service. Those who are spiritually tuned, find the place ideal for *sadhana* (practices relating to spirituality). Whether a devotee or a casual visitor, one cannot miss the *Prasanti* or supra peace at Prasanti Nilayam.

This came to me forcibly on an occasion during the *Dasara* celebrations in Puttaparthi, when over 60,000 people had gathered. Some of us had walked up the slope behind the Prasanti Mandir to the shade of the Banyan tree, planted by Sri Sathya Sai Baba. The serenity and calm there were so enchanting that we suddenly became unaware of the surging mass of humanity, just a stone's throw away. Surely, Prasanti Nilayam is a paradise of absolute peace and serenity.

When I sauntered on the hill and had a bird's eye view, I was impressed by the many-sided development and growth of Prasanti Nilayam - the dairy *(gokulam);* industrial units, the Shiva-shakti temple which marks the sanctified spot of the place of Sri Baba's birth, the Mosque nearby; the Harijan colony and more particularly the educational complex (or the Sathya Sai Vidyagiri). It became obvious that the supra peace there provides the ideal atmosphere especially for the children studying in the Easwaramma High School and the students of the Sathya Sai College, whose education blends academic instruction with spiritual discipline. The mystical radiations, purity and calm of the place are also ideal for the healing of the sick at the Hospital there.

The *sarva-mata-aikya stambha* (Pillar of unity of all religions) erected on the fiftieth birthday of Sri Sai Baba at the entrance to the stage of the spacious Poorna Chandra auditorium, exemplifies the Sai insignia and stresses the fundamental unity behind the diversity of all faiths. The Poorna Chandra auditorium is a marvel, since it is the only hall of its kind in Asia, planned like a huge hangar, with pillars only on the sides and with a capacity for seating 30,000 persons.

Today, Puttaparthi is the Mecca of all Sai devotees. Visiting it as often as possible is a must. For, each spot there recalls to the mind the many *leelas* (sports) of Sri Sathya Sai Baba. Thus, a *kalpa vriksha* (wish fulfilling tree) on a hill near the Chitravathi river is a sacred tree, since the young Sai used to pluck from its branches any fruit desired by devotees. The very same tree yielded to his touch mangoes, grapes, oranges, apples, pears or plums!

Many devotees go there often to seek inspiration and guidance for their spiritual progress. They stay in the township abiding by the guidelines which help in maintaining the sanctity of the place and providing the correct atmosphere for *sadhana* (practices relating to spirituality).

The Sai Organisation in Puttaparthi and elsewhere is run by the Sri Sathya Sai Central and State Trusts as well as the Bhagawan Sri Sathya Sai Organisations, of which Sri Baba is the founder President. The seva organisations have units at the State, district, town and other unit levels called *Samitis*. There are Samitis in different parts of India and a network of corresponding organisations in 64 countries of the world and the number is steadily growing. Prasanti Nilayam will host the 1980 World Conference which will be attended by over 10,000 delegates representing the Presidents of Sai Organizations round the globe. Truly, Prasanti Nilayam* of Puttaparthi has become internationally renowned

---

* The postal address is "Prasanti Nilayam P.O., Anantapur District, Andhra Pradesh. Pin Code: 515134.

as a sacred place radiating purity, serenity and peace.

After the first visit, I have been to Puttaparthi on several occasions and each time I have felt as though I have returned from another world of absolute peace and bliss. Recently, I went to Puttaparthi on the evening of July 21, 1980. The next morning, I found that even by 7 a.m., large crowds had forgathered on the grounds in front of the Prasanti Nilayam. The verandah of the Nilayam was also full of devotees.

At 8.15 a.m., Sri Baba came out bright and radiant, making all those assembled bloom like flowers in response to the welcome rays of the morning Sun. He asked several people to proceed to the interview room and I was one of the thirty one persons to be chosen; somehow, all of us were able to fit into that quiet, little room.

Sri Baba asked two boys seated near him, "Are you ready?"

"Yes, Swami!" said the two boys in one voice. They were dressed and looked alike.

Sri Baba made the boys move closer to him and asked the parents of the boys to sit on either side.

"Today I am a priest!... For I am going to perform the thread ceremony of these

boys," he said. "But priests only chant *mantras* and ask for *dakshina* (fee)!"

Every one laughed and Sri Baba said sweetly, "I will not only tell you the *mantra*, but I will also give you the meaning, which priests will not!"

Looking at the two boys, Sri Baba asked, "What are your names?"

"Sanjay Melwani and Mahesh Melwani," they answered.

"For two boys who are identical twins, the names are in no way identical!" remarked Sri Baba. "They should have been something like Sunil and Anil!"

"Never mind! Names do not matter!" he said, as he moved his right palm in circles and materialised some *vibhuti* (ash) for the boys.

"I will tell you the *Gayatri mantra* but you must first know who *Gayatri* is?" said Sri Baba. "*Gayatri* is the *Chandasam Mata*, the mother of the Vedas... *Gaya* means *prana* or life and *Gayatri* is that which protects life... Man takes his second birth when he begins to chant *Gayatri mantra*; when he does *veda adhyayanam* (recitation of vedas) he has the third birth and the fourth birth is when he learns Brahma *tattwa i.e.*, *Brahma jnana* or knowledge of *Brahman*. A brahmin is thus no one special who eats a lot, on special days! He is one who has the supreme knowledge of *Brahman*", said Sri Baba. He then materialised two sacred threads that were both folded and tied up. He first opened out one thread and asked the parents of the boys to hold the two ends. As they did so, Sri Baba pointed out that the sacred thread is made of three threads with a knot in one place. "The three threads signify *tri kaala* (the three phases of time: past, present and future), the *tri-gunas (Rajo, tamo* and *sattva*) and the *tri-lokas* : *Bhuh* (earth), *Bhuvah* (atmosphere) and *svah* (beyond the atmosphere or Heaven)." Sri Baba said *Gayatri* is *pancha-mukhi* (with five faces).

Oṃ Bhūr
Bhuvaḥ Svaḥ
Tat Savitur vareṇyam
Bhargo Devasya Dhīmahi
Dhiyo yo naḥ pracodayāt

One of the boys said, "Swami! We say *Brahmārpaṇam**... before taking food. Is that mantra not the same as *Gayatri*?"

---

* *Brahmārpaṇam Brahmahavir*
Brahmāgnau Brahmaṇā hutam
Brahmaiva tena gantavyam
Brahmakarmasamādhinā

(Bhagavad Gita, Chapter 4, Stanza 24)

(For the meaning of this stanza see footnote on page 37).

"No!" said Swami, "That is a prayer you offer to God, the cosmic power, to remove *doshas* (blemishes), if any, in the food prepared and to help in digestion of the food... But the *Gayatri mantra* is an appeal for the removal of the darkness of ignorance and for the illumination of the intellect."

Sri Baba made both the boys wear the sacred thread and repeat after him the *Gayatri mantra*. He patiently corrected slips and repeated the *mantra* till they were able to pronounce every word correctly. The way Swami taught the *mantra* with love and patience was a model for every teacher in the world in teaching students.

Thereafter, Sri Baba called upon the bride and bridegroom to come forth! As I wondered who they were, the two boys and their parents made way for an elderly lady

---

(Everything is an offering to God
Provisions used for food are essentially God
Fire used for cooking is God
The process of cooking is also God
The work that consumed food helps to do is also God).

Aham Vaisvānaro bhūtva
Prāṇinām Dehamāśritaḥ
Prāṇōpānasamāyuktaḥ
Pacāmyannam Caturvidham

(Bhagavad Gita, Chap. 15, Stanza 14)

(Becoming the fire of life I (God)
Enter into the bodies of all creatures ,
Mingling with the upward and downward breath
I digest the four kinds of food).

and gentleman to come forward. They sat near Sri Baba who said, "I will now celebrate the *shastiabdapoorti* (60th birthday) wedding of the couple."

Suddenly his right hand moved in a familiar way and two wedding rings appeared at the same time and both the rings had the picture of Sri Baba engraved on them. Sri Baba asked the lady to put the ring on the finger of the right hand of the husband and the husband to put the ring on the wife's finger. In both cases the rings fitted perfectly!

"Do you know why the 60th birthday is celebrated?" asked Sri Baba and proceeded to give the answer: "By that time, man is expected to have discharged his responsibilities to his office, society and family and also achieved full control over anger, jealousy and all sensory desires. The *shastiabdapoorti* is to celebrate the achievement of such mastery over the senses." Sri Baba also spoke about the eternal nature of spiritual relationships and said that "the real 'I' is the self within and 'Real self is the selfless self."

Addressing their son Srinivas, Sri Baba said, "I know you see many pictures!" He then asked the boy who had been stunned by Swami's statement: "Can you say why film stars act in pictures?"

"Because they get money," replied the boy in a low voice. "Actors cry on the silver screen since they are paid to do so!... Why should you pay money to see pictures and weep?... Now consider this!... A film star cries on the screen because her husband died... Later, she goes to see the same film, with her husband and weeps, being moved by it... Now, which of these is real?..."

Turning to the father of the boy Sri Baba said, "Films have a very bad influence on our youth. As a result, they waste their youth.... Misuse of youth is evil" he said. "Youth also love to talk too much.... This reduces their physical energy and affects the memory power; that was why *maunatva* or silence was practised in days of yore. Youth should learn to respect the mother who gave them their body, the father who helps them to develop and the guru or teacher who indicates to them the proper line of development."

Sri Baba told the boy, "You were here with Swami so long today because of your father's wedding... Don't worry, I will celebrate your wedding also!"

Sri Baba then turned to the sister of the boy who said, "Swami, I want to join M.Sc."

Sri Baba said, "First finish your MRS!..." He then asked Srinivas whether he understood the meaning of MRS and Swami smiled when the boy explained, "Yes Swami! MRS means getting married and becoming the wife of somebody, a Mrs.!"

Swami asked those who came in connection with the thread ceremony to adjourn to the next room for a private interview. Afterwards, the *shastiabdapoorti* couple and a few others were also given private interviews.

The flow of charm, compassion, grace and love from Sri Baba flooded every one in the interview room. Towards the end I said, "Swami, you take so much trouble for the the sake of all and do not mind in the least all the time you take again and again to tell us about the fundamental reality and forever to shower your love and grace."

"That is no trouble at all!... But you would have seen that those I talk to get so much *ananda* (happiness) and their *ananda* makes me happy too! I am here only for the happiness of all", said Sri Baba, who lives every moment of his life only for others.

On 23-7-1980, I was again on the verandah of the Prasanti Nilayam; at about 10.30 a.m. Sri Baba came out of the interview room. As he walked towards his car, he looked at me and said, "Come!" I instantly followed and as I got into the car my heart drummed against my ribs! Such was the joy I experienced that moment as it was my first experience of sitting in Sri Baba's car and by his side. Mr. Chakravarthi of Hyderabad and Major Talwar of Bangalore were the other two occupants of the car.

The faces of people who lined up on both sides of the road lit up like lamps at the very sight of Sri Baba; they threw flowers at the car and some of them tried to touch the moving car in a bid to pay their respects to the *avatar* inside. Sri Baba asked the car to stop at the Gokulam, which has a beautiful statue of Lord Krishna with a cow and calf. Sai Gita, which has also made its home in Gokulam, trumpeted away, mad with delight at seeing Sri Baba.

"Enough Gita! That'll do!... Gita!..." Sri Baba kept repeating, sweetly responding to its elephantine affection.

Sai Gita raised its trunk thrice and saluted Sri Baba and also touched his feet with its trunk. The affection of the animal truly transcended human levels. Sri Baba told us how the now majestic Gita was first brought in a van as an eleven-day-old baby.

Then we followed Sri Baba into a shed where he patted with affection one of the cows (Holstien Fresian breed) and said, "This cow yields about 30 litres of milk a day." There were several cows and calves in the shed (pure Jerseys and mixed breeds) and

Swami mentioned how the Gokulam had started with just two cows. (The Gokulam was inaugurated in August 1975 on *Krishna Janmashtami* day - the birth day of the divine cowherd, Lord Krishna). The cows are milked by college students at 4.30 a.m. and 3.30 p.m. every day.

We stopped at another shed, where Sri Baba lighted the fire for two stacks of paddy husk for the large-scale preparation of *vibuthi* (or ash) to be sold in shops. Thereafter, we went for a little drive and while returning, the car stopped at a new construction - the hostel for college students.

Sri Baba's alertness, briskness, circumspection and concern for others are worthy of emulation. Even as he glided along, (Sri Baba hardly walks but only floats gracefully) he told Mr. Chakravarthi, "Beware of that protruding pole there, you will hurt yourself!" He asked the man in charge why there was delay in the progress of work. When he got the answer, "Swami! We have yet to receive the cement", he remarked sweetly, "Yes! It is our mistake... We will make it available."

"This hostel will accommodate 1000 students," said Sri Baba and went into the dining hall and kitchen, where he gave instructions for the construction of ovens. He mentioned that the location and design of the kitchen was such as to prevent smoke or the kitchen odours from coming into the dining halls.

We next visited another construction in progress. "This is the new school building for the tiny tots," he said. We went in and Sri Baba showed us a fairly large room saying, "There are 20 such class rooms." After a visit to the spacious dining hall, we followed Sri Baba to the first floor which had two wings, like the wings of an aeroplane (the whole building is the shape of a plane). Sri Baba said, "This will be the dormitory where the children will live and the second floor is where the teachers will live and look after the children of this boarding school." The school has an excellent location next to the Easwaramma High School (named after Sri Baba's mother) and opposite is the newly started Sri Sathya Sai Junior College for Science, Arts and Commerce. How wonderful! I thought, since a child which got into the primary school building at a tender age could emerge as a full fledged, adult graduate, by just walking through two adjacent buildings!

As the car drove into the side gate of Prasanti Nilayam, where the canteen is located, Swami pointed to a new circular building and said it would be the Hostel for those who come from abroad. He then asked the car to stop at the Poornachandra Auditorium. We followed Sri Baba who showed us new, three-dimensional murals pertaining to all religions - murals that had replaced the paintings that were there before. I felt that the murals heightened the beauty of the magnificent auditorium.

At the entrance to the Prasanti Nilayam, Sri Baba stopped, since a lady with a Tibetan spaniel had earlier requested him to bless her dog. The lady gushed away; "Swami! This dog has just returned after a pilgrimage to Badrinath and other holy places and finally it is now in Puttaparthi..."

Sri Baba smiled as he asked, "Will visiting all holy places change the qualities of the dog?"

I thought about the wonderful philosophy contained in that simple question: pilgrimages to sacred spots should result in the upliftment of the pilgrims.

"It is only in the depth of silence and peace that the voice of God can be heard."

—SRI SATHYA SAI BABA

YOUTH ON SRI BABA

"Youth is wasted on the young"

—BERNARD SHAW

Sri Sathya Sai Baba has a soft corner for youth in general and students of his educational institutions in particular. The youth on their part find in Sri Baba a charismatic and dynamic mystic, who is a living example of the concepts of self-abnegation, selfless service and soul force in action.

The impact of Sri Baba on youth came to me in a telling manner when during May 1979, I talked to a random group of students of the Sri Sathya Sai College as well as of the Summer Course on Indian Culture and Spirituality. This chapter presents the questions I asked the young people and their answers, in their own words.

* * * * *

Sandeep Shastry, a nineteen-year-old student of the second year B.A. class at the Sri Sathya Sai College of Arts, Science and Commerce, Kadugodi, Whitefield, said, "My father is in an United Nations job as Head of a Civil Engineering Project in Kabul. I studied there upto the Higher Secondary (Pre-University Course) in an Indian school.

"I joined this college in Bangalore and have spent two years here. Kabul is a completely westernised city, with all its attendant comforts and style... I enjoyed all those luxuries and used to taste alcohol now and then!... Going to school was more a way of spending time... I never took either education or the teachers there seriously. I used to be terribly self-centred and never cared for others... But today, I feel and act differently. A gradual change has come over my views, behaviour and attitude towards life... Earlier, I had thought life is only for enjoyment but now I know there is greater meaning to life."

"How come you have changed? After all, in terms of the curriculum, is not the Sai College just like any other college?" I asked.

"True, but here my attitude and that of my friends towards studies is more intense... more concentrated. The atmosphere here promotes studies as something more than just passing examinations."

"Do you live in the College Hostel?"

"Yes, I live in the hostel."

"Do you like it?"

"Yes! Because I like the way we live in the hostel... We, boys from different countries and varied background, stay together and help each other sincerely in an atmosphere of give and take."

"Who was responsible for your joining the Sai College?"

"In 1977, when my father asked me to join a college in India, *I myself* instinctively chose the Whitefield College, although I would have got admission in any of the Delhi Colleges, since I had scored high marks."

"How did your first encounter with Baba go?"

"The very first time Baba saw me, he said '*Oh! you are from Kabul!*' I wondered how Baba knew this!... For, though my father is a devotee, he had never had any personal contact and so when Baba next mentioned: *your father works for U.N.*, I got even more flabbergasted! I felt Baba knows about things without any one having to inform him!... Four months after I joined the hostel, I was once laid up in bed with malaria and had fever which touched 105°F. Baba gave me some *prasadam* which I ate, and lo! that very night my fever subsided."

"Later, Baba asked me to play the key role in a drama titled *Bhajana vinaa* (without *bhajan*...). The role I enacted in the drama was my own past life and it produced a great impact on me and my friends... Six months later, I went to Kabul for two weeks, when strangely enough I felt disgusted with the life led by the people, which indeed was the very style of life I had led before!... Thus, I began to realise the impact of the education and hostel life in Bangalore and *I am convinced that I can be happy only when I live a simple and disciplined life, as taught by Sri Sathya* Sai Baba."

"Don't you think Baba has sort of hypnotised you?"

"No!... Not at all! For, the change in me has been gradual. Without my knowledge, a change in attitude has come over me... For instance, I now take more interest in my studies and enjoy sharing things with others. Do you know that thirteen of us live in one room in the hostel? I could have never tolerated this before! I would not have also found it comfortable...

"Another change that has come over me is that I feel concerned when some one else falls ill and I take interest in that person's welfare. Such things never used to bother me!... Also, I take more interest in my parents and keep in touch with them by writing regularly, because of the education I have received here... I had never been in the habit of even cleaning my room, but now I feel happy to sweep with a broom the halls in the hostel..."

"How do you think you would behave in the outside world once you are out of the Sai College?"

"In the outside world I would live in such a way that my life is a message for others. The life and the discipline in this college and the hostel would certainly help me to do this..."

"Would you feel happy if the world ignores you and not bother about the example you set?"

"I won't bother!... I am optimistic about the ultimate future, thanks to Baba..."

* * * * *

Amit Singh (19 years) a student of the II year B.Sc. class at the Sri Sathya Sai College of Arts, Science and Commerce completed the Higher Secondary examination from the St. Xaviers in Delhi. Thereafter, he joined the Bangalore Sathya Sai College.

Talking about his hostel life, he said, "I get up at 4.45 a.m., have bath, do *suprabhatam*, then go for a brisk run or jogging and have coffee at about 6.15 a.m. I study for about 1½ hours before breakfast. Thereafter I attend college at 10 a.m. sharp. Till 10.30 a.m. we have prayers *(bhajans)* and thereafter classes till 1 p.m. We resume after lunch at 2 p.m. and go for games at 4.40 p.m.... After studies and dinner, I go to bed around 10 p.m."

"Don't you find this routine rigorous?"

"No! I have got used to it. I sleep early and get up early. In the hostel, I also do *chapathi* rolling, vegetable cutting, etc. I am also on duty at the *Pragyan Pradarshan* (Spiritual Museum) and explain the exhibits to visitors."

"Have you not felt it boring to stay all the time in Whitefield? Have you not felt like moving out and meeting other people, say, for some gossip?"

"I have never felt the need to go out... The influence of Swami and the general discipline here hardly give us the time or the chance for idle talk or gossip... All because Swami has been such an uplifting experience for us..."

"Do you really think so? I feel Swami is sort of hypnotising students like you. What is your feeling?"

"It is wrong to say that we are being hypnotised. *It is not a question of Swami holding us, but rather our wanting voluntarily to hold on to Swami, because it is so reassuring!...* Please note that at no time have we lost either our consciousness or our rational approach. In hypnotism, we would have had no control over ourselves, for it would be a case of influence over the mind... *But Swami takes hold of our hearts!*"

"Tell me, do you find any special merit in the Sai system of education?"

"In the Sai method of education, student-teacher rapport is intimate, like in the *Gurukulas* of yore... Our teachers are intensely interested in our welfare and education."

"In practical terms what has Sai Education taught you?"

"Well, if I were to start work in the world today I would not call others bad and consider myself superior... I will try not to waste my time but do my job in a dedicated manner. By making good use of my time, I will make others see for themselves how time can be utilized without waste."

"Has there been any change in your food habits?"

"I have become a vegetarian without any one telling me. The Sikh community has the custom of eating meat and they ask for explanations as to why I have become a vegetarian... Then I tell them I am trying it out for myself and it is benefiting me."

"I dare say you are aware that quite a few persons attack Sri Baba for their own reasons

How has this influenced you and the other students?"

"Most such attacks are based on ignorance... It will have no influence on us, since we know the truth about Baba... Actually the influence of Sri Baba on us has been nothing but salutary. Even in my own friends I have seen a great change in outlook and I know how wonderfully impressed the parents are because of their children developing true character and values..."

"Even when Baba is not physically present, his spiritual dimension works wonders on us."

* * * * *

Twenty year old Ravi Kumar is a student of the Final B.Sc. class at the Sri Sathya Sai College of Arts, Science and Commerce, Bangalore. Asked to state the difference between the Sathya Sai College campus and other places, he said, "The involvement of the teachers in the lives of all the students is the difference... By involvement I mean not only the teaching but the way in which they try to see whether we have understood what has been taught... Also the simple lives led by our teachers, who do not have any expensive habits, make us feel close kinship with them. Our teachers also do social work with us... They just don't supervise... They follow all the rules and regulations we follow... like getting up for *suprabhatham,* attending *bhajans,* etc."

"Do you have moral instruction classes at college?"

"We have moral classes every Thursday when we study about all religions in the world. What we hear in the moral classes we find exemplified in the daily life of Swami."

"Are there any novel features about your campus?"

"The *bhajans* or prayers from 10 to 10.30 a.m. every day are a novel feature that makes our minds receptive to the education in the classes. Also, there is a great sense of unity prevalent amongst the student-teacher community in the entire college, because we all have only one objective: *i.e.* to please Swami."

"What was your reaction when you saw Swami for the first time?"

"Even at first sight, I felt Swami was some one great. In the college and the hostel I have felt his real interest in our lives. Earlier, I had my own conceptions of him... For the first 2 years, I only considered him a great personality. But then I gradually found that Swami was able to purify my mind as well as the minds of those around me. So I felt sure he was some one unique and superhuman."

"Don't you think this could be just an illusion or self-deception on your part?"

"Definitely not!... But even if it were to be an illusion it is a happy one and I am satisfied and happy with it, for I have only become the purer for it."

"How do you say you have become purer?"

"Because I nowadays try to control my anger even when provoked... I have become aware of the jealousy and ego in me and I always make a conscious attempt to rid myself of these evils..."

"Can you say why our youth are attracted to Swami?"

"Swami has a very handsome and arresting personality... Also there is a lot of curiosity to see him, because they have heard about his miracles. However, Swami's real attraction for youth is not these things, but the love he has for them and his talk which they are unable to forget, since he speaks straight to their hearts."

"We never forget what Swami says, even after years, and when we remember something said by Swami on some previous occasion, we get so much happiness even at the recollection of it. *It is the inner power Swami radiates which I think is responsible for his attraction.*"

"How would you answer those who criticize Sri Baba needlessly?"

"The answer is simple. Students like me should lead an ideal life as taught and practised by Swami. *Words are not enough to silence doubting Thomases...* Only deeds will silence them... So we have to show them *Satya* (truth), *dharma* (righteousness), *shanti* (peace) and *prema* (love) in our actions. Let me illustrate this with an example. Every year for the Summer Courses new students from different parts of India come to live with us in the hostel. In the beginning they are a bit rude and their conduct leaves much to be desired... But even after a few days they change completely after seeing the way we live and behave... I have observed this personally... I mean the effect of a good example."

* * * * *

K. S. Narahari, who is nineteen, is a Final B.Sc. student of the Sri Sathya Sai College in Whitefield, Bangalore. He joined the first Pre-University course in 1974 and passed both the years with a first class. He then joined B.Sc. and got the 3rd rank in the University during the first year. This year he expects to get the 1st rank.

"Why did you join the Sai College?" I asked.

"My parents are devotees and I used to go with them to see Baba. Even as a child I was inclined towards spirituality and religion.

"Though my parents asked me to join this college, I was also keen about it. Even if they had not asked me, I would have still joined this College. This was the reason why I did not apply to any other College, in spite of getting 80% marks in the SSLC examination. Something compelled me to join this College and I am happy I have done so."

"What was the main attraction of the College for you?"

"The main attraction is Baba, who answers my heart's call..."

"Are you sure you have not been brain washed in this manner?"

"No fears!... Even when I had not seen Swami or heard his speeches, or gone near him, I had felt drawn towards him.. I have not even read any of his books till now... Still, Swami's attraction has been there for me, even without seeing him and this has become stronger after seeing him. I attribute his attraction to some unseen power within him, which I am able to experience but not explain."

"What do you think of Swami's miracles?"

"I do not think anything of them for *the biggest miracle for me is Swami himself.*"

"What is the result of Swami's influence on you?

"After 5 years at this College and Swami's influence, I feel that I have improved within."

"What do you mean by within?"

"I mean that there is a change in my thinking and outlook..."

"How? Can you give some instances?"

"Previously I used to think of a multiplicity of Gods, but now I feel that there is only one God. Also, I have improved physically. I had bad habits like getting up late in the mornings. Now I get up at 4 a.m. and I find that six hours sleep is sufficient. Such changes in habits have helped me to remain in the pink of health and not be affected by cold, fever, etc. This has also been the experience of other boys who have stayed with me. A boy by name Narayana Sharma had asthma trouble. I used to tell him as a senior boy that if he got up at about 4.30 a.m. and took a cold water bath he would get relief and to his surprise·he found it helped him considerably in overcoming his breathing trouble... Spiritually also I have improved."

"How do you say that you have improved spiritually?"

"The other day I gave the tailor 2 shirts for stitching. He promised to give them in 2 days and he delayed it for a fortnight. I felt like troubling him by delaying the payment... but then I remembered Swami telling us never to hit back... Soon I began to think, that the tailor must have had his own problems and that I should not be mean. So I paid the tailor, remembering Swami's dictum that when you trouble any one, you only harm God because God is in every one, be he a tailor or a votary of any other profession."

"Is there much difference between your college hostel and other hostels?"

"Our lecturers live with us and make their lives an example for us. *We do not have servants in the hostel... We maintain it ourselves and keep it clean.* We also help in cooking and serving food. We live as one happy family, caring for one an other and sharing everything we have."

"Our lecturers also get the books for us and teach us. They give extra coaching when they find we are weak in a subject, but refuse to take any money for such service. Even at 12 in the night they are prepared to teach us... Their concern is that sincere! They give us opportunities to ask questions and do not put us down even when we ask inconvenient questions."

"Do you find any difference in the working of your college and hostel, when Swami is away and not residing at the Brindavan campus?"

"The college and hostel function in the same way, whether Swami is physically present there or not."

"If some one attacks Swami on any count how would you react?"

"I would ignore the attacks on Swami, for if I hit back, I will not be following Swami's teachings."

* * * * *

Anil Kripalani, an eighteen year old Pre-University class student of the H. R. College of Commerce and Economics in Bombay got the opportunity of joining the Summer Course on Indian Culture and Spirituality in 1979.

I asked him how he got to know about the Summer Course.

"My sister told me..."

"How did you get selected for the course?" I asked.

"I wrote the examination conducted by the Sri Sathya Sai Seva Organisation in Bombay and was selected. I was one of the eight students selected by that centre."

"Did you have any prior knowledge or ideas about Baba and his mission?"

"Yes!... I joined the Bal Vikas classes at the age of ten and when I was fourteen, I joined the Pre-Seva Dal classes, which I am still continuing."

"What did you learn in those classes?"

"In Bal Vikas classes I learnt how to chant *slokas* and how to pray. In the Pre-Seva Dal course I read the book *Summer Roses on the Blue Mountains*. I listened to lectures on Baba's philosophy and life besides the life of other saints like Swami Vivekananda."

"Have all those classes done anything to you?"

"Of course! I have learnt how to respect my parents and teachers and I have developed the habit of thrift. The classes have helped me to concentrate on my studies."

"When did you first see Baba and where? And what was your reaction?"

"I saw Baba first in 1970 at Dharmakshetra in Andheri, Bombay. Even at that age of ten, I felt drawn to him though I am unable to explain why."

"Have you been close to Baba?"

"No! Not physically... But somehow I always sense his close presence in spirit. So I hesitate to do anything wrong since I feel that Baba is for ever watching me!... He has changed me in many ways: I used to be very mischievous, disobeying my parents and often behaving in a childish manner. But today, I am different... I am also more responsible towards my home duties and my parents... More than me, my parents have been able to see the influence of Baba on me."

"I also changed my food habits and given up eating meat because I have begun to respect animal life. Nowadays I try to control my anger and I do social work during my spare time. Also, I do not waste money any longer."

"Has any one made fun of you for trying to follow Baba?"

"Occasionally people have told me that I have taken the spiritual path at too early an age! I do not agree but generally I do not discuss with others either about Baba or what I do spiritually, since this is my personal business. I feel, I should avoid discussions which will not serve any useful purpose."

"The problem of students today is the generation gap. Many feel the generation gap between them and their parents... However, with Baba students do not feel any generation gap. They understand the value of things Baba stresses, like good company *(sat sangh)* and spirituality... For, Baba's teachings are really practical.

"I have consciously followed some of Baba's teachings... Thus, in a practical way, I have worked with some blind students. I have read out to them history books and explained various happenings of the past. I have also helped them to move from place to place. This may not be a big act of service... But even this, I would not have done at this age and stage of my life, but for Baba.

"Baba is a super super power, who appeals to youth to the extent of transforming us... We are convinced he is super-human, because *we feel his influence even when he is not physically near us,* though of course we like also to see him whenever possible."

* * * * *

Twentyone-year-old Sanjeev Chaudhry of Chandigarh is a student of the M.A. class of the Department of Economics in the Punjab University. Asked how he came to learn about Swami and the Sai movement he said, "My contact with Swami and the Sai Organisations is primarily because of the Summer Course on Indian Culture and Spirituality."

"When did you hear about Swami first and when did you see him?"

"I heard about Swami in 1974 and saw him for the first time in 1977. When I saw Swami for the first time it was just a glimpse in a moving car, but even so, it was electrifying.

"I was not so much fascinated by his physical personality, which of course is impressive, but rather by something that seemed to emerge from inside him and envelop his eyes with a strange power which I had never seen anywhere else. The first glance we exchanged gave me a sensation which seemed to purify me internally. I felt the very atmosphere around him was charged with sacredness.

"During the last 3 years, I have come into contact with Swami only now and then. The physical proximity is of course highly elevating. Strangely enough, *even when I am physically away from him, I feel his spiritual presence. Therefore I can really say that Baba is closer to me, the farther away I am from him.* This may appear strange to others but it is very real for me... That is what it is!"

"Have people made fun of you, for following Baba?"

"Yes! Some people made fun of me initially. They used to taunt me saying 'What is so special about that man that you should be obsessed with him always? What do you really get through association with him? How do you know, you have not been tricked into believing Baba? "

"What was your answer to such taunts?"

"I told them I had been a confirmed atheist but Baba gave me a new understanding and took me on the Godward path. So, I know for myself that I have not been tricked. Also, *nothing has happened to me as an overnight metamorphosis. It has been a gradual change that Baba has wrought in me.*"

"You talk as though Sri Baba is some one very special?"

"Yes of course! Baba is very special, because no one else has been able to instil in me the significance of life and living. I am convinced that all talk against Baba is based on sheer ignorance of what Baba is and what Baba stands for. *Sri Baba's mission has great relevance for youth.* He provides the much needed direction to young people like me. Without Baba's influence, I would have been frittering away my time, energy, money and youth in useless pursuits..."

"What do you think about Baba's miracles?"

"What took me to Baba were his miracles, but soon his teachings and his spiritual powers made such a great impact that I consider his miracles no longer important."

"Are you definite that Baba has not mesmerized or hypnotised you?"

"I am sure I have not been hypnotised, because I am a logical, thinking person, quite sure of the things I do and want to do. I have seen the external world and what goes on there and I have voluntarily decided therefore to pursue the Sai path... Actually Sri Baba's attraction for me has been gradual, progressive and continuous. Had it been brain washing or hypnotism, his appeal would not have lasted this long let alone increase with passage of time. Abraham Lincoln was not wrong when he said : You can fool all people for some time or some people for all time but not all people for all time.

"If any one traduces great persons like Baba it is more disservice to mankind than to Baba. For it is likely to keep away several people who might have either got solace or benefited spiritually from his inspiring influence."

"How would you talk about Baba to those who do not know anything about him?"

"I would simply tell them: To understand life go to Baba. You will then understand

Truth also in a practical way. I would also tell them about Baba's irresistible appeal for all and particularly for the youth. In Chandigarh, I live in a hostel, and *I see my friends drinking, smoking and taking to drugs for the simple reason that they do not know what else to do!* In our University 55% of the students in the hostel drink regularly! *I feel only Baba can change and save these students.*"

"Can you tell me about the best features of the Sathya Sai Hostel?"

"Yes! First there is an invisible string of love that binds us and makes us all work in a co-ordinated and co-operative way. Unlike other hostels in which I have stayed, this hostel is always kept clean and the entire maintenance is in the hands of the students. There is no litter anywhere and everyone is extremely responsible."

* * * * *

Deepak Mukhi, who is nineteen, is a graduate from the Hindu College of the University of Delhi. He said that he had heard about Bàba from his aunt and had gone to Puttaparthi in July 1976 when he saw Baba for the first time there. "But Baba never looked at me and this disappointed me a great deal... However, later, when he did direct his glance towards me, I experienced an overwhelming feeling as though my heart was bursting!... I have now known Baba for over three years and believe in him fully."

"Don't you think you could have been deluded into believing in Sri Baba?"

"No! For initially I was sceptical. What I didn't like about Baba were his miracles, because I had been reading the gospel of Ramakrishna, who had said that when you acquire *siddhis* you should not use them to materialise objects.

"Later, after seeing and experiencing Sri Baba I discovered that miracles were not a part of his real personality but only an expression of his love. Further I found, that whenever I prayed to him with true devotion, there was instant response."

"What is your view about the discipline in the Sai hostel?"

"I found the discipline in the hostel very stringent but at the same time rewarding. *It helped me to overcome laziness which I must say has become a predominant nature of today's youth.* At first, I also hated the rigour of the summer course but soon got adjusted to the extent of feeling fine with it! I did social work too every day and now I am sure I am going to miss it, once the course is over. This appears strange even to me, since I had never imagined I would go to villages and dig sewer drains for others, particularly as I am from an opulent home."

"How did you find your lecturers and fellow students?"

"I found the company of the students with me very interesting. Several of the people living in the hostel and attending the course inspired me by their selflessness. They made me realise my duty to think about others.

"As for the lecturers, they guide us very effectively. To give an example, a lecturer at Brindavan came with us for social service work. I found that he never pushed any student to do any work, but he did the dirtiest of jobs himself with great dedication. I think, this is the most effective way I have come across of getting others to do their duty. It is a silent but very powerful approach to get us moving on the right lines in doing social work or for that matter, any work.

"Again, two nights after we landed, the hostel warden had an informal meeting with us and asked if there was anything we found wanting or difficult. This showed the organisation's concern for us students in a practical manner. Of course, Swami himself looked after us and distributed some items like ice-cream. That he personally did this to over

1000 students touched us and gave us an indication of his great love and patience."

"Have you learnt anything special at the summer course?"

"I have known from this course more about all religions and all faiths and how whether one is a Christian, a Muslim or a Hindu the same God dwells in all."

"Did the course have any personal impact on you?"

"During the entire period of the course we have been absolutely pure... We haven't fooled around with ourselves. We haven't had any lapses or bad impulses or thoughts let alone having to fight them! This has been the result of the discipline of good company *(sat sangh)* and Swami's evening lectures. Several of my friends who used to get distracted by the other sex have felt the same way. A friend of mine used to be steeped in pornographic literature and was deeply immersed in bad habits. He had been trying to control himself without success for the past one year. He confessed to me that *for the first time he has been able to remain clean and pure in thoughts* for a month. He is very happy about it and so am I, as his friend."

* * * * *

Ashwin Shirali (18 years) of the II year B.A. class of the Sriram College of Commerce,

Delhi University, said "I wrote the examination and was selected to attend this summer course."

"When did you first see Sri Baba and do you firmly believe in him?"

"I saw Baba nine years ago... Then my father was working in Bangalore and I was a student of the St. Joseph's School there. When I saw Baba first, it was more to accompany my parents who used to visit Whitefield. Actually I used to be critical of him till a year ago, mainly because of controversies around him and my friends making fun of Baba.

"About an year ago, on July 28, I had a dream in which Baba appeared and showed his love and spiritual power. The dream was so powerful that I could not forget it for a long time. Then I began to analyze myself, read his books and soon I knew how wrong I was in my understanding of such a powerful personality."

"Can you tell me why this summer course has an impact on youth?"

"The summer course has a great impact primarily because of the presence of Sri Baba in our midst. I found Baba helpful in breaking the barriers we create between ourselves and others. I always used to consider doing social work as something filthy and degrading. But today, I do not dislike but actually love social work in particular and all work in general not only because I am now convinced about it but also because I want to please Baba. I know that serving society is the only way of pleasing Baba."

"What is it that you find special about Sri Baba? And has he been of personal help to you in any way?"

"There is something about Sri Baba which is nice to experience but which I am unable to describe. I can call it spirituality or a wholesome mixture of love, gentleness, kindness, understanding, etc.

"I have already given up drinking and smoking and have decided today never to take to these, as I find spirituality far more intoxicating and satisfying. But for Baba, I would never have come to this firm decision."

"Are you not under a spell cast by Sri Baba?"

"No!... on the other hand, I feel my true nature or all the better qualities in me are slowly coming to the surface. If it were a spell there would be no action, nor would there be the reasoning faculty functioning inside me... nor would I make far-reaching decisions. Baba has only forced out of my mind several wrong impulses.

"During the first year of my college I had bad company. I tried drinking and smoking innocently. At the summer course I saw how Sri Baba stressed the importance of *sat sangh*. He also taught this to us in a practical way, for I had good company at the hostel and consequently only good thoughts always. I have never had before, the type of wholesome atmosphere I had at the summer course."

"Do you think Sri Baba's influence on you will continue after you return to your home in Delhi?"

"Somehow I feel that Swami's influence has been more on my heart and so whether he is physically present or not I will continue to get inspiration even by thinking of him. *My feeling is that Swami is a superhuman force and by following him I will become a better human being.*"

* * * * *

Ajay Pant from Lucknow, U.P. is twenty years old and a student of the B.A. (Part I) class at the Canning College of the Lucknow University. He said that it was by accident that he joined the summer course, after writing an examination. "I was never a devotee of Baba nor did I have any idea of the details of the summer course. My sister is a staunch devotee to the extent of her talking to a photograph of Baba and getting results! She had hurt her brow and was not feeling too well. She had to write the test organised by the Sri Sathya Sai unit in Lucknow. As she complained that she felt a little dizzy, I offered to take her to the hall where the test was arranged. When I went inside I suddenly felt an urge to write the examination. I talked to the convener and he permitted me to do so. The examination paper was easy as the main question was to write an essay on the Bhagavad Gita, Koran, Bible or any avatar. I then promptly forgot all about it.

"On April 29, my birthday, I got a letter saying that I had been selected for the summer course. Though I felt happy I was not very enthusiastic... you see my father is a retired Lt colonel and I did not feel like taxing him to make the trip to Bangalore. So I went to Mr. Shah, the District President of the Sri Sathya Sai unit in Lucknow and told him the position. Mr. Shah explained to me that I had not to pay any fee for the summer course and that the boarding and lodging also were free... As for the fare to travel to Bangalore, he, as a devotee, would give that to me."

"Do you have any regrets that you attended this course?"

"None at all! On the other hand, I think the course is unique for it has inspired me to try and lead a good life.

"I have always believed in two powers—myself and God," continued Ajay. "On 15th May this year, a boy I knew very well died in a scooter accident after sustaining a compound fracture that led to the coagulation of his lungs with fat globules. That was the first death I had ever seen... I even saw him cut up and stitched after the post mortem. The doctors said that only God could save him and I wanted Baba to save him. I kept a letter to this effect under his pillow, but when he died I tore it up!

"After attending the summer course, through Sri Baba's lectures, I have realised the inevitability of death. I have also come to know that if God had saved that boy I would have had a false picture of that reality... *Sri Baba has made me understand that it is ignorance not to accept the reality of death.*"

"Are you fascinated by Sri Baba's miracles?"

"I am not fascinated by Baba's miracles and materialisations. But I am not against them because I think there is need for these in the world of today. People want miracles in order to get convinced about mysticism and spirituality."

"What is your reaction to the social work programme?"

"I have got great satisfaction and a sense of achievement in doing the social work. I have begun to understand that this is the only way of paying back our debt to society... If I don t do social work I will feel like an unemployed youth."

"What do you think of your life in the Sathya Sai Hostel?"

"I stay with ten others in a dormitory but this has given me a feeling of brotherhood with different types of persons. I noticed in the hostel how well the students of the Sathya Sai College who stay there permanently behave, as compared to students like me from various States, who come to attend the summer course. These boys never use harsh words, are always polite and go out of the way to help any one and every one. This has to be seen to be believed! Thanks to the hostel discipline. I have become more active, regular and organised in my personal habits. I have also come to realise that studies and what we learn are of no avail unless they are put into practice."

"What is your genuine impression about Sri Baba?

"Baba is the most modest and the most lively of persons I have ever met. He is able to establish a personal rapport with every one in spite of having innumerable devotees and this is by no means physical... For even those who have never seen him feel that Baba is just for each of them!"

"Do you think the impact of the summer course on you will last?"

"I am sure the impact will last. Frankly speaking I am a human being and may be I may fall a prey to temptations. But I know it is good to follow the path of duty, devotion and discipline as in Brindavan. I can only say I will make an honest attempt to be good and make others happy, under all circumstances."

* * * * *

Seventeen-year-old S. Murali completed the Pre-University course from the Loyola College, Madras. He said, "I am attending this summer course for the first time and before I came here I did not have an idea about it."

"Don't you think the course has been strenuous?"

"I did not feel that the course was strenuous. It was also not easy, at the same time... But I did enjoy it greatly.

"I have learnt something about different religions and culture. I had no idea at all about our heritage and I am happy to have got an introduction to this... I have felt for the first time a happiness and peace of mind which I have not felt in my college before."

"Did the hostel life have any impact on you?"

"Yes! It has made me an extrovert for I am an introvert by nature... On self analysis, I find that this change has happened because of the company here which is totally different from the type of company I had in Madras. The point is that here all the boys practise common goals sincerely and this attempt has forged a new brotherhood in action.

"I have now got used to getting up early in the morning and have shaken off my indolent ways. I have also started doing social work which I had always considered dirty earlier... I feel convinced now that every one must do a job of social service."

"Don't you think your old ways will surface again the moment you go back?"

"The danger is of course there and may be I may not get up at 4 a.m. after I get back, but then I am sure I will be a better person than before... By better... I mean I'll be less selfish, I'll always control my temper and pay more attention to my studies!

"Swami is a remarkable personality... No one else has made the impact he has made on me. I feel he guides me invisibly from inside me... I would like to spend my holidays by attending such courses in the future also."

* * * * *

Fifteen-year-old O. P. Rohit is doing the Pre-University Course at the D. A. V. College, Amritsar (Guru Nanak Dev University). "What aspect of the summer course has appealed to you most?"

"I have liked most the social service part of the course. In Punjab, because of our family position I used to feel hesitant to do any community work. Even in my own house I considered it below my dignity to serve a glass of water to others. I never used to oblige even my mother by doing some essential shopping for the family. But at the course, though I don't know how, a great change has come over me. I no longer mind doing any type of social work, after seeing many of my companions from very rich and influential homes, doing the toughest and most menial of jobs with great enthusiasm and sincerity. I have not even played strenuous games before. So at first, I found it difficult to plough and cut drains with an axe but soon I learnt to do these jobs with ease. I realise that it is all a matter of the mind.

"The hostel here is very different from the hostels in Punjab, where there is too much indiscipline with boys taking drugs, smoking, drinking and gambling. There they not only keep their rooms filthy but also their minds by reading vulgar books. Naturally they are rowdy in their behaviour. Here it is just the opposite and we experience much quiet that is conducive for our studies.

"I have now come to realise the purpose of life. I feel that material comforts are not that important... I will try to always remember the main point stressed at the course that the same soul or divinity is inside all and so we must give up hatred of others as otherwise we will be hating God! Not to hate others is only a negative quality. So, we must love others which indeed is more becoming of human beings."

"What other impact did the course have on you?"

"I will always try to speak less and thereby conserve energy. I will be careful to choose good company, since I have understood how important this is."

* * * * *

Ravindranath S. D. who is seventeen has finished his second PUC from the St. Philomena's College, Mysore.

Asked about the summer course he said, "The discipline has been fantastic. I had never believed that such discipline was possible!"

"I think the course will be useful to me for life. I have liked the community here which is refreshingly different. Every one here is so very helpful and interested in you that you really feel fine!

"I have learnt that this life can never be full of happiness and that worldly pleasures are temporary. I have realised the necessity to think of a higher power always if one is to have peace of mind. All the lectures interested me and I discovered many new things like the unity of all religions. *I have learnt to appreciate spiritual books which I used to consider a bore earlier. I may find the useless trash I used to enjoy before, a bore in future!*"

"Are your parents devotees of Sri Baba?'

"I do not come from a family of devotees. No one else in my house is a devotee of Baba.. The first time I saw a photograph of Sai Baba I got interested, but when I read a few of his books I became an instant devotee."

"How would you evaluate Sri Baba?"

"I feel *Sri Baba is a leader we young people can look up to, since he is a symbol of love, humility and truth in practical life.*"

"After attending the summer course I have developed a desire to join the Sathya Sai College. Even otherwise I will only follow the

Sai path and teachings. Even if Baba wants to leave me, I cannot leave him."

* * * * *

Dilip Kumar is a nineteen-year-old student of the final year B.A. course of the Ravenshaw College in Cuttack (Utkal University) of the Orissa State. I asked him how he joined the summer course and he replied: "I wrote the examination held for recruiting students for the course and got selected."

"In Cuttack do you live with your parents or do you live in a hostel?"

"I stay in a hostel even in Cuttack, in the same way as I have stayed in the Sathya Sai Hostel for the summer course. I must say that I find great peace at this hostel which is totally lacking in the hostel I stay in Cuttack. There is very good discipline in the Sathya Sai Hostel, because every one is actively cooperating and working for the maintenance of such discipline. *I fina a happy determination on the part of all the students here to be always disciplined.*

"In the hostel and college where I study in Cuttack, we students try to have more fun, for we find studies boring. We gossip a lot, go to pictures and hotels and read different types of cheap fiction which stirs our passions. On the other hand, here in the Sathya Sai Hostel at the summer course, we have been engaged in work from dawn to dusk and we have had hardly any time even to gossip and our mind has been completely tranquil and pure."

"Why do you think people at the Sathya Sai Hostel are so determined to maintain the place well and keep to discipline?"

"Here all the inmates feel that the hostel belongs to us and we have to take care of it, whereas in Cuttack for instance, we want others to take care of the hostel for us..."

"How have you found the lectures at the summer course?"

"I have learnt quite a few things from the lectures. I had many wrong ideas before... for instance, I did not realise that Indian *dharma* cut across caste differences and that Hinduism has a universal message."

"Has the summer course made any difference to your personal style of living?"

"Of course!... I used to get up rather late every day but now I find the whole day becomes more meaningful when I get up early in the mornings. Then again though I always used to respect elders and teachers even before, I find I have been rather formal. I have learnt that respect is something that should come from within. Previously I used to while away all my leisure time, and now

I have decided to utilise time properly since Sri Baba has convinced me that time wasted is life wasted... I will also pray to God regularly.

"In the villages I have cleaned drains and roads and for the first time, I have talked to villagers. I feel it is wrong to look down on villagers or for that matter on any one, since the message of Baba has made a dent on my mind."

"What is the message of Sri Baba that has influenced you?"

"The message that the same God is present in all of us..."

"Have you not done any social work before? And if so, what is so great about the social work you did as a part of the summer course?"

"It is not like that!... Previously I used to do social work but then I was doing it as a kind of favour to others and I was also doing the work with definitely superior airs... But at this course I have learnt to do social work in all humility and mainly as a service to God."

"What is your impression about Sri Sathya Sai Baba?"

"I had previously seen only some photographs of Sri Baba... but after seeing him in person, I find the photos do not bring out the real Baba. Apart from his physical charm, all of us at the summer course have found in Baba a very simple and humble person who gives us more than motherly love and fatherly care."

"Don't you think you will go back to your old self once you leave Whitefield?"

"I have found Baba's discourses so appealing that even after I go back, *I will never forget his message. So, even if I err, I will try to correct myself.* Baba's teachings are practical or easy to practice. For instance, Baba has made me understand that when you are *alone* and everything around is silent, you are not really alone, but in the company of God... Now I have been able to experience at this course the charm of this lonely silence through practice. *In future, I am sure, I will no longer feel bored when I am alone.*"

"Have you witnessed anything strange or unusual either at the summer course or in your hostel life at Brindavan?"

"What I consider very strange or unusual about the hostel life is the total absence of fights, quarrels, abuses and misunderstandings amongst the students."

"Didn't you feel the generation gap between Sri Baba and yourself? You are 19 whereas he is 52."

"Neither I nor my friends at the summer course felt any gap between Sri Baba and ourselves. On the other hand, my friends and I were convinced that Baba knows all the problems of youth. He has also a good sense of humour. When I asked him how to control anger, he joked: 'Drink a glass of ice cold water and cool it off...' He then told us that if we cut out desires from the mind, anger will automatically be cut out. For anger appears only because of unfulfilled or thwarted desires. When asked how to behave correctly with girls, Baba said: 'Think of them as you would of your own sisters and your thoughts will become brotherly and good'."

* * * * *

Eighteen-year-old Shastri Maharaj, who finished the Grade 13, from the Gordon Graydon High School in Mississauga, Ontario, Canada, attended the summer course. He said that his father is an instrument technician, working in an oil refinery in Canada and added, "I was born in Trinidad (West Indies). My great-grandfather, a Sanskrit *pundit* in Rajastan, went there as a teacher.

"My sister suffered from asthma about five years ago in Trinidad. We had just heard then about Baba. One night when my sister's suffering was acute she said, 'If Sai Baba is God let him give me his Grace.' We then got for her Baba's *vibhuti* from a devotee. She swallowed the *vibhuti* and soon stopped coughing and had very good sleep for the first time. Later, when we met Baba, he told her, 'That was not asthma... That was aesinopheles!' "

"Where did you see Baba first and what was your reaction?"

"I first saw Baba in August 1979 in a hall in Ooty. His personality was distinctive and his physical form was so unlike what I had ever seen before... I was in tears of joy."

"How did you like the discourses of Sri Baba?"

"The daily discourses of Baba have given me instant inspiration and happiness."

"What have you learnt from the discourses?"

"I have learnt humility and begun to accept the world as one family, but above all I have learnt to be disciplined... Discipline is new to me because in the schools in Canada very little stress is placed on discipline—moral, spiritual and physical. For instance, boys carry cigarettes to the classes. You can see the packets in the pockets. Also boys and girls move too intimately in class rooms and halls. They are also aggressive with one another. They tend to be prejudiced against one who does not see eye to eye with them on even a small thing!... But over here, every one is more tolerant of each other and you can see true understanding at the summer course... The social work has given me the attitude of handling jobs like cleaning a drain in the same way as other routine jobs!"

"Did you like the food served at the hostel?"

"At first I had some problem but I soon learnt to be more tolerant and try out foods which I had not eaten before."

"Has the course done you any good?"

"Yes! I have become more appreciative of my parents and they will find a new son, when I go back to them. I realise that I have been too talkative and so will try to talk less in future... I will try simple living without depending on too many accessories. I am quite determined and will put my best effort to live up to Baba's teachings. I feel that I have become more self-reliant and am confident about being able to look after myself well. I will use my spare time to sing *bhajans* on the glory of God."

"Away from Baba, don't you think you will be away from his influence?"

"Whether Baba is physically near me or not will in no way affect performance of my duties on the right lines. *His influence is not the influence of his physical form alone.*"

* * * * *

Neliesh Paul, who is nineteen has completed the intermediate course from the Dayanand Anglo-Vedic College, Lucknow, affiliated to the Allahabad University. He said that he first saw Baba in Puttaparthi in 1971, "but Baba did not have much impact on me then... His influence has however been gradual and subtle. I like Swami's *bhajans* since the names of all Gods figure in them."

" I have had experiences which make me feel Baba's omnipresence. Controversies about him do not bother me in the least. I feel wherever I am I will have his blessings if I am on the right path. Here my friends are very good and very helpful in nature... In other places, unless people want something from us they do not bother about us."

"I used to see too many pictures and read bad books but I don't see much in such things today. In short, my old ways of running after pleasures is no longer that interesting!"

* * * * *

Sanjeev Varma, who is twenty years old, has done the B.Sc. final examination as a student of the Hans Raj College of the Delhi University. "I feel that for the first time in my life I have made the best use of my time at the summer course."

"Why do you say that?"

"Because Delhi University life is artificial, routine and mechanical. We keep talking all the time with friends. Where can all such irrelevant and aimless discussions lead us to?... I realise how much time we have really wasted. I used to smoke a lot but now I have given this up permanently.

"I had no faith in Baba till a year back, but today I have full faith because I got fascinated by the aura I saw around him. The first time I saw him in Delhi I felt he is no ordinary mortal. Then I read books about him. Later, *when I heard him talk, I found he was always so much to the point that every sentence and every word he uttered was convincing.* My faith has nothing to do with Baba's miracles. It is more due to his teachings rather than even his physical form which of course is highly attractive.

"Baba will continue to influence my life since his message to me has mathematical exactness and scientific precision. Some one told me that Baba has done some magic on me!... But I do not agree because magic is something of a low level and *we cannot link cheap magic with lofty Baba*. Actually, I am sorry I didn't come under Baba's influence earlier.

"The summer course has been a turning point in my life. I could never get up early in the mornings, but now I do so automatically. I have also conditioned myself to regular hours of eating."

(Please note: The educational qualifications of all the students referred to in this Chapter are as on May 1979).

A student smoked but denied it when questioned. Sri Baba then materialised a photograph showing the boy smoking in the very place he had done so. Thereupon the boy pledged never to smoke again.

—A true incident.

WAS HE THERE ?

"There is only one God and He is everywhere."
—SRI SATHYA SAI BABA

It happened in Whitefield, Bangalore during the summer course on Indian Culture and Spirituality organised in 1977 for students from all parts of India.

I had been asked to speak on the Indian heritage. I was happy as the thousand-strong student audience was highly receptive and disciplined. An added attraction was that Sri Sathya Sai Baba occasionally attended such lectures.

I thought to myself how nice it would be if Sri Baba were to be present when I spoke... But I decided neither to request him nor even give any indication of my wish. After all, if he could divine my thoughts, he should know!

A few days before the talk, Sri Baba asked me about the date and time of the talk. Forgetting my earlier resolution, I requested him to attend my meeting and he instantly agreed. On the appointed day, (Wednesday, June 15, 1977) I went 15 minutes in advance. Soon the bell rang and Mr. Sachdev, the organiser, introduced me to the audience and called me to speak. Sri Sathya Sai Baba had not come and I felt rather disappointed. However, I went ahead with my talk, after congratulating the gathering for being the very model of a model audience. For, the usual experience one has is of members of an audience conversing amongst themselves, even as a speaker addressed them, resulting in the situation of the speaker and the audience speaking almost simultaneously!

Realising how talks on spirituality, particularly around 12 noon, tended to produce soporific effects, I spoke in the lighter vein. The theme of the talk was on how Indian youth often gaped at things foreign and aped the West blindly, whilst those abroad looked to India for light and spiritual guidance!

I narrated the story of a young man from India who hailed from a poor but religious family. Nevertheless, he had nothing but contempt for spirituality, religion and the Indian heritage, even though his father was a Sanskrit scholar and *pundit* of great learning. The boy went to the United States for higher studies with the help of a merit scholarship won by him. He did an excellent job of study there and incidentally also picked up many American things like the typical American accent, etc. He came out with flying colours in his studies and landed a good job in the USA, on a handsome salary.

After a while, the young man fell in love with an American girl and asked her whether she would marry him. She said, "Of course!... I would be delighted...! I like India and you can teach me everything about the religion, spirituality and culture of India."

The young man was completely nonplussed, for he had no idea of even the ABC of Indian spirituality and culture!... He then made enquiries as to where he would be able to learn at least the rudiments of Indian religion and culture in the USA. Some friends introduced him to an American, who had spent a long time in India and had specialised in the subject of Indian culture and spirituality.

For the first time, the young man learnt from the American *pundit* several simple things like how the word *OM* is made up of *A*, *U* and *M*, how it is the primeval or first sound and so forth. He made discoveries about ancient Indian philosophical truths with the help of his American teacher who, at long last, he discovered to his chagrin was none other than a student of his own father, the *pundit!*

The way the story was received by the audience convinced me it had made an impact, and so I followed this with another story of a similar situation in a totally Indian milieu. Ram was a little boy who lived in South India. His parents who were enormously fond of Ram, took good care of him. As a part of his health care, they established a routine of administering one ounce of castor oil to the boy, on the last Sunday of every month. Ram hated this regimen and so to escape from it, on the last Sunday of a particular month, he ran away to the house of his friend, Krish.

Krish was the son of his school teacher and it so happened that it was castor oil administration day in the teacher's house also! Krish had been protesting vehemently that he would not touch the castor oil and it was at this time that Ram entered.

When the school teacher saw Ram, his eyes lighted up and he told Krish, "Look! What a naughty boy you are, Krish!... You are raising such a rumpus to drink this castor oil... Now look at Ram!... He is such a good boy!... See how quietly he will drink this castor oil!" Saying that, his teacher asked Ram to drink the castor oil. Ram felt hopelessly caught; silently cursing his fate, he gulped the oily liquid without a murmur!

I dealt with several aspects of Indian culture and heritage and ended on the note that deep study of the subject would make people set out on the great voyage of discovering the truth about themselves. In fact the letters SAI underlined this basic need for Self Analysis in depth!

The audience response gave me the satisfaction of having communicated my thoughts. However, the satisfaction was incomplete. since Sri Sathya Sai Baba had not been present at the meeting. I made no secret of my feelings to my wife, who had also attended the lecture, as we drove back. I felt that after the promise he had made to me Sri Baba should not have kept away!

It was with the same gnawing grouse that I went for Baba's evening discourse. The evening programmes were a regular part of the month-long course and comprised *bhajans*, followed by two students presenting summaries of talks given to the summer course and culminating in Baba's address.

Sri Sathya Sai Baba was always in time for the functions and entered the hall from the main entrance. It was his wont to walk around and greet the audience before going up to his seat on the dais. Sometimes, he would talk to a few people or just linger at some places and then walk up to the dais.

That evening Baba entered the hall and did not go anywhere else. He came straight to the row I was seated and said, "You made a good speech this morning... That is how one should speak to students!"

As I stood dumbfounded, he moved away to greet a devotee but soon came back and said, "That story about the American student and the boy who drank the castor oil really came off well!... The other examples you gave were also good and amusing. You quoted Swami several times!..."

I was completely confused, confounded and beyond myself with happiness. I told him that it was astonishing that Sri Baba could say all that without being present at the meeting. He said that it was nothing astonishing, but "*sahajam*" (i.e. quite a normal thing) for him! Justice Eradi and Mr. Chakravarthi wno had also attended my talk in the morning, were there then and shared their astonishment with me!

The matter did not end there! I must mention an amusing sidelight, which was narrated by my wife as we were driving back home from Whitefield.

Sri Sathya Sai Baba's soft conversation had been barely audible in the ladies' row. His sister, Parvathamma, had been sitting next to my wife and had heard Baba use words like "...Good!... nice!... that really came off well... That is how it should be done!... Excellent!" and had come to her own conclusions.

She asked my wife what she had prepared and sent to Baba, for him to have liked so much! She had concluded that we must have brought lunch for Baba from our home and that it had won his appreciation! My wife then told her about the lecture!

* * * * *

It happened again at the summer course held in 1978. I had been one of the speakers, though this time I spoke on *Mass Communication in Spirituality*. Sri Baba did not attend my lecture but in the evening came straight to the place where I sat and said, "I liked the humorous *gurram* (horse) story in your talk today." Evidently he was there too!

I had used the story referred to by Sri Sathya Sai Baba to illustrate a point in the talk. The horse in question belonged to an *ashram* and had been trained to respond to spiritual communication. Thus, to ask the horse to walk slowly, one had merely to say GOD IS GOOD! To make it trot faster the message was : GOD IS LOVE ! To make the horse gallop one had to utter the words : GOD BE PRAISED! And to stop the horse the code word was AMEN !

A new rider bought the horse and mounted it. He said GOD IS GOOD and the horse began to move slowly. He felt happy and said GOD IS LOVE when the horse began to trot merrily. After a while, he said, GOD BE PRAISED ! and the horse started galloping. Soon it galloped with such speed that the rider got scared. He also noticed that the horse was going up a steep hill and nearing the narrow tip. He immediately shouted STOP ! STOP ! having forgotten the code. He finally recalled the word, after making a desperate bid, and shouted AMEN just in time, bringing the horse to a dead halt at the edge of a precipice on the tall hill. He looked down below from that high point and felt deeply grateful to God for having saved him from a precipitous fall. In the great relief and joy he experienced he exclaimed: GOD BE PRAISED !

* * * * *

The first book written by my wife, entitled *Art Hobbies*, had been programmed to be released. My wife wanted Swami's blessings for it and took a rough copy that was just out of the press to Brindavan.

It was a clear and bright Sunday morning in December. She went to the darshan shed but it was over-crowded and she was unable to get a proper place to sit. With difficulty she managed to get a little space in one of the middle rows. She felt disappointed for, had she sat in one of the front rows, there would have been better chance of Swami noticing her. She sat with the wrapped-up book, herself wrapped up in the thought: "Will I be able to get the book blessed by Swami, before its official release in the city, at a scheduled public function?"

Swami came for *darshan,* but he never went to the side where my wife sat. After moving about for a while, he went and sat on his usual chair, listening to bhajans. My wife was sorely disappointed, for after that, she knew, he would normally walk back to his residence. She asked herself, "Why have I not been lucky enough to get his blessings?... Why can't Swami take another round and visit the section where I am squatting?" Her head bent (probably to hide her long face!) she was lost in thought.

Suddenly, a bunch of roses fell on her lap. She looked up startled and lo! Sri Baba was just a few rows away! Yes! he had got up and walked to the area where she sat. She looked up with joy. Sri Baba was not looking at her, but signing a photograph for a lady.

My wife heard some whispers around her: "Oh! Swami has given her flowers. How blessed indeed!" Her fingers clutched the flowers as her eyes followed Sri Baba. Suddenly Sri Baba headed straight in her direction. Standing in the empty pathway, a few yards away, he stretched out his hand and said, "Give me your book!"

Amazed, she got up as the other ladies made way for her to walk up to him. She was very happy as she handed over the book.

Swami leafed through the pages and asked her with a smile, "Is this book for me?" She nodded her head and explained that the book had a purpose. It would be useful for Home Science students and others who want to make profitable use of their leisure time. As Sri Baba looked through a few more pages, he gave my wife permission to do *paada namaskar*. After blessing her, he moved off, his hands still busy turning the pages of the book. After a while, the book got tucked away safely under Baba's arm!

As my wife stood watching Sri Baba, her mind grappled with several questions: "How did Swami know I had brought the book?... How did he know that I wanted his blessings so much?... And how did he know that I felt he might not bother to take the copy of the book with him, when I brought it from the press?"

Was he there too?

* * * * *

Whitefield, 28th October 1979... On that day, between 9.45 a.m. and 11.45 a.m. Swami was in the interview room talking to a group of scientists and professors of Management.

At the same time, in a distant corner of the Brindavan campus, a small group of devotees discussed threadbare arrangements for a public function. I was in that group and made several suggestions. Everyone expressed views on how the function should be arranged and there was keen discussion for about two hours.

In the evening, the same group went to Swami to tell him about the morning's discussions. But before any one could speak, Swami smiled and repeated *verbatim* what each one of us had said about the arrangements!

We were all speechless because at the very time of our discussions, Swami had been talking to a group in the interview room.

Was he there at both places at the same time?

* * * * *

My wife and I were once called by Sri Sathya Sai Baba for an interview along with Mr. V. K. Narasimhan, Editor of the *Deccan Herald*, when there was a stimulating discussion on many interesting points. Before we took leave, Mr. V. K. Narasimhan mentioned to Sri Sathya Sai Baba that my wife had written various articles, etc. Sri Baba smiled and said, "Yes!... I know about it... Not only that!... I also know about the functions she attends... Recently she went to a college to light a big lamp?"

Amazed, I asked, "Swami, how did you know?"

He laughed outright and asked my wife, "Did you not go to the Jayanagar College and light a lamp there?... Swami knows!" he said.

Sri Baba referred to a College Day function at the R. V. College in Jayanagar, Bangalore, some months back, where, as the Chief Guest, my wife had lighted a huge artistic lamp, at the entrance to the college. I had doubts as to whether the College Principal had sent an invitation to Sri Sathya Sai Baba for the function, but on checking up found that she had not done so!

So,... was he there too?

* * * * *

"How do you get to every place Swami?" I once asked Sri Sathya Sai Baba. There was a muffled smile on his visage as though he had been caught at a favourite game!

"Oh!" he said, brushing aside the question, "When Swami wants he always sees and hears!"

WHAT IS DEVOTION?

"Devotion does not mean worship of the Lord as an emergency measure."

—SRI SATHYA SAI BABA

August 28, 1977; Whitefield, Bangalore, 6.30 p.m. I had the *darshan* of Sri Sathya Sai Baba and was about to return. Dr. R. S. Padmanabhan who was there suggested that I stay back to attend a meeting of college hostel students, at which Sri Baba would be present. I was happy I did so, for I listened to Sri Baba's discourse on *bhakti* or devotion which I have reproduced from memory.

Real devotion should always be absolute and unconditional. It is common for people to be devoted and think of God in times of danger, stress and need. Thus, a student might get suddenly devoted to God just a little before his examinations! But such devotion becomes conditional *i.e.* for the purpose of achieving a goal. *Ananya Bhakti* or selfless devotion is that devotion which wants and wills for a union with the Absolute, for its own sake. It is for this reason they say that real happiness consists in union with God. Such happiness is different from mere emotional rapture and is indeed a state of extinction of all otherness.

The *gopis* (the milk maids of Brindavan) who loved Krishna typified this kind of devotion with the result whatever they did was done in the form of an offering to God. There is the story of how once when the *gopis* were selling their wares, instead of calling out "Milk for sale", "Curds for sale" and "Buttermilk for sale" they called out, "Oh! Krishna, Oh! Murari! Oh! Giridhari!"... "Oh! Govinda!... Damodara!... Madhava!"

Some curious onlookers asked "Oh! Are you selling idols of Krishna?... We want to buy them." Not even fully aware of what they had said, the *gopis*, immersed in the Lord's name and memory, opened their baskets. And lo and behold! They found the baskets full of Krishna dolls! The onlookers were baffled!

The *gopis* are always quoted as examples of whole-hearted or undivided devotion to God. Amongst the *gopis* there was neither jealousy nor lack of understanding of any type whatsoever, since each one of them felt communion with Krishna. Jealousy raises its ugly head only when some one has something which the other person does not have! In the case of the *gopis*, all of them were so devoted to

Krishna that they all had Krishna imprinted on their hearts. In this state of communion with God, each *gopi* was supremely happy and so, no one was jealous of another person, and all lived in an atmosphere of perfect love and dedication, basking in the ecstatic thought of the Supreme. It is said that the *gopis* used to blame the creator for making their eyes wink, particularly as it prevented them from beholding Krishna continuously and to their heart's content, as He played with them at Brindavan!

According to Sri Sathya Sai Baba, "Like the *gopis* one should always think of the Absolute and do one's jobs in such a way that the thought of divinity becomes one's life-breath. All the duties and activities carried out by a true devotee should be performed as offerings to the Almighty. Man must realise that he is an agent or instrument of the Divine and is guided by him."

A question may be asked whether God can be seen in a scientific way. For scientific research, different instruments are used. With different types of lenses and depending on the objects on which these are focused, as well as the "intelligence" of the eye viewing it, the external universe becomes more and more clear. Can God be seen in a similar fashion? For this, the instrument of the mind containing the lens of love, should be used with wisdom or the inner eye, to see God who is omnipresent.

The Absolute or Consciousness or God is everywhere. The consciousness is found in the largest of things and in the minutest of matter. (*Aṇoraṇīyān mahato mahīyān*). God is all-pervading, with all, beyond all and in all. Therefore, when a devotee offers pure, unselfish and absolute devotion or *bhakti* to God or chants His name forgetting himself, he is able to chain God or imprison God in his heart. The Lord is said to have declared : "*Mad bhaktāḥ yatra gāyanti tatra tiṣṭhāmi Nārada*" (Where my devotees sing, there I remain, O! Narada). A *bhakta* or devotee therefore scores over a learned *pundit* or a sanskrit scholar, or one who is proficient in all the *Vedas* or *Vedangas*. Thus, a *bhakta* is better than a man of great erudition, who in spite of all his learning, may remain farthest from God.

This could be illustrated by an example: When soup, (or *sambar* as it is called in South India) has to be made, one collects different ingredients like *dal* (pulses), tamarind, chillies, chilly powder, etc. In the same manner, *japa* (meditation), *bhajans* (devotional songs), *poojas* (prayers) and the reading of the holy scriptures are just the raw materials, which have to be processed in order to realise the Ultimate. However, although the raw materials for the *sambar* may be wonderful, if the proper vessel is not used and if that vessel is not properly tinned and cleaned, in spite of one getting the best raw materials, the *sambaar* or soup will get spoilt and people will be in a soup!

Similarly there is no use of a man's meditation and learning, if his heart, which represents the vessel in this case, is not "cleaned" of all selfishness and is also not coated with love. With more and more of growth, man's heart should become purer and expand with thoughts of the Supreme, enabling him to have equanimity of mind and constant bliss in daily action.

There is the story of Santa Sakku Bai who was devoted to Lord Krishna. Unfortunately, both her husband and mother-in-law never let her out of the house and strictly warned her not to see Krishna at any cost. So, Santa Sakku Bai who could do nothing about it, directed all her thoughts to Lord Krishna as she went about her daily chores.

Once, it so happened that both her mother-in-law and husband had to leave their village to attend a marriage and on that occasion Krishna appeared before Sakku Bai. She was so overjoyed and elated that she wanted to make some offerings to the Lord. She went in and searched in the kitchen, but there was no butter, curd or milk—the things which Krishna loved dearly. She did not know what to do and ran to the courtyard, where she located a banana bunch. She brought the bananas and in her ecstasy, removed the skin each time and after handing it over to Krishna threw the pulp away! Krishna however fully enjoyed what she offered. After a while, she realised her mistake and begged Krishna's forgiveness. She said she would now offer him real banana pulp. Carefully, she removed the skin, threw it off and requested Krishna to accept the pulp. Krishna who ate a little, spat it out saying, "No good!" Thereupon Sakku Bai said "Oh Lord! When I offered you the skins of the banana, you ate them with such relish but when I gave you the real pulp, you spat it out! Could you kindly explain the reason?"

Krishna answered, "In the beginning you displayed full devotion for me, but later your devotion got diluted, focussed as it was on the pulp of the banana." Such indeed is the true nature of devotion, in which everything becomes an offering to God and so even the mistakes get automatically swallowed!

Devotion or *bhakti*, for the sake of *bhakti*, without any thought of return, *bhakti* for the sake of communion with the Absolute is the surest and the best way of experiencing the divine.

One easy way of devotion is through love of one's fellow-beings and society. When love of others becomes the life-breath of individuals, they automatically commune with the divine and get all *shakti* (vigour) and experience real happiness.

There are the five elements—fire *(agni)*, water *(jala)*, air *(vayu)*, earth *(prithvi)* and ether or sky *(akasha)*; and five senses—*shabda* (sound), *sparsha* (touch),. *rasa* (taste), *roopa* (form) and *gandha* (smell). Now out of the five elements, water lacks one of the senses *viz. gandha*. Therefore it has horizontal movement. Fire lacks two of these senses *viz. rasa* and *gandha* and therefore it goes high up into the air. Air lacks three of these senses *viz. roopa, rasa* and *gandha* and has movement in all directions. The sky has only one of the senses *viz. shabda* and so it is more expansive and subtle. Thus, as the sense attributes diminish, the spread becomes wider and that is the reason why God is omnipresent and all-pervading, since he is beyond and above all attributes. This also illustrates how when one becomes freer and lighter, one is able to commune increasingly with the Absolute.

There is need therefore for realising that God is every where and Absolute :

Tvameva mātā ca pitā tvameva
Tvameva bandhuśca sakhā tvameva
Tvameva vidyā draviṇam tvameva
Tvameva sarvam mama Deva Deva.

(That God is the mother, the father, the relatives, the friend, the knowledge, the wealth and everything). With this realisation, devotion should be developed, through love for others, which is the best way of achieving union with the Absolute.

As I returned home, the recipe of Sri Sathya Sai Baba to take human beings near God kept recurring in my mind : "Love others and realise God." I was reminded of what Jesus Christ had said about those who say they love God and do not love their brothers. Such people, according to Christ, are liars: For he that loveth not his brother whom he hath seen, how can he love God, whom he hath not seen?

On another occasion, Sri Sathya Sai Baba discussed the true nature of devotion and stressed that it should be pure, sincere and intense. He then narrated a story to explain such devotion as shown by the *gopis*.

One day, Lord Krishna told Narada that there was nothing to beat the devotion of the *gopis*. Narada was not convinced and wished to have some proof.

Lord Krishna suddenly complained of a bad headache. Narada and the others tried to assuage his pain by rubbing some potion on the forehead but the pain did not decrease. On the other hand, it increased and Krishna was in great agony. Narada and the other sages got worried. They asked Krishna, "Pray tell us the remedy for your headache.

"Nothing else except the dust from the feet of my devotees will cure my headache"; said Krishna. The statement shocked every one. None dared apply the dust from their feet on the Lord's forehead.

"How can we do that?" They argued. "A wretched fate will befall us if we commit such a crime and we will all definitely go to hell !... We dare not do so." They all said so and the Lord continued to suffer from acute headache.

Narada then set out to find other devotees who would give the dust from their feet to remove the Lord's pain. Nobody came forward. Finally Narada went to the *gopis*. As soon as he told them about the dust required to cure the Lord's headache, all the *gopis* sat down, showing their feet to sage Narada. "Take the dust from our feet Narada and rush to the side of Krishna... Cure his headache... The Lord should not be allowed to suffer like this! Why are you tarrying?... We cannot bear to think that Lord Krishna is suffering from a headache." Thus they all wailed in unison.

Narada felt aghast: "Do you know what you are saying?... Dust from your feet for the Lord!... Do you know that for such disrespect you will all go to hell?"

"Oh Narada, hurry up! What does it matter if we all go to hell and suffer?... What matters is that the Lord's headache should be cured. Our fate is of no consequence, if only we can cure his pain. We do not mind doing anything even if the worst befalls us, as long as we are able to serve the Lord!... Our lives are only for him!"

In a flash, Narada realised what true devotion meant and how ecstatic was the devotion of the *gopis* for Lord Krishna. Indeed, how beautiful can life be, when it is really lived totally for the Lord, like the *gopis!*

At a meeting in Puttaparthi, Sri Sathya Sai Baba dealt with the subject of true devotion and narrated a story about Akbar and Tansen.

The great musician, Tansen, one of the nine gems of Akbar's Court, sang melodies specially for Akbar. Tansen's music was so good that it brought down the clouds and the rain from the skies; at times even snakes were charmed by his melody. Akbar greatly enjoyed Tansen's music and was very happy with him.

On one occasion, while Akbar was walking incognito in the streets, he was attracted by the songs of a *dasu* or a street singer. The music was so fascinating and irresistible that Akbar kept following the singer unconsciously, for a long, long time.

The music of the street singer made Akbar feel a rare rapture that touched the deepest recesses of his heart. Never before had he heard such music which thrilled his heart and soul !

The next day when Akbar saw Tansen, he said, "Tansen... yesterday I heard great music sung by an ordinary street singer and I was greatly moved by it. You are one of the greatest of musicians and I have enjoyed your music, but never have I felt so moved to the very core of my heart and soul by your music. Can you explain this?"

Tansen thought for a while and replied, "Oh King ! The street singer was addressing his songs to God, whereas I am looking at your face and singing to make you happy !... Naturally such music cannot compare with music that finds divine inspiration." Akbar felt insulted but realised the truth of Tansen's words. Music as an offering to God or as a form of devotion is unparalleled.

"Devotion to God should not be confined to your pooja (shrine) room. It must enable you to see God in everyone — even your enemies. The end of devotion is the realization of the omnipresence of divinity."

—SRI SATHYA SAI BABA

SRI BABA ON TEACHERS AND EDUCATION

"If one student turns bad, it affects only that person; but if one teacher fails in his duty, thousands of students are affected."

—SRI SATHYA SAI BABA

It happened in 1977, at the Summer Course at the Sri Sathya Sai College of Arts, Science and Commerce, Whitefield, Bangalore. A large number of students were on the stage of the college auditorium with Sri Baba.

I was in the audience seated next to the eminent scientist, Dr. Bhagavantham and I said, "Look! how the boys vie with one another to be as near Sri Baba as possible... How nice it would be if likewise students in our universities are close to their professors, Vice-chancellors and Chancellors!" Dr. Bhagavantham's reaction was instantaneous: "No Vice-chancellor or Chancellor in the country dare go that near any student these days!" His remark symbolised the unrest and indiscipline amongst students and the yawning gap between teachers and the taught in many an educational institution.

The term *Educate* is derived from the latin *Educere* meaning to lead out or to draw out that which is latent or hidden. So, education must bring out the best in the inner core of each student.* According to Sri Baba, this is just what the true education of Bharat imparts, namely *Atma Vidya* (or knowledge of the *atma* or soul) as against *Angla Vidya* (English or Western Education). Modern education in India still follows the pattern introduced by the British, about which Macaulay said in 1835, "the aim is to produce a class of persons Indian in blood and colour but English in taste, opinions, in morals and intellect."

As against the Indian tradition of initiating children into education by making them write and learn the letter "Om", today several children are first taught nursery rhymes like "Ba Baa Black sheep" and "Three blind mice", thus blinding them from the start to the hoary culture of Bharat.

In ancient times, boys and girls used to be instructed by teachers with profound knowledge of Indian culture and spirituality.

---

* In the course of a discourse to students, Sri Baba said, "A student is one whose duty is to study. He is called *vidyarthi* because he seeks *vidya*. What does *vidya* mean? *Vid* means *light* and *ya* means *that which gives*. So education means proceeding from darkness to light *i.e.* from the ignorance of the *atma* (soul) to the awareness of the *atma*.

Modern preceptors are often ignorant of the true significance of religion and Indian culture. How can such preceptors make the hearts of the little ones thrill to the nobler and eternal values of life?" asks Sri Sathya Sai Baba.

"Some modern teachers are obsessed by western culture and civilisation. They question the validity of the Vedas and teach history, giving it an anti-Hindu bias! It is because of neglect of spiritual education that there is so much unrest amongst students, who indulge in anti-social activities and bring disgrace to educational organisations

"Teachers should rise above imparting bookish knowledge and doing a job of formal teaching. For, this is tantamount to giving students information without inspiration. Teachers have a sacred role. They are like sculptors who should sculpt the uncut rocks of children's minds and shape them into persons of exemplary character. Children and students are often innocent and pure at heart. It is only the elders and teachers who give them wrong ideas!"

Everyone should first understand the differences between worldly and spiritual education.

Worldly (Material) Education	Spiritual Education
1. Caters to the mind and intellect.	1. Goes direct to the heart.
2. Promotes desires and attachments leading to a state of *ashanti* (lack of peace of mind).	2. Helps to eliminate desires and gives detachment and *shanti* or peace.
3. Develops the ego, produces anger and unhappiness.	3. Deflates the ego and produces tranquillity and happiness.
4. Makes one unduly happy when successful, and utterly desperate when unsuccessful.	4. Teaches the method of facing both success and defeat with an equal mind.
5. Helps to conquer aspects of the outside world.	5. Helps to conquer oneself.
6. Gives information and knowledge.	6. Gives humility and wisdom.

"The home situation is also important for proper upbringing of children. If parents go to clubs, play cards, smoke, gamble, drink and quarrel, how can they ever prevent their children from developing such evil habits? Teachers should occasionally visit the homes of the children under their care and tell the parents that if they do not mend their ways, their children cannot improve.

"Teachers to have the right impact on children and their parents must first set good examples," says Sri Baba. "Teachers should never forget that their personal lives and example make the greatest impact on students... Who should teach the teachers?... Teachers should realise that as the water in the tank, so it is in the taps. Parents and teachers should make charity, love, sacrifice, and honesty fashionable.

"Education should train students to respect their parents, co-operate with them and earn their blessings. It is the duty of teachers to see that along with a degree, students acquire the nobler values of life. The educational system of a country is the bank on which the nation draws a cheque whenever it requires strong, reliable, skilled workers. If it goes bankrupt, as ours has very nearly gone today, it will be national disaster. If the system is over-hauled and lubricated, the next generation will be assured of good leaders and what is more, good followers," says Sri Baba.

"Personal relationship between the teacher and the taught is essential to promote harmonious development of the personality of the students. Teachers should help students to get rid of bad habits, bad thoughts and evil talk and promote in them the concept of *dharma* in every walk of life and human endeavour. It is important that all teachers should work together as a team and themselves develop exemplary character for emulation by students. When rural students get back to their villages, there should be some method by which they continue with *saatwic* qualities; to enable this, spiritual centres should be started in villages. Loving kindness must well up naturally and spontaneously from teachers and flow towards students. They should always try to give a total picture of different subjects to students. When one teaches the basic facts about physics, one should also teach the realities of metaphysics. When one teaches botany and the wondrous secrets of a tree, one should also talk about the Creator who created the tree.*"

Sri Baba does not believe in compulsion "Any work that is done should be only because of conviction from within. It must be remembered that violation of God's laws is the main reason for the absence of peace in

---

* This reminds one of the poem by Joyce Kilmer which begins with the lines, "I think that I shall never see
A poem lovely as a tree;" and ends with:
"Poems are made by fools like me;
But only God can make a tree."

the world. The present day poverty and helplessness of people and even natural catastrophes like earthquakes and floods are due to people not following the principle of *dharma* laid down in the sacred scriptures.

"Since welfare and peace of the world are our main concern, the primary duty of teachers is to work for the revival of that *dharma*. This can be done by training students on the right lines and providing the missing link of spirituality in their education and daily living. If schools, colleges and universities function well, *Sanatana* (eternal) *dharma* will become an integral part of education as in days of yore and there will be happiness and peace everywhere.

"Changes in the educational system for the sake of change are the order of the day, but such changes relate to external features. As a result, the desired results are not obtained in spite of any number of rapid reforms. Only changes motivated by spirituality or the reality of the inner life can give permanent results and peace. Teachers who are torch bearers of the future should never forget that *the end of education is character*," stresses Sri Baba.

Since the general system of school and collegiate education does not equip students to face the challenges of life, the Sai system of education has been oriented to supplying the missing link of spirituality and developing the *inner personality* of students.

In a nut-shell the attempt is to infuse soul power into education through :

(1) Removal of the illusory idea that happiness consists in money, knowledge, comforts, position and reputation;

(2) Revelation of how happiness is a state of mind that can be so cultivated that both good and bad, as well as pleasure and pain will be accepted with the same equipoise;

(3) Bringing out the inner personality of students so that the best in them is placed at the service of the community;

(4) Attracting students to the cultivation of *pragnan* (spirituality) along with *vignan* (science) and induce the practice of spirituality in daily living;

(5) Making students give up gossip and practise limited speech;

(6) Introducing students to the sweet experiences of meditation and yoga, or of the joy of inquiry into one's own reality;

(7) Placing students on the path of self-confidence, self-satisfaction, self-sacrifice and self-realization;

(8) Fostering a spirit of tolerance and humility so that they will always look at the good points in others and their own faults;

(9) Promoting the performance of all duties with discipline and devotion and instilling in students the concept of *dharma* in every walk of life and every endeavour.

Results are achieved *inter alia* :

(1) Through an opening prayer each day in the school or college, and by all praying together wishing all people and the whole world well.

(2) Through teachers becoming disinterested seekers of truth and setting examples of simple living and high thinking;

(3) Through teachers living in the hostel with students and leading a highly disciplined life, to enable such discipline being imbibed naturally and subconsciously by the students;

(4) Through teachers doing social work along with students, as an offering to God and setting an example of being

always ready to serve and unwilling to be served; and

(5) Through regular study of classical texts on spirituality, biographies of saints, world religion, etc. as a part of moral instruction.

Sri Baba attaches the greatest importance to the nursery and primary education of children since "the memory power is very good during the early years." He emphasises the point by saying, "You elders remember very well the things you learnt in your childhood days. The slokas you learnt from your grandmother can be recited by you even now."

Sri Baba stresses how important it is for elders not only to train children on the right lines but also to provide the right examples. "Thus, if there is a phone call for the father, he should not ask the child to answer : 'Father is not at home!'... For this will become the first lesson for the child on how to tell lies!... The child is the father of the man and it is imperative to see that the child imbibes the right values at every stage of its growth."

The present author had the occasion to visit the Sri Sathya Sai School run by the Rajmata of Nawanagar in Jamnagar. He saw the school children participate in prayers and *bhajans*, learn music, dance, the floral arts, gardening and crafts, in an atmosphere of love and discipline. The Jamnagar school is one of several Sai schools, where children get individual attention and full mead of affection from teachers dedicated to their job. At a time when young minds are wax in reception and marble in retention, they are inspired to follow the moral code :

Satyam vada (Speak the truth)
Dharmam cara (Follow *dharma*)
Mātṛdevo bhava (Respect mother)
Pitṛdevo bhava (Respect father)
Ācāryadevo bhava (Respect teacher)
Atithidevo bhava (Respect guest)

Such values inculcated at an early age build the foundations for national discipline and *shanti* or peace.

In short, *Sai Education* helps to bring to the surface the perfection and goodness innate in human beings and train them to do their worldly duties with discipline and devotion, in a selfless manner. The chain of Sri Satya Sai educational institutions which derive inspiration from Sri Baba have also become centres of national and religious integration, emphasising the fundamental unity underlying all diversity. Here the youth from different regions of India as well as various parts of the world, representing different faiths and varied strata of society, study together, work together, play together and sing *bhajans* together, imbibing a world view of all religions, a wider horizon of Indian culture and tradition, intuitive knowledge of the basic reality of the *atma* and moral values.

Besides running model schools and colleges,† seminars and special training courses are organised for teachers in colleges and schools. In March 1978, a seminar on moral and spiritual education in colleges was held at the Sri Sathya Sai Arts, Science and Commerce College, Whitefield. Several educationists and college principals participated in the seminar. Sri Sathya Sai Baba, inaugurating the seminar, said "The main reason for deterioration in discipline is because the human mind is being allowed to deteriorate. All the time is spent in bad thoughts and bad actions with the result man's animal instincts have come into the open every-

---

† The Sri Sathya Sai College of Arts, Science and Commerce, Prasanthi Nilayam, Puttaparthi, Andhra Pradesh; the Sri Sathya Sai College of Arts, Science and Commerce, Whitefield, Bangalore, Karnataka; The Sri Sathya Sai College of Arts and Science for Women, Anantapur; The Sri Sathya Sai College for Women, Jaipur; The Sri Sathya Sai College for Women, Bhopal; Smt. Eswaramma High School, Prasanti Nilayam, Puttaparthi; Sri Sathya Sai Vihar, Ootacamund; Sri Sathya Sai School, Jamnagar; Sri Prasanthi Vidya Mandir, Kotah, Rajasthan (Middle School); Sri Sathya Sai High Schools at Muddenahalli and Alike, Karnataka; and Sri Sathya Sai Kendriya Vidyapeeth, Sri Sailam, Kerala.

where. Sri Baba exhorted teachers to play their sacred role of building values and morals by inspiring students to *see things with their own eyes, experience with their own hearts and think with their own minds.* If education is to be useful in daily life it should promote sacrifice and discipline. Educational Institutions should never become the abode of Goddess Lakshmi (Goddess of Wealth) but should always remain the abode of Goddess Saraswathi (Goddess of Learning)."

In February 1980, Sri Sathya Sai Study Circle was formed to bring together all teachers and educationists interested in serving humanity through education. Members of the Circle* started their activities with the decision to make special efforts to instil in young minds healthy appreciation of the universality of all religions and the virtues of duty, discipline and devotion.

In addition to providing the right motivation to teachers and educationists, Summer

* The Study Circle comprises a cross section of the intellectual elite of Bangalore, scientific institutions like the Indian Institute of Science, Institute of Management, University of Agricultural Sciences, National Laboratories, etc., besides educationists from several colleges and schools. Dr. S. V. Pappu of the Indian Institute of Science, Bangalore is the convener of the Study Circle.

Courses† on Indian Culture and Spirituality are organised by the Sri Sathya Sai Central Trust specially for college students (including those not studying in Sri Sathya Sai Colleges) to enable constructive use of vacation time. Such courses have drawn participants from all over the world. The seventh Summer Course held in Whitefield, Bangalore in 1979 was attended by 1000 students (650 boys and 350 girls) from different universities and institutions in India and abroad.

The month-long Summer Course on Indian Culture and Spirituality was envisaged to integrate cultivation of the spirit with education and to make young people aware of the great Indian heritage as well as the real values of life. For, to quote Sri Sathya Sai Baba, "Our students have forgotten their *inner power*, which is many times more potent than brute force. Soul power promotes an integrated, harmonious and balanced personality."

Boys and girls stayed in dormitories, in separate hostel buildings, strictly adhering to discipline and the daily routine. Regulations ensured that there was no socialising. It was

---

† Delivering the valedictory address of the 1978 Summer Course, Mr. A B. Vajpayee, then Minister for External Affairs, Govt. of India, suggested to Sri Sathya Sai Baba to conduct such classess on spirituality for politicians of the country to infuse values in politics.

unbelievable in modern days that so many boys and girls could live side by side, in the same campus, without one even looking at the other - all quietly minding their work, in an atmosphere of gentle harmony and peace. Silence, cleanliness and keeping to time were compulsory. The students resided with their teachers, as in *gurukulas* of yore.

Every day, the students were up by 4.30 a.m.; after morning ablutions, they joined in the OMKAR or chanting of the OM (the primeval *pranava)* twentyone times. This was followed by *suprabhatam* (or the early morning song) to awaken the God resident within every heart. After *suprabhatam*, they joined in *nagarsankirtan* or group singing around the campus. After breakfast and by 8 a.m. they all got ready for the daily programme of social service for about three hours, in nearby villages.

In their white uniforms, carrying various implements and brooms, they chanted *bhajans* in praise of the Lord. As they proceeded for work in this manner, they showed the spirit in which such social work should be done *i.e.* in all humility and with the attitude that "Service to man is really service to God." The social work included repair of roads, cleaning up of clogged village drains (that acted as breeding ground for mosquitoes and pests), improving the general sanitation and the running of a mobile medical camp.

Catering for the entire assembly was in the hands of the students, who also planned the menu and willingly took up chores like cutting vegetables, rolling *chappatis* and cleaning utensils. After lunch, the students got ready for their academic lessons on Indian culture and spirituality, which lasted till five in the evening.

Planned with meticulous care by literary stalwarts like Dr. V. K. Gokak, the curriculum of the course embraced a wide range of subjects on Indian culture; art; philosophy; world religions; great saints of the world; systems of philosophy; .yoga and sacred texts, with special accent on the *Bhagavad Gita*. The students listened with interest to lectures delivered by eminent men like Dr. Bhagavantham, Professor N. Kasturi, Justice Bhagavathi, Justice Kailasam, Shri R. R. Diwakar, Shri Nakul Sen and others, lectures which imparted to their sensitive minds a global view of all religions and stressed the validity of the message of the ancient scriptures in inspiring individuals to practise spirituality in daily living.

After tea, the students reassembled in the auditorium, for the most eagerly awaited daily programme of the evenings - the discourse of Sri Sathya Sai Baba. The programme began with *bhajans* by a group of students, followed by two students (a boy and a girl) giving the summaries of the day's lectures. At the end of his discourse, Sri Baba sang *bhajans* and was joined by the audience in one voice.

The Summer Course kept the students continuously busy from dawn to dusk and served to demonstrate the proper use of time. Sri Baba often tells the young people that "Time wasted is life wasted." Even Sundays, the days of rest from lectures, were devoted to elocution contests and other extra-curricular activities.

One might ask the legitimate question whether the Summer Course and the Sai system of education have the desired impact on young people. The chapter on "Youth on Sri Baba" throws light on this question. However, in discussions with several students of Sai Institutions, I found that youth have been considerably motivated in the proper utilization of time and control of excessive talk. Sri Baba has often stressed that the bane of modern youth and the student community is "too much talk." The students in olden days never spoke more than 3 or 4 words in a day... When you go on talking, you not only lose energy, but you also lose the respect of others who will call you a bore!... When you observe silence and speak only when necessary, your memory power increases and you are helped to discover your soul power." says Sri Baba.

I talked to the teachers to find out whether admission into Sai institutions is restricted to the children of devotees and whether teachers experienced any constraints, like, say, a compulsion to openly show reverence to Sri Baba. The answers given by Professor D. Narendra, Principal of the Sri Sathya Sai College of Arts, Science and Commerce, Whitefield, were highly revealing in this regard.

Professor Narendra said, "There are many students in Sai institutions who are not children of devotees. The students are drawn from different backgrounds including the neighbouring rural areas. Special attention† is given to students of rural areas to enable them to catch up with urban students, coming from well known schools.

Professor Narendra mentioned that "Sri Baba does not expect anything from the lec-

† When I visited Puttaparthi, I saw a lecturer of the Sai College there giving special lessons in English grammar to some students of the college, from the rural milieu. The lecturer mentioned how Sri Baba had been keen that this should be done to bring up the rural students to the same level as their urban brothers.

turers except the discharge of their duties with sincerity and love. He does not expect and does not like any show of reverence."*

"Long before I came to work at the Sri Sathya Sai College of Arts, Science and Commerce in Whitefield, I had read Sri Baba's books and listened to his discourses. I was struck by the profundity of his knowledge and the depth of his scholarship. The moment I started working with Sri Baba, I developed great reverence for him, because of his encyclopedic range of mind, his objectivity, his ability to see all points of view, and his insistence on following all conventions and regulations. Whenever we teachers have gone to him with problems, he has always given solutions that touch the core of the problems and are so obviously just to all concerned," said Professor Narendra.

"What did Sri Baba tell you, when you first joined as Principal of the College?", I asked.

---

* Once at a college function when the teachers had brought garlands, Sri Baba lovingly reprimanded them saying, "Why all this waste? If you had wanted it so much, you could have brought just a small flower as a symbol. Why waste money on so many garlands?" A lecturer, Mr. Nanjundiah, mentioned that when he took a few fruits and a large garland as offering to Swami, he said, "*Bangaaru,* this becomes a weighty burden for me and is unnecessary from your point of view. Your doing your best for the students is the best form of respect you can show me."

"The day I took charge, Sri Baba told me: 'You are coming to a rural college which is full of poor students from villages... You must try to serve them sincerely.' I found later, that 70 per cent of the students of the college were from the adjoining rural areas," said Professor Narendra.

"What is the impact of Sri Baba on the teaching fraternity?", I asked.

"Frankly, all of us teachers have felt that Sri Baba releases a certain kind of creative urge in each one of us with the result we do our best and constantly try to excel ourselves. Even the feeling that Sri Baba is there acts as a kind of inspiration and a constant incentive to give of our best. In addition Sri Baba has taught us by his own example how to have a sympathetic and loving approach to students but at the same time ensure discipline and be strict," said Professor Narendra.

On another occasion, I happened to meet Mr. A. V. Balesham, a Telugu *pundit* from an elementary school in the Medak district of Andhra Pradesh. Mr. Balesham had attended along with 599 others, an orientation course in spiritual education for teachers at Brindavan in Whitefield. Asked to give his reactions, he said, "We came with many misgivings... We were worried what inconveniences we would face at *some* Sai Baba College in Bangalore, when we were asked to attend this orientation course, but after arriving in Bangalore we felt happy, sinee we were made so welcome and given not only good food but also much food for thought, through lectures and particularly the discourses of Sai Baba. Most of us have as a result been doing some re-thinking on our profession. What have we been doing all along? Why have we been doing what we have been doing in such a mechanical manner? How can we become more effective instruments for inspiring children? Such questions kept recurring in our minds."

Mr. Balesham said that during their usual teachers' training course, all of them had studied child psychology and all about teaching the child. "But only after this orientation course has an awakening come over us about what we had been missing in our career, *viz* the spirit of selfless love for the little ones."

Asked if he had known Sri Sai Baba before, Mr. Balesham said, "Personally I am not thinking at all in terms of the personality of Sri Sathya Sai Baba. I admire the way in which he demonstrates that his life is his message as well as the exemplary training he has given to the Sai College students. We have to acknowledge the great good he is doing for the cause of education and the wholehearted manner in which he has extended his co-operation and help to this movement of revitalising education at the grass root level."

Om! Saha nāvbhavatu...Saha nau bhunaktu
Saha Vīryam Karavāvahai
Tejasvināvadhītamastu
Mā vidviśāvahai

—*Upanishadic Verse*

"*May He protect us both* (*teacher and the taught*) *from obstacles from known and unknown sources. May He invigorate us and infuse the power* (*to enjoy the teaching*). *And may there be no misunderstanding between us* (*the teacher and the taught*)."

A GROUP INTERVIEW

"When one lamp lights many lamps, all shine with equal brilliance."

—SRI SATHYA SAI BABA

It was a Wednesday in January 1973. Mr. V. K. Narasimhan and I had been to Whitefield. Most unexpectedly, Sri Sathya Sai Baba asked us to join a band of devotees from different parts of the U.S.A. and Australia who had all been called for a group interview. There were twentysix of them - the majority of them eves - and all of them trooped into his interview room, a rapturous expectation writ large on their faces. Their happiness and impatient joy seemed to stem from the very bottom of their hearts and their beaming faces revealed boundless reverence and unqualified devotion for Sri Baba.

One cannot describe in words the spontaneous and wondrous change that comes over devotees summoned by Sri Sathya Sai Baba for an interview. This constitutes the summation of their prayers and the supreme happiness that not only fills them but also spills out has to be seen to be believed !

Sri Baba closed the door of the room and saw to it that everyone squatted in comfort, in the manner of a loving mother looking after her children. Then he sat on his chair and looked around in a glance that manifested pure love - the love which he preaches and lives.

A hushed silence and rare peace pervaded the room. The devotees on the floor, and one of them in the wheel chair, had all widè open eyes as they gazed and gazed on Sri Baba's physical form, making full use of their proximity to him. Sri Baba's eyes rested on each of them and his looks spoke of deep concern for every individual.

Sri Baba smiled and asked whether any one had questions to ask. An American seated close to him said, "Baba, you are our Master, our Guru..."

Baba nodded his head and said with sweet humility, "No!... I am not your master... I am the servant of everybody..." Greatly touched and a trifle perplexed, the American said, "No... If you are not our guru, you are our Father."

Baba leaned forward, as he shook his head, saying, "Oh! Yes! ... In a way, father, mother, or brother or any one else you may think of!" He then outlined the concept of the spiritual family, which is permanent or immortal, as opposed to the ordinary family, which is impermanent. This spiritual family* comprises *truth* as *father; love* as *mother; peace* (or *shanti)* as daughter; *wisdom* as *son* and *detachment* as *husband* or *wife*. "*Sneha* or friendship is symbolised by the yogi", he added.

The group were eager to clear many lingering doubts. "How can I control my mind?", asked an Australian.

"Such a question was asked of Krishna by Arjuna in the *Bhagavad Gita*", said Sri Sathya Sai Baba, and added, "Check or control your thoughts... particularly thoughts that are not good. Thought control leads to mind control... What an individual thinks about becomes very important to him. That is why it is said, thoughts become things... Spiritual discipline enjoins strict control over one's thoughts so that the mind is always kept in a serene state and not allowed to go astray... All the sense organs lure human beings only

---

† Later, when I discussed the concept of the spiritual family, Mr. V. K. Narasimhan said, "Sri Sathya Sai Baba's delineation of the spiritual family is an improvement over that given by Yudhishtira to a *Yaksha* in the *Mahabharatha*. Asked to describe his six relatives, Yudhishtira said *satyam* is *mata* (truth is the mother), *jnaanam* is *pita* (wisdom is the father), *dharmam* is *braatha* (dharma or righteousness is the brother), *dayaa* is *sakhaa* (compassion is the friend), *shanti* is *patni* (or peace is the wife) and *kshamaa* is *putra* (forgiveness is the son)."

because of the commands and orders of the mind. That is why, the mind has always to be kept in check and always pure."*

"Baba, please tell us how to keep our hearts white or pure", pleaded one of them.

"The heart is always pure or white"... said Baba in a loving, gentle tone and added, "Now look at my handkerchief. It is white, but due to constant use, it becomes dirty. So I send it to the washerman. The washerman does not make it white. He only removes the dirt from the white cloth by washing it. Likewise the desires of man cover his heart. Wipe away the dirt of desire and your heart will always be pure and clean."

The group was overwhelmed by the simple and direct manner of Sri Baba's exposition.

"How can we make love come out of the heart, Swami? Please educate us", asked another.

"No effort is necessary... You pour water for a small seedling but you do not make any special effort to make it grow! For it grows of its own accord... This is also true of your heart.

---

* I was reminded of what Marcus Aurelius had said, "Our life is what our thoughts make it"; and what Gautama Buddha had said: "The mind is everything; what you think you become."

"Fill your heart with love for others and don't do anything else... You will find that this love will flow out on its own to make others happy... If it is selfish love, your heart will contract, but if it is selfless love, your heart will expand and love will continuously come out of it, with effortless ease. The quality of inner, selfless love is not strained... It flows like the gentle rain from the Heavens... Love is life... Love is everything... Love takes you to God."

As Baba spoke about the transcendental nature of true love, the group experienced a tremendous surge of love flowing from him to them in abundance.

"Swami, you have said that morning time is good for meditation. I can't find the time then... I have to look after my husband and my patients... What should I do?", asked a doctor in the group.

"*Bangaaru,**" said Sri Baba in a low voice, "When you have work, such work and service to others becomes worship. When you do your work as an offering to God, that work becomes the best form of prayer. You then live your life as a divine pilgrimage and therefore as an offering to God."

---

* meaning: *the golden one!*

"Baba, do you think that we should start a Sai Centre at our place?", asked a member of the group.

"There is no compulsion... You don't *have* to do it!... There is no pressure at all, but if it gives you pleasure, go ahead!", he said with tenderness.

Another devotee's face was filled with tears. Mr. V. K. Narasimhan looking at that face, exclaimed, "Baba!, that lady seems to be in pain...: She is crying !"

Sri Baba smiled and said, "No, you are mistaken ! Those are not tears of sorrow !... Those are *bliss-drops* or tears of great joy !..."

"Swami, I would like to serve society and make my life useful ...Could you please outline some programme or give a formula?"

"The formula is very simple", said Sri Baba. "You can be of the greatest service to all, if you follow the maxim : *Be good, Do good* and *See good.*"

A lady from Australia spoke next. She said, "Whenever I am engaged on a service project, I feel I see you there actually helping me... Are you really present or is it some kind of ego which makes me think that I see you there?"

Sri Baba smiled. "The moment you serve others or do jobs without thinking about yourself, your ego vanishes... And if you always think of me, naturally I am with you!...

"When you think of God and do your work you become an instrument of God... And of course the instrument is as important as God's grace itself... For example, if some one wants to dig with a crowbar, he cannot do so, unless the crowbar is straight, strong and sharp... So too, you, the instrument in this case, have to be good and pure and have God's grace to be effective."

Sri Baba conversed in a very lively, simple and captivating manner. He spoke mostly in English. Sometimes he quoted Sanskrit verses or spoke in Telugu, which Mr. V. K. Narasimhan translated into English for the benefit of the devotees.

One of the devotees asked: "I want to do *yoga*. What is your advice?"

"What is *yoga*? Will you tell me?", countered Sri Baba.

"Yoga is union...Swami", she said.

"No, it is more than union, it is *oneness*... In union two things join together. The highest philosophy stresses just one and you must understand this."

The conversation again drifted to the subject of meditation. Sri Sathya Sai Baba explained, "You are asked to meditate, because this helps you to focus your mind on one form, or on one image to which you pray... But the mind is a monkey and has to be controlled. Once the mind is trained in one-pointedness, it will be able to see the one in the many, though normally it only sees the many in the one and is unable to fathom the essential unity in all diversity.

"We often say : This is my body, this is my mind, my intellect, etc... We know that the body, mind and intellect are not permanent. We also know, that something, that owns all these three, is permanent... *i.e.* the soul. So you must not waste your time but spend it to discover that which is permanent and residing in you."

"No Swami ! We don't waste time", butted in a devotee.

"Oh, I suppose in 24 hours you sleep for 12 hours, and gossip the remaining 12 hours !"

Every one laughed and Swami quoted a Telugu verse to illustrate the value of time.

"Time should be used to discover the God within you. You can discover that God easily, when you live in love. Love everyone. Start the day with love (selfless love) and end the day with love - that is the way to God.

"Selfless love is Godly or divine... Selfish love is earthly or human", he added.

Sri Baba asked a devotee in a wheel chair, "What would you like to have? Tell me."

"You! Swami", he replied instantly.

"What a lovely answer!" remarked Mr. Narasimhan.

Suddenly, Swami's right palm circled in the familiar way and he materialised a silver ring. He took the right hand of the devotee and slipped the ring on the 3rd finger. It fitted perfectly.

"You see this ring has the right American fit!" said Swami.

Everyone laughed and saw Swami's right hand circle again and materialise enough *vibhuti* for 12 ladies. Eight other ladies had not got the *vibhuti*. So he circled the palm again and this time produced enough vibhuti for distribution to 8 persons. For the lady who continued with her "blissdrops", Baba materialised a silver ring that perfectly fitted her finger. Her joy knew no bounds.

A devotee asked, "Meditation is so difficult!... How can I do it easily, Swami?..."

"Well... Meditation is the easiest of all things. When you think that it is difficult, this thought itself makes meditation difficult. Man has even reached the moon, but with effort he can reach God more easily. Where there is a will there is a way..."

"Baba... Please tell us how to see the light inside?" The question was from an old lady.

"With the help of the inner eye... Now, in this room, when you open your eyes, you see so many people. But when you close your eyes, you see darkness. Now what is it that sees or feels the darkness. It is the inner eye.

"When you are inside a temple standing before the image of God, you often close your eyes and pray. This is because you feel instinctively that the inner eye alone will reveal God to you."

There was a moment's silence. Then one of them said, "You have given us so much information about the way to reach God...."

There was a smile on Sri Sathya Sai Baba's face as he said, "What is the use of information? I want your transformation."

As the group dispersed, I noticed that every one had radiant smiles and the bliss on their faces was as visible as the morning sun.

SRI BABA ON THE RAMAYANA

"If we do not understand Rama as an ideal human being, how can we understand him as God?"

—SRI SATHYA SAI BABA

Sri Sathya Sai Baba inaugurated a national Seminar on the Ramayana at the Sri Sathya Sai Arts, Science and Commerce College in Whitefield in May 1977. Distinguished scholars from several States of India participated in the Seminar which was arranged as part of a month-long Summer Course on "Indian Culture and Spirituality." The aim of the Seminar was to stress the unity in the diversity of the interpretations of the great epic *Ramayana*, which is the epitome of Indian culture.

Sri Sathya Sai Baba told the thousand and odd delegates who attended the seminar that it was essential "to sow the seeds of the high ideals and moral values of the Ramayana in the hearts of the people and allow them to grow." In his daily lectures, both to the seminar as well as the month-long course, he dealt with different aspects of the

Ramayana and exhorted youth to absorb the sacred values and high ideals contained in the Ramayana and implement them in their daily life.

Each character in the Ramayana symbolised values as well as good and bad tendencies. Each character had to be studied and understood in the correct light, so that mankind could emulate the good and reject the bad, after realising the pitfalls in them.

A study of the different characters in the Ramayana will show that even bad characters were not all bad. There were several good points in them, but the bad aspects resulted in their downfall, thus giving the lesson of the danger of bad qualities, which have to be avoided. Rama and Lakshmana were all good; Vali was also good in many ways. Even Ravana had his share of noble qualities, but the overall impression that has remained is about the bad aspects of Ravana.

Long after the Seminar, several of the instances given by Sri Sathya Sai Baba lingered in my mind. Discussing the character of Sita, Sri Baba said, "Women have to learn much from Sita. Sita gave up her jewels, her fine clothes, a life of luxury and everything else in order to accompany Rama to the forest. However, while in the forest, the desire for the golden deer crept into her mind; that desire kept her away from Rama, for many many years! Had only Sita not hankered after the golden deer, she would not have been separated from Rama." Sri Baba finally summarised this by saying *Kama* (or desire) and *Rama* cannot co-exist!

"This instance teaches us how we should learn to control the mind and not hanker after worldly things, if we wish to be in constant touch with the divine," he said, and added, "Desires lead to bondage and bondage leads to sorrow. When desires are controlled and bad thoughts are eliminated, not only does the individual progress, but he also gets extra energy and strength to serve society."

In all the lectures, Sri Sathya Sai Baba stressed that "Every action has reaction, re-sound and reflection." People experience good and bad, only as the consequence of their *Karma* or action. People will reap as they sow! To illustrate this Sri Baba referred to Sita who, misled by the sound of Ha! Sita... (sound uttered by Maaricha) requested Lakshmana to rush and protect Rama.

Lakshmana pleaded with Sita not to believe Maaricha's tricks. In a huff, the angered Sita questioned Lakshmana's motives and went to the extent of saying that Lakshmana perhaps wanted Rama to die, so that he could marry her! Her words exceeded all limits of decency and greatly hurt, Lakshmana went on the errand unwillingly...

Several months later, after all the waiting, when Rama saw Sita for the first time, not only did he not talk to her, but he also suggested that she could choose to be with Lakshmana, Bharatha or Shatrugna! Sita did not deserve such harsh words from Rama, but the brash manner of Rama was only an echo and reflection of her unkind and harsh behaviour once towards Lakshmana. Sita was the incarnation of Lakshmi and the embodiment of several wonderful qualities. All this did not absolve her from paying the price for some harsh words ! This is where the Ramayana teaches how a little wrong, even when committed unwittingly, has to be paid for and cannot be set off against other virtuous acts and deeds !

Giving another example of how actions always boomerang, Sri Sathya Sai Baba said that Dasaratha's separation from his sons at the time of his death was a reaction, the result of the curse of the parents of the young boy whom Dasaratha had killed although unknowingly with his knowledge of *shabda vedhi.** Actually, Dasaratha had mistaken the sound of the boy filling his pot with water

---

* That is, sending an arrow to a spot from where sound emanates.

as the sound of an elephant drinking water. The boy was fetching water for his blind parents, who when informed of this tragedy cursed Dasaratha that he too may suffer from pangs of separation from his son. Dasaratha could not help the punishment, since the curse had to run its course !

King Dasaratha never looked upon his kingship as an opportunity for self-aggrandisement but used it only to render exalted service to the people. Dealing with King Dasaratha's character, Sri Baba said that one night, when the king felt thirsty he got up and poured water from the jug into a glass. As he did so, he noticed that his fingers trembled a little. Dasaratha thought about it and said to himself, "If I am unable to control even my fingers and therefore unable to have full and absolute control over my own body, how can I exercise control over my kingdom?"

The next morning, Dasaratha called sage Vasishta and others and said that as he was not in the pink of health the time had come for him to step down from the throne. He requested them to arrange for Rama's coronation, saying that unless a person was cent per cent fit as a king, without even the slightest signs of physical weakness, he could never do full justice in serving the people.

"If only people could take a leaf out of Dasaratha's example in the present day, how wonderful it would be!", concluded Sri Baba.

Yet another fact stressed by the Ramayana is that without divine grace, one's best efforts will not yield results. To take the case of Sri Rama, Dasaratha nominated him as the successor - a nomination which was widely acclaimed by the people. The auspicious date and hour for the coronation were also fixed by the priests. However, at the last minute, Kaikeyi made Dasaratha agree to exile Rama and crown Bharatha, and so the coronation of Sri Rama was not to be ! Kaikeyi thought that Bharatha would be happy and become the king, but Bharatha implored his mother not to send Rama away, on the ground that he would be unable to bear the separation from Rama, but she did not yield. Bharatha refused to become the king, even though Rama's coronation was cancelled and Kaikeyi begged him to rule the country. Ultimately, the *paduka* or foot-wear of Sri Rama were the ones destined to occupy the throne for 14 years ! As for Rama, such was the state of his mind that he was happy he was going away to the forest, thereby upholding the sanctity of his father's words. He did not even for a moment feel sad that he had not ascended the throne. This instance shows Rama's equanimity both in adversity and pleasure and also demonstrates how God's will alone is final.

"The Ramayana expounds the technique of imparting knowledge about the nature of *atma*" said Sri Sathya Sai Baba, and narrated an incident. Sita, Rama and Lakshmana once went to sage Bharadwaja's ashram. As the men were all seated on one side and the women on the other, Sita joined the ladies and sat with them. And Rama sat with the rishis. Since Rama and Lakshmana lived in the forest and also wore bark, they too looked like rishis. So, the situation was such that no one could easily spot them out. On the other hand, Sita could be easily recognised.

As the rishis discussed the Vedas, the women talked amongst themselves in whispers. They asked Sita, "Has your husband come with you?"

"Yes! For... I cannot come alone,"... said Sita.

"But where is your husband?", they asked

Sita was silent. The rishi *patnis* or wives of the saints were not satisfied. Pointing to a person nearby whom they thought to be Rama, they asked her, "Is this your husband?"

"*Neti...Neti...* (Not this... Not this person)", said Sita. They pointed in that fashion to several others, one by one and Sita kept saying, "*Neti, Neti...* (Not this!... Not this!). Finally, when they pointed to Sri Rama, Sita did not say anything, but bent down her head. Her silence indicated that it was Rama.

"Thus, in the spiritual effort to realise the *atma*, the technique or method of '*Neti, neti*' (Not this... Not this) or rejection of what is not and arriving at the truth in silence is unique", concluded Sri Baba.

Sri Sathya Sai Baba narrated a story from the Ramayana to explain how people often look at things with coloured glasses. Thus, Tulsidas, writing about the beauty of Sri Lanka (Ceylon), described how pure and white the flowers there were and how exquisite was the scenery. Hanuman, who was by his side, sought to correct Tulsidas instantly, saying that what he wrote was not the truth. Hanuman averred that he had gone and seen how everything in Lanka was red, and how even the scenery looked blood red and not at all pure white! Tulsidas refuted what Hanuman said and because of the altercation between two devotees, Rama had to appear on the spot.

Rama explained to Hanuman that Tulsidas wrote from the very depth of his heart and really saw the flowers as white and the scenery as pure and exquisite. Then Hanuman began to argue with Rama also. (After all Hanuman's mind was that of a monkey!) He emphatically told Rama tht he would never agree with Tulsidas, since he had witnessed the scene and seen things for himself. So he felt it his duty to oppose untruth.

Thereupon, Rama explained that at Lanka Hanuman's mind and thoughts were in a state of agitation and in that condition of anger, his vision had become red. So everything looked red to him at that time!

"This story tells us not to look at problems with blood-shot eyes and minds clouded with passion," said Sri Sathya Sai Baba, and added, "When individuals are overcome by passion, jealousy, lust, greed, anger and desire, they do not see things in their true colours. What they see is more a reflection of the state of their own mind."

Hanuman was however the quintessence of devotion to the extent of every hair in his body always murmuring the words "Rama, Rama". He was also a very innocent person and all he cared for was to be always near Rama.

When they were all back in Ayodhya, there were grand celebrations. At the conclusion of the celebrations, every one returned home. Hanuman did not have any home to go to and so stayed close to Rama.

Late at night, Sita appeared with a jug of water and both Rama and Sita retired to their chamber. Hanuman followed them. Sita went inside but Rama stopped Hanuman at the door.

"You cannot come in, Hanumanta", Rama said affectionately.

"Why not? Sita is there", asked Hanuman.

Rama patiently explained, "Look at that sindoor (red mark) on her forehead. It gives her the right to be in my bed room. Sita is not a different person. She is my better half."

Hanuman felt distraught and rushed out to find some *sindoor* and apply it on himself. As it was night time, all the shops had been closed. Hanuman however broke into a *sindoor* shop. Though he found the *sindoor*, he saw no mirror to apply it on his forehead. Also, he thought if a little sindoor could give Sita the right to be in Rama's bed room, then why not besmear his entire body with *sindoor* so that he would never be separated from Rama! So with his entire body covered by *sindoor*, he made his appearance before Rama!

Yet another instance of Hanuman's *bhakti* (devotion) and yearning to be with

Rama was seen at a time when everyone requested Rama to be given chances to serve him. Sita and each one of Rama's brothers asked for different jobs of work like serving food to him, accompanying him tc different places, etc. Hanuman went through the list of jobs all the others had asked for and racked his brain to think of some work that would enable him to be with Rama always. Finally he asked Rama to give him the job of "snapping" his fingers whenever Rama yawned!

Rama smiled, for he knew Hanuman would follow him everywhere saying that a person might yawn at any time and at any place! He however agreed to the request, in view of Hanuman's intense devotion.

Sri Baba said that Hanuman's actions were always innocent and pure. At the time of the coronation of Rama, Sita gave a pearl necklace as gift to Hanuman. To the chagrin of Sita, Hanuman pulled out one pearl after another from the necklace shook each near his ears to find out whether the echo of Rama's name emanated from it. When he did not hear the sound of Rama, he discarded the pearls as useless! On the other hand, since every cell in the body of Hanuman breathed the name of *Rama*, there was no place in his body for *kama* (lust). It was because of this that he remained unaffected and pure, even when he came across several women in Ravana's harem in Lanka, during his search for Sita.

Hanuman was a scholar of the Vedas and Shastras and the repository of virtues like humility and devotion. He belonged to the glorious rank of messengers who spared no effort to achieve success in tasks entrusted to them by their masters. Hanuman was always imbued with both devotion to Rama and self-confidence, and these were the positive and negative points which helped the divine current of Rama to flow in him.

Talking about Ravana, Sri Sathya Sai Baba said that Ravana had mastered the four Vedas and six Shastras and was therefore symbolically represented as having ten heads. He had acquired powers through prayers but in spite of his devotion to God he suffered from jealousy lust and hatred. This resulted in his committing many sins, culminating in the ruin of his kingdom and his dynasty.

Throughout the month-long course, Sri Sathya Sai Baba explained how "The Ramayana helps to stress the sacredness of Indian culture and underline values that help every one to lead a good life. It will particularly enable Indian youth to appreciate the spirituality of India which constitutes the soul of Indian culture."

Sri Baba advised students and the youth to follow the example of Rama, particularly Rama's quality of restraint in speech. "Students today talked a lot and this was not good for them. Excessive talk weakened nerves and retarded memory power. The value of silence is so great that it provides equanimity of mind, which state alone confers divine strength. The virtue of silence was practised by rishis like Vasishta to conserve energy and attain realisation.

"Instead of frittering away energies and precious time reading obscene books and seeing sensual films, youth should read carefully the Ramayana, Mahabharata and the Bhagavad Gita to imbibe precious character-building values. Like Lakshmana and Hanuman, students should become servants of God and this they could do by serving society selflessly. Only then could they become leaders of modern India which in turn would become great because of their selfless service. Young men should strive for upliftment of the poor through work, worship and wisdom and never succumb to the evils of wine, women and wealth", concluded Sri Baba.

"When one harbours jealousy, anger and ego, he becomes Ravana. When one follows the path of love, truth and dharma, he becomes Rama."

—SRI SATHYA SAI BABA

SERVICE TO MANKIND THE SAI WAY

"Whatever service you render to others is service unto God Himself."

—SRI SATHYA SAI BABA

The importance of social service is generally realised but it is not often that such service is looked upon as a duty as well as a privilege. Sri Sathya Sai Baba says that human beings should not only help one another but also feel happy doing so. Anyone who is devoted to God must also be devoted to God's creations. That is why helping others becomes a sacred duty. Concern for others is the basis of all religions. So, the best and only religion in the world is the religion of love.

Sathya Sai workers are brought up in the belief that selfless service to the community is service to God. Sri Baba often reminds them that *pleasure is an interval between two pains* so that those in pleasure will always rush to the help of those in pain, as a way of offering prayers to God. Besides work, service is worship and even a small amount of selfless

The entrance to Prasanthi *Mandir* in Puttaparthi

The main Temple at Prasanthi Nilayam in Puttaparthi

Feeding of the poor at Puttaparthi (Sri Baba can be seen in the circle)

Sri Baba visits prisoners at the Thana jail

Sri Baba leads a cow to the *Gokulam* at Brindavan Whitefield (above) and

social work by students of the Sri Sathya Sai College of Science, Arts and Commerce, Bangalore

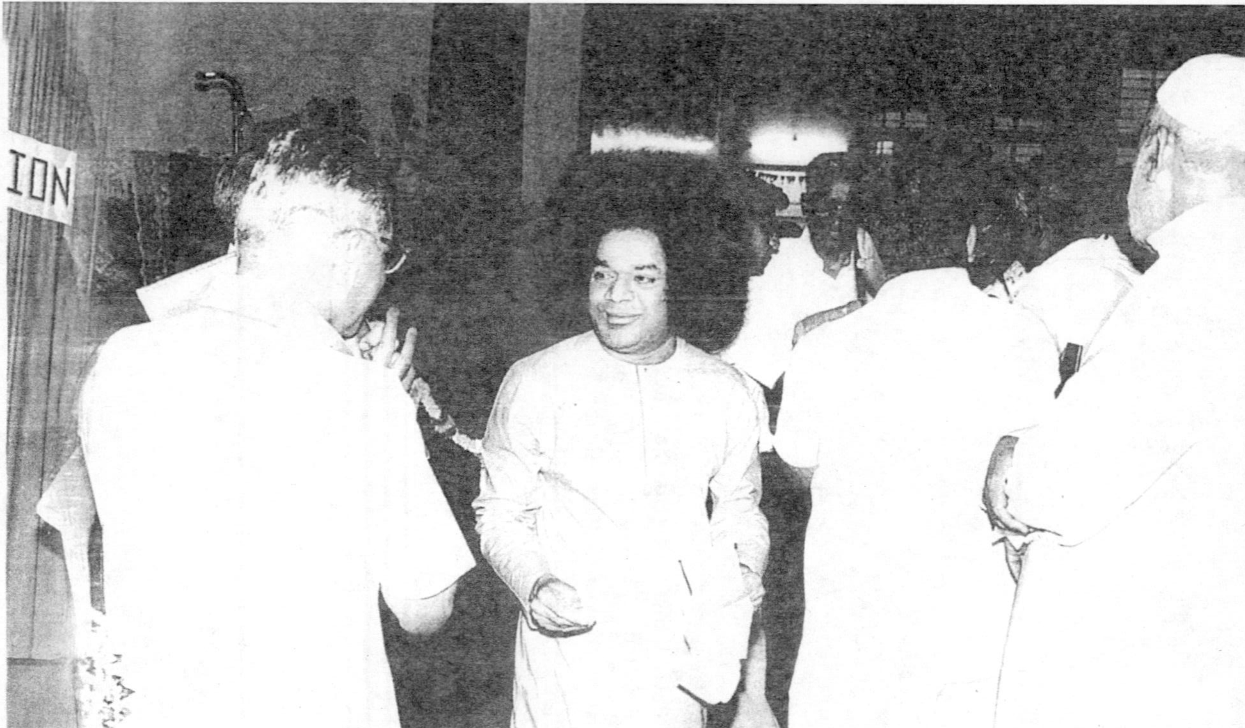

Sri Baba at a seminar on spiritual education arranged for Principals of Colleges.

Pouring of holy ash on the statue of Shirdi Baba.
Sri Karunyananda holds the pot.

Sri Baba makes a point during a discussion.

Children of the Sri Sathya Sai School of Jamnagar at prayers (above) and at science class (below).

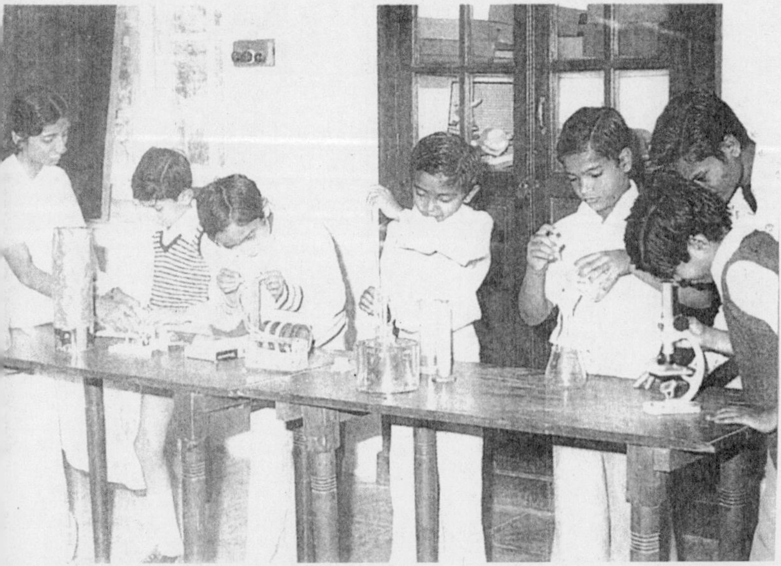

Bhajans by Sri Baba

Nagar sankeerthan by students of the Summer Course

When Sri Baba amazed the author (See chapter on "Was He there?")

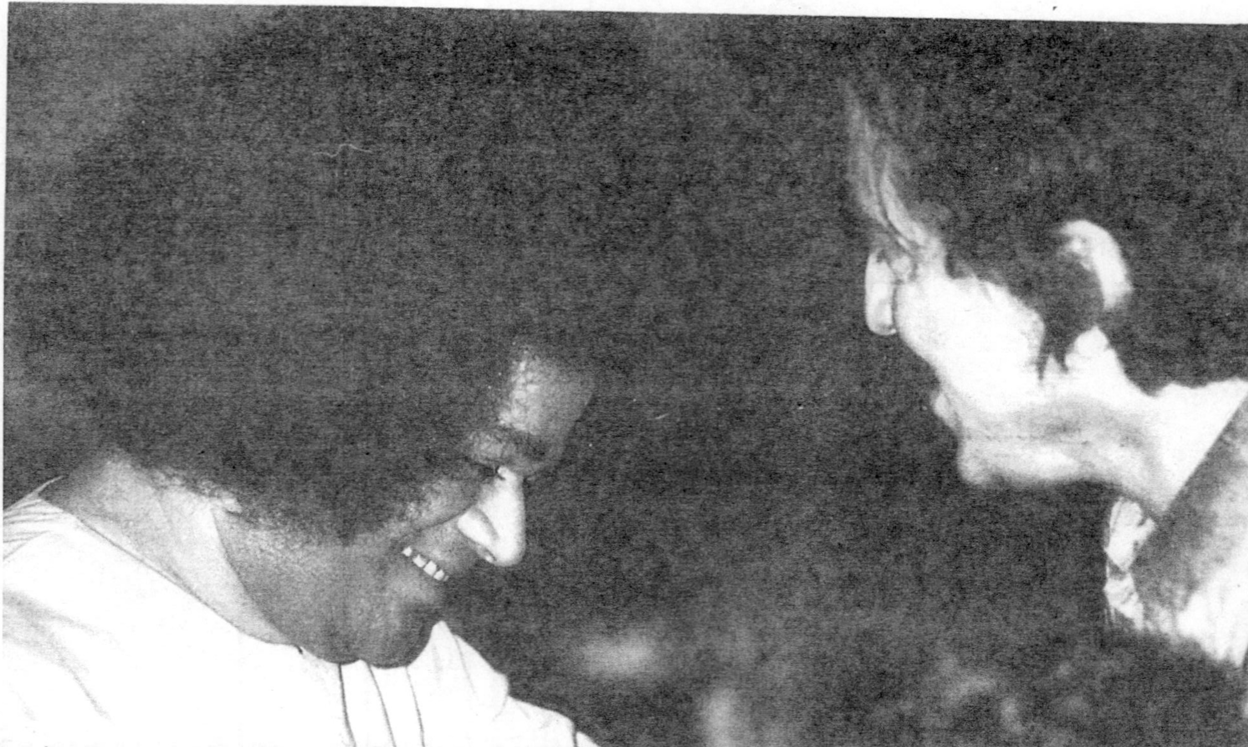

service is better than months of mere meditation. Indeed, *manava seva is Madhava seva.**

"The river flows permanently, but its waters are for the benefit of others. The tree bears fruits, but only for others. The cow gives milk only for the calf and others. Thus, the river, the tree and the cow all silently teach the lesson of how to live for others or how to serve the God embodied in others," says Sri Baba.

"When a person serves society sincerely and is no longer self-centred, the ego in him vanishes... And *exit* of the *ego* from a person's heart makes room for God to *enter* it," explains Sri Baba and stresses that "practical help or service to others should always be rendered to the best of one's abilities and without expectation of any reward, either immediately or in the future."

An example of how humanitarian service should be rendered was provided by volunteers of the Sri Sathya Sai Seva Dal unit when they promptly rushed to the aid of victims of a cyclone** and tidal wave that played

---

* *Service to man is service to the Lord.* The same idea is conveyed by the lines:

"Yo mām sarveṣu bhūteṣu santam ātmānam īśvaram
Hitavarjam bhajate māndyād bhasmanyeva juhoti saḥ.

This means, that whosoever worships God without caring for suffering humanity wastes his effort.

** *See Footnote on next page.*

havoc in the coastal areas of Andhra Pradesh (South India) during November 1977.**

When the first news of the cyclone disaster reached Prasanthi Nilayam, at Puttaparthi (in Andhra Pradesh), the All-India conference of the Sathya Sai Organisations was in progress. On that occasion, Sri Sathya Sai Baba suggested to his devotees to do their best for the amelioration of the suffering of those affected by the cyclone, and his call had a spontaneous and massive response.

A relief fund was started, with one lakh of rupees contributed by Sri Sathya Sai Baba, from his Central Trust, and within hours, donations poured in from devotees. Eleven lakhs of rupees were collected within a day, proving that money and resources will always be contributed, if only people have faith in an organisation and its ability to deliver the goods in the right manner.

Besides being the main reckoning force in collecting funds, Sri Sathya Sai Baba rushed a team of 200 men and 100 lady volun-

---

* Cyclones are also known as hurricanes in some parts of the world. A cyclone is a vast, violent whirl of air and the turbulent sea provides it with a continuous source of moisture.

** The cyclone broke loose like Hell one November night and a gale speeding at over 150 kilometres per hour coupled with tidal waves left a trail of death and destruction unprecedented in the living memory of the Andhra Pradesh State.

teers from the Sri Sathya Sai Seva Dal unit with the main guidelines of "service with love" and *sadviniyogam* or the proper reaching out of help.

The team, which was one of the first organisations to go to the area, found the area ravaged by the cyclone and tidal waves a scene of utter desolation. All trees had been uprooted; electric and telegraph poles had got twisted like straw ropes dragging down kilometres of high tension wire; huge trees had fallen across roads; telecommunications had broken down; mounds of rubble, blown-away huts and heaps of corpses littered the general landscape. Fields of harvest had all been thrashed flat; wells and tanks had been muddied with salt and silt from the sea; thousands of head of cattle and other livestock besides people had been washed away. The survivors were so numbed by what had happened that they were in a daze.

It was with effort that the Sathya Sai Seva Dal volunteers recovered from the initial shock, and organised relief work for the stranded, starving and thirsty people left behind in the wake of the calamity. They established 5 main centres in Barrenkula and Kottamajeru of Krishna District, as well as Gundupalam, Aduvaladevi and Garapavaram in the Guntur District, to cover 65 villages and hamlets. They chose areas near the sea, as other service organisations did not work in those remote locations. Places chosen in the Krishna District bore marks of the havoc caused by tidal waves, while the areas in the Guntur District gave evidence of damage through cyclones. Thick with dead bodies of human beings and cattle, several areas looked macabre and heart-rending!

The Satya Sai Seva Dal volunteers began the relief operations with the odious job of removal and disposal of the stinking bodies and carcasses strewn all over, in addition to spreading disinfectants, to clear the stench that filled the air. Enthused by their example, the initially reluctant villagers also joined them in this job.

Jeeps and other vehicles could not be used due to absence of level ground and roads. So they went about on foot and did their work round the clock. On-the-spot study revealed that mere donation of utensils or foodgrains was of little avail since people lacked even the physical or mental stamina to do any work. They were so utterly dejected and hopelessly forlorn in their outlook. They seemed to have lost even the will to live!... So dazed were they, with the immensity of the tragedy they had witnessed: their loved ones killed or washed away, their homes reduced to nothing, their crops ruined and their fields turned into watery graves!

"Has all this really happened before our eyes or is it an illusion? Oh God! Let it only be a nightmarish dream and not a reality!" they wailed again and again.

The Sathya Sai Seva Dal volunteers had to use iron-control and will power not to break down themselves, face-to-face with such acute agony, suffering and despair! Inspiration from Sri Sathya Sai Baba helped the volunteers to do their utmost for the people and alleviate suffering. "Hearing or reading about such natural calamities is abstract... Being an eye-witness of human suffering or spending days in the midst of large-scale tragedy gives a totally different dimension of the brutality of an immense calamity," said Mr. Ramana Rao, leader of the Sri Sathya Sai Seva Dal volunteers.

The volunteers organised community kitchens initially for feeding 8000 persons, but soon the figure rose to 14,000 persons daily—a monumental task indeed for the volunteers who were later amazed how they had ever been able to accomplish the job. They did it only because of the spiritual orientation that *God* is worshipped when *suffering humanity* is served - a concept dinned into their minds by Sri Baba.

In Barrankula village, the Seva Dal volunteers reconstructed 58 huts providing both materials and manual labour. A team of 16 doctors - all Sai devotees, went most willingly and provided medical aid to the people. They worked unsparingly from dawn to dusk and looked after the health of over 20,000 persons by launching immunization measures. A Sathya Sai medical camp was set up at each centre.

At the outset, new clothes (3000 *saris* and 3000 *dhotis*), 650 blankets and 2200 children's garments were distributed. The children's garments were made by the students of the Sri Sathya Sai College for Women in Anantapur. Gradually, the Sathya Sai Seva Dal volunteers visited the temporarily sheltered people and presented 2500 sets of cooking vessels, plates, *tumblers** and water containers, to enable the families to cook food, once they were able to get the provisions.

In one village, the Seva Dal volunteers worked round the clock to desilt a well and chlorinate it and make the water safe for use. They kept the supply of drinking water going regularly through several improvisations, till the Army arrived with mechanical equipment.

The Seva Dal volunteers besides silently attending to the relief work continuously, also visited homes of villagers to assess their

---

*tumblers=glasses.

needs and gather opinions, when they heard echoes of the thought: "Our faith in God has been restored."

In addition to material relief, the volunteers provided spiritual succour to the dazed survivors, through organisation of group *bhajans*. The devotional *bhajans* (songs surcharged with devotion and addressed to God) proved most effective in changing the atmosphere of eeriness and gloom into one of elan and hope.

Natural calamities and cycles of misfortune are a part of life. Nevertheless, such events pose a test for man's humanity and help to underline his obligation to fellow human beings in distress. It is on such occasions that the light of human love should shine forth through service to lead those in trouble from darkness to light. This indeed is the *Sai philosophy* of *social service with love*.

But then how many people are in a position to help others? Indeed one must have something with oneself, before one can share it with others. Many are neither educated and wealthy nor in positions of authority to be of help.

Sri Baba says no one is really handicapped in this respect. One may lack material power or money, but no one lacks the quality of love. Love is ever present in everyone's heart and must be allowed to flow out constantly.

The easiest method of making this love come out is by loving God who has created this universe. And any person who really loves God will automatically love all God's creation. So, he will do social service as an offering to God.

Sometimes it has been asked why Sri Sathya Sai Baba does not stop or control natural calamities like floods and cyclones instead of asking his workers to rush to the succour of the affected victims, since "he is considered an *avatar* come to save humanity."

Sri Baba's reply is that this would go against the *karmic* law of cause and effect and also negate the working of laws. Even if something is stopped or repressed in one place the effect of that repression will be seen as an eruption somewhere else. "Once people are able to transcend the cycle of cause and effect they will automatically be able to command and control nature," is his firm affirmation. In the meantime people can be made to forget the worst pains of the worst disasters by basking in the radiant love of fellow human beings.

"*Paropakara* is the term used for *seva* (or service) in vernacular languages. *Para* is commonly considered to mean *others*. Actually *para* means something much higher. We refer to our gross body as *dehatma* and call the life principle in us *jeevatma*. But the real entity of the self in us (the *atma* in us) we refer to as *Paramatma*. *Para* in this context connotes the *divine reality* or the God dwelling within. Thus *paropakara* truly means not just service to fellow beings, but service unto *Paramatma* or God Himself," explains Sri Baba.

> *"You, who are lower than even a worm, how dare you speak of showing pity to creatures?... No, no it is not pity to creatures that is to be shown but service to them in the consciousness that they are verily God Himself...."*
>
> *—Sri Ramakrishna Paramahamsa.*

WHY SPIRITUALITY?

"Spirituality cannot wait : now is the right time."

—*SRI SATHYA SAI BABA*

What is spirituality? Spirituality is the quality of being spiritual. The term spiritual refers to the *spirit* or the *soul (atma)* in contrast to the elemental body, or *matter*. People sometimes get the doubt: *Why should I be spiritual, when I am quite all right as I am?* For those who can afford and enjoy all worldly pleasures, such comforts become an end in themselves. They continuously spend time and burn all their energy, pursuing pleasures with the sensory organs. They identify themselves totally with their body, mind and intellect, and remain unaware of the immortal entity of the soul resident within their body. It is this ignorance that makes them conscious of only the body all the time and lead a fu l r material life.

The relentless pursuit of more and more money, fame, position, power and pleasures is with a view to enjoying happiness. Yet full happiness often eludes the grasp of people.

Very successful businessmen and film stars get tired of life and even commit suicide! Top-notch industrialists and millionaires suffer from chronic restlessness and the best of intellectuals feel downright miserable, on several occasions. Executives and men in power suffer from both tension and hypertension, due to a surfeit of problems and worries. In this manner, from time to time, people find themselves at the end of their worldly tether. It is when they experience such emptiness in the heart that they begin to wonder about the real significance of human life on planet earth. At that stage, self-enquiry provides relief, particularly as the approach is scientific. Self-enquiry begins with the question WHO AM I?* One may answer the question by giving the name of one's body. Sri Sathya Sai Baba narrated the story of a boy in a town who got the news that his father in the village was very unwell. So the boy rush-

---

* Bhagavan Ramana Maharishi of Tiruvannamalai, S. India, stressed the need for people to always ask themselves the question : "Who am I". The quintessence of the life and message of Sri Ramana is for such a constant and searching enquiry into oneself, as a step towards the realization of *Brahman* or God. An interesting incident at the Ashram of Sri Ramana illustrates this. A short and frail devotee called Dikshitar, never spoke much to others and was full of humility. Another devotee, well built and tall, once got so very angry with Dikshitar that he raised himself to his full height and shouted "Don't you know who I am?" Dikshitar replied so meekly "That is the very purpose for which all of us are here at the Ashram."

ed to the Railway station, bought a ticket and got into the train. As soon as he reached his village, his relatives announced that his father had died.

He dashed home and wailed, "Oh! dear father! Why have you left me?" Finding the boy in great agony and grief, a saint who happened to be there, pointed to the dead body and asked "Who is this?"

"That is my father!" said the sobbing lad.

Thereupon the saint asked, "Then why do you say your father has left you?... If you say that the body there is your father then your father has not left you!... He is still there!..." Puzzled, the boy exclaimed: "Yes! That is true!"

Thus, if one is only the human body, the body remains even after one's death. So, one is certainly not the body!

Again, one may think that one is the mind and intellect. In answer to the question *who am I?* one may say, I am a writer or an architect or an engineer... However, some introspection will show that one existed even before one became a writer, an engineer or an architect! So one is certainly not the mind or intellect!

"*I* is often confused with *my*", says Sri Sathya Sai Baba. "For when I say: This is *my* book or *my* car, it means that the book or car belongs to me and that *I* am not the book or the car. Similarly when I say this is *my* body, it means the body belongs to me and that *I* am not the body."

The great adventure of the journey into the world of the spirit begins with the realization that man is not the body, not the mind and not the intellect. Man then tries to master the body and the senses and to gradually understand the differences between the joys of worldly life and the happiness of the spiritual path.

JOY OF WORLDLY LIFE : THE PATH OF *PREYA* (Pleasant material life)	HAPPINESS OF SPIRITUAL LIFE : THE PATH OF *SREYA* (Good life of the spirit)
1. Worldly pleasures (caused by name, fame, wealth and sense enjoyments) are connected with the external or *seen* world and external objects.	1. Spiritual joy is connected with the *unseen* world within man, or the world of the spirit.
2. Promotes consciousness of the body and makes one forget the real self.	2. Removes body consciousness and makes one aware of the real self.
3. Gives superficial satisfaction and is temporary.	3. Gives inner satisfaction and is permanent.

4. Weakens the body, tires it out and causes harm.	4. Strengthens the body, never tires and never harms.
5. Palls after a while; comes in fits and starts and so the joy is discontinuous.	5. Never palls and has no end. So the happiness is continuous.
6. Promotes selfishness and greed.	6. Promotes selflessness and sacrifice *(tyaga).*
7. Makes one unhappy even when all necessities are more than met.	7. Makes one happy even with the barest of necessities, in tune with Sri Sathya Sai Baba's interpretation of the statement *"Less luggage more comfort, makes travel a pleasure."* (The *luggage* refers to *desires* and *travel* to *life's journey).*
8. Increases the desire for things leading to worry and want of contentment. According to Sri Sathya Sai Baba, "The poorest man is one who has many desires."	8. Cuts out desire and leads to contentment. As Sri Sathya Sai Baba says, "The richest man is one who has no desires."
9. Often followed by bad reactions. Sri Sathya Sai Baba says, *"Pleasure is an interval between two pains."*	9. No after effects of any kind, and leads to perennial happiness.

10.	Does not give peace of mind (but only pieces!)	10.	Gives peace of mind, "the peace that passeth all understanding."

The best life is the life which blends spirituality with daily living. Man who is always trying to satisfy his cravings and desires with his senses lives close to the animal level in the world and follows the path of *preya* (pleasant worldly life of sensory stimulation). When man rises above *preya* and follows the path of *sreya* (good, divine life) he progresses to his real higher self.

I once asked Sri Sathya Sai Baba, "When should one begin a spiritual life?"

Sri Baba answered, "Young age is the best time to start, for the body is full of vitality and strength and the mind is fresh and full of vigour. It is at this stage that spiritual truths have to be implanted for best results. Unfortunately the common tendency is to generally advocate spirituality for people after retirement, after they become too old. At that age when the body is old and weak, how can he think of God in all earnestness and with the freshness characteristic of youth?"

Spirituality starts with *mind* over *matter*. But not many bother to find out even the meaning of the words mind and matter. People ask the question, "What is mind"? and philosophers in pure jest reply "Does it *matter?*". Scientists ask, "*What is matter?*" and get back the answer: "Never *mind*". The mind is nothing but a *bundle of thoughts* and *desires* while *matter* is what the human body is made of. Control of the mind is essential to ensure triumph of the spirit over the body and get peace of mind.*

"It is unfortunate," says Sri Sathya Sai Baba, "that the mind of man is filled with knowledge about everything else *except* the knowledge about his own mind... That is the main reason why man's mind often functions like a mad monkey.!"

Man should be careful with his thoughts since thoughts have great power. When man thinks, it is in the form of mental pictures and he develops habits based on the pictures he continues to have in his mind. To play about with all types of thoughts is to play with fire; for the actions of man are influenced by thoughts that are stored as images in his mind.

---

* Scientific research, referred to as bio-feed-back, is based on study of both mind and matter, with the help of electronic gadgets that amplify and measure the minutest of physiological changes. Bio-feed-back has confirmed the control of the body, or matter, by the mind—a fact demonstrated by saints thousands of years ago.

That is why man really becomes what he thinks.

According to Sri Baba, spirituality has to permeate all fields of human endeavour. It is easy for one by reading books and listening to spiritual leaders to get good thoughts and some idea of the spiritual path. However, this would be of little avail if one does not try seriously to practise spirituality in daily life. *Everybody seeks happiness, but few realise that the way to get permanent happiness is through practice of spirituality.* The kingdom of God is within man and it is up to him to discover it for his own happiness. As Jesus Christ said, "The Kingdom of Heaven is within you and whosoever knoweth himself shall find it."

For those who ask for tips to practise spirituality in daily life, Sri Sathya Sai Baba says, "Do your duty in a humble and selfless manner, without any jealousy, ego and hatred... Spirituality is nothing more than living with a pure mind and a pure heart and doing all work as an offering to God. When people live their lives in this manner, every activity becomes natural, spontaneous and devoted, leading to fulfilment... So, *do good, see good* and *be good*, for that is the way to God."

"Some talk of *socialism* and other *isms* as a panacea for all the problems of mankind.

While doing so, they lose sight of the basic fact that every crisis brews first in the minds and hearts of people. Man's inhumanity to man stems from selfishness, cunning, greed, anger, hatred and desires for which the only cure is the medicine of spirituality, with its democratic prescription : "All men are equal, because divinity of the *Atma* (or soul) resides equally in all."

Sri Baba says, "God is in everyone and people should try to have a vision of this divinity." Once a person sees God in the other man, he will not cheat him, as it would amount to cheating God, he will not fight with him as that would mean fighting with God; he will not be cruel to anybody as that would mean being cruel to God. As man begins to think of the divinity in every *jiva* (living being) the connection between man and man becomes *atmic* or soul-linked and universal brotherhood becomes a reality.

Such *soul-ism* is the benign teaching of Sri Sathya Sai Baba, according to whom, "only the knowledge of the self (or the soul) will help mankind to lead a happy, peaceful life and build a new world order by cleansing it of all its impurities."

THE ROLE AND GOAL OF RELIGION

"Character is three-fourths religion. So, a truly religious person is a person of character."

—SRI SATHYA SAI BABA

Many wrong conceptions prevail about religion; a great deal is written and said against religion, much of which is designed to traduce it and challenge its authenticity. It is therefore very important for everyone to understand the truth about religion objectively.* To do so, one should not be cynical like the college student who prayed: "Oh God !, if there is a God !, save my soul, if there is a soul !"

The literal meaning of the Làtin word *religion* is to *unite again with God; re* meaning *back* or *again* and *ligio* (derived from *ligare)* meaning *to unite* or *to bind.* Religion has been defined in various ways by different people. Religion is essentially a means of making man search for the soul or the God within

* According to C. Rajagopalachari, "It is not merely wrong to display the detective police mentality when studying a religion... It incapacitates one even to understand it."

him. It is the science of the inner nature or the latent divinity in man. All religions have the goal of self realization. To achieve this, each religion prescribes its own formula for the worship of God. Religion is the means to an end and all the different rituals and modes of worship are aimed at realising the divine consciousness in man. As Swami Vivekananda said, "the book from which to learn religion is your own heart".

Much harm has been done to the cause of religion by some who lash out at atheists, rationalists and those who malign God men. Fortunately; only some misguided persons indulge in such a pointless exercise; for innate in the religious attitude is tolerance and no really religious person will deny the right to atheists and others to continue in their own beliefs. Hinduism,* the age-old religion of India, is a vedic religion, and the *vedas* (derived from *vid*, to know) clearly state that as the world is very wide, each person is free to pursue his own path, without causing any conflict amongst God's creations. If some do not want to believe in religion or God, they should be left alone. For nothing is gained by

* "The Hindu religion has divine roots which gave it the inherent strength to withstand several onslaughts on it in the past," says Sri Sathya Sai Baba, and adds, "The term *Hin* means *to cause harm* and *du* means *dooram* or *distant*. So the Hindu religion means that which makes harm distant."

bruising any individual's rationalistic or atheistic leanings.

Yet another reason for the unpopularity of religion is the undue emphasis given to orthodoxy and ritualism. The truly religious texts always strip religion of dogmas and unnecessary rituals. For example, the *Bhagavatam (Skanda* III, *Chapter* XXIX - *Sloka* 21-22) commenting on the ritual of image worship declares :

> "I, the soul of all being, am always present in all beings. Ignoring me, who am there, this mortal man performs the mockery of image worship."

With the birth of modern science, there has been decline in religious faith, since people are unable to see God with their eyes and scientists do not have any proof of God in laboratories. But then, while the scientist may say that religion has been unable to prove the existence of God in a test tube, how about the inability of science to prove the non-existence of God, in a scientific manner? In a discourse at Puttaparthi, Sri Sathya Sai Baba stressed in the lighter vein the need for giving at least the benefit of the doubt to God! He said that analysis of the atheistic statement: GOD IS NOWHERE affirms God's existence by first saying **GOD IS**, before adding the words NOWHERE! Also, the same statement through a little juxtaposition will read GOD IS NOW HERE!†

Sri Baba told the story of a person who accused another of wasting ten minutes every day by praying to God, in view of the lack of proof about God's existence. The other person retaliated stating that in the event of proof later becoming available about the existence of God, he would not have wasted at least ten minutes every day, whereas the other person would have wasted all his life without remembering God!*

It has been sometimes said by critics that different religions are promoted only because these offer a good means of livelihood to many people. It has also been said that the absence of God-fearing people would constitute a threat to the profession of priests and for this reason, faith in religion is promoted by different religious organizations.

Nothing can be farther from the truth. One could put forth the counter argument that any activity for human good will always

---

† Sri Sathya Sai Baba explained the same idea on another occasion by saying, "GOD is NOWHERE, if you are not prepared to see, but otherwise GOD is NOW HERE!"

* Bertrand Russell, though an agnostic, admitted that in spite of whether there is a God or not, belief in God and religious practices have done much good to the people of the world.

provide sustenance to a few. The profession of doctors is an example and if efforts are made to strengthen faith in medicines and cure diseases, one cannot argue that this is being done only to ensure a living for doctors! On such considerations, doctors should never cure patients!

A leading magazine commenting on a talk at a world religious conference wrote that if faith in religion and belief in God existed mainly in villages, why were people in villages exposed to poverty and hunger? Is it that the more one believes in God, the more poor and hungry one becomes? Here too one could raise several counter arguments, and ask for instance, why urban people who have faith in medicines and doctors should suffer from diseases like high blood pressure, diabetes and cancer? Why should their faith in medicines and doctors be so cruelly rewarded with diseases like cancer? The way people run down religion saying that God-fearing and pious people only serve to patronise priests is like saying that those who observe health norms and take medicines and vitamins do so only to patronise doctors! Even as those who suffer from disease develop faith in medicine and doctors for a cure, those who suffer from a surfeit of sorrows cling with faith to religion and the divine physician or God.

Some critics say that man has made God in his own image mainly due to frustration and illusion. Creation of such a God may help man, in assuaging ruffled emotions, but this takes away all his initiative in finding out remedies for different maladies of society. As a result, the only cure of application of science for mankind's progress and the introduction of social justice through revolution gets neglected. The well known statement of Marx that religion is the soul of soulless conditions, the heart of a heartless world, the opium of the people adds grist to the mill of such thinking. It is argued that people are made to continue in a state of poverty and ignorance through religion and statements of the type "Blessed are the poor, for, theirs is the Kingdom of Heaven".

These arguments are fallacious in the extreme. For no religion ever advocates resignation to fate and leaving things to chance. Emphasising the need of religion for man, Sri Sathya Sai Baba says that people should use their brains and their hands to do their chosen jobs of work, to the best of their abilities, without bothering about the results or rewards, which should be left to God. Faith should go hand in hand with hard work and man must have his hands in society and head in the forest. He must use all his faculties and do his work in utter humility, mainly as an offering to God. Then work will truly get transformed into worship.

Some critics argue that a religious attitude will make people neglect the starvation and suffering of human beings. This too is wholly untenable, since no religion ever teaches the neglect of fellow human beings. Every religion prescribes its own steps for the realisation of God and for service to society.

In the west, religion has become a subject for academic study, since it has been found to be a positive approach in guiding people to righteousness or *dharma*, which alone can guarantee real progress of nations and the world. *Yoga* or union with God, as described in the *Bhagavad Gita* is propounded by all religions and is generally understood to mean *proficiency* and *perfection in action* (*yogaḥ Karmasu kauśalam*).

A concept of secularism, as enshrined in the Indian constitution, is some times invoked to argue that no President, Prime Minister, or Minister, or for matter, citizens of the country, should associate themselves with Gods and Godmen, and that Government should not promote religious matters. There can be no worse interpretation of the concept of secularism, which does not mean irreligion or *no* religion but connotes rather respect for *all* religions. India being wedded to a concept of secularism has the unique advantage of promoting all religions and/or the religion of one's own choice. The main point about secularism is that religion remains personal.

There is an increasing tendency on the part of self-styled reformers to malign religion in general and Godmen in particular and talk against cults being built around religious leaders. Little do such persons realize that in this way they set in motion another cult that could be described as the anti-religious or anti-Godmen cult. Undoubtedly, personal or class interests might have sullied the case for religion occasionally, but then, which is the field that is totally devoid of charlatans and perverts? At best,an exception which proves the rule should be disregarded in investigations of truth.

It would be wrong to either ignore or neglect religion on any superficial score and on the ground of guarding secularism. If world integration is to be no empty phrase, no one should try to arouse animosity or decry any religion. Religious intolerance is the result of ignorance, hatred and petty jealousies; also, religious dogmas that go against society should be eschewed as they do not represent the true spirit of religion.

There is no question of indigenous or alien religions, since all religions have the same goal. "If the mind of man is good, what can be wrong with any religion?" asks Sri Sathya Sai Baba. According to him, "All religions demand that their followers be good, see good and do good. No religion approves of untruth and injustice... Thus, in essence, they are all one and have a common goal while in details they may differ and follow different paths to reach the common goal. God is one and only one, without any equal but worshipped by different people in diverse forms and different names. *(Ekam sad viprāḥ bahudhā vadanti* : God is one but is called by many names). Form and name are transient and change with time. The unchanging truth, beauty and love, continue to hold the devotion of followers of all religions.

In India, several religions have co-existed for centuries and it is ever gratifying to see in the same milieu a Church, a Mosque, a Gurudwara and a Hindu temple, since such a situation provides living testimony to the co-existence of all faiths and of the right of people to practise the faith of their choice. Mahatma Gandhi gave the correct secular definition of religion when he said that the essense of religion is morality. Jesus Christ too recognised no religion outside good conduct.

Sri Sathya Sai Baba says there is only one religion and that is the religion of love.

Religious leaders state the truths without demanding acceptance or obedience, leaving it to people to come to their own conclusions because of their conviction that Truth is greater than authority. Viewed from this angle, one can be in full agreement with Mahatma Gandhi's approach: "I reject any religious doctrine that does not appeal to reason and is in conflict with morality... I exercise my judgement about every scripture including the Bhagawad Gita. I cannot let scriptural text supersede my reason." Thus, correct appreciation of the true meaning and role of religion alone will enable religion, and the spirituality informing it, to permeate the daily life of people.

Right conduct and conscientious performance of duties are more important than prayers, because such is the essence of the offering of prayers to God. Seeing God's image in a temple or Church is less important than having the vision of God in all God's creations. A spirit of reverence is essential to understand any religion. It is totally wrong to start with suspicion and think that saints and religious leaders are not genuine but only interested in self or sect-advancement and that people in general are deceived to shower reverence on them! Religion is not something which people can be forced to accept.

Sri Sathya Sai Baba stresses that "the seeds of all religions are in the *Sanatana Dharma* (Eternal Truth) of vedanta* (religious philosophy)". "Any misunderstanding between religions is but a very small family affair", says Sri Baba and adds. "The Vedic *Dharma* is the great grand father, *Buddhism* is the son, *Christianity* is the grandson and *Islam* is the great grandson." Study of the teachings of some religions like Islam will prove this. The term *Islam* means *surrender to God* and Prophet Mohammed's teachings are for all and not for Muslims alone. The Holy Koran emphasises how God is the benefactor of all humanity; it stresses that belonging to a creed is less important than living a good life and performing good deeds. Prophet Mohammed spread Islam by practising the tenets he preached. Without imposing his teachings on others, he set a good example of tolerance and respect in dealings with non-Muslims. Again, the simple religion of the Jews, Judaism, stresses tht supremacy of the moral life and the importance of right conduct over right belief. Guru Nanak, the founder of the Sikh religion ,preached the existence of

---

* *anta* means *end* and the Upanishads are referred to as *vedanta*, since they occur at the end of the Vedas.

one God, and Lao-tse, the founder of Taoism propounded the return of good for evil. Thus, the same truths have been expressed in a variety of ways, in different languages, under different circumstances, by founders of different faiths and a fundamental unity lies behind the apparent diversity of terms and names like Allah, Jesus, Vishnu, etc. So there is no point in conversions from one religion to another.

The Sai insignia is a symbol of the importance and equality of all religions. It stresses the universality of the approach of Sri Sathya Sai Baba which is aimed at making Hindus better Hindus, Muslims better Muslims, Parsees better Parsees, Christians better Christians and so on.

Indeed the RELIGION of Sathya Sai is LOVE OF all RELIGIONS.

The Sai Symbol

"If God did not exist, man would have to invent Him." —*Voltaire.*

ART AND SPIRITUALITY

"All sundaram (beauty) must lead man to ***sathyam*** *(truth) and all sathyam to shivam or bliss (which is auspiciousness itself)."*

—SRI SATHYA SAI BABA

Art is beauty and beauty is art. There are 64 arts *(kalas)* of which the more prominent ones are painting, dance, architecture, music, poetry and literature. The sheer melody of beautiful music charms people and even tames beasts. The beauty of a flower, the colours of a painting, the rythm of a dance, the form of a sculpture, the lyrical charm of a poem, the expressive architecture of a building - all help to elevate the mind of man to heights of joy. Keats echoed this thought when he said, "A thing of beauty is joy for ever."

How is art related to spirituality? The answer can be found in Leonardo da Vinci's statement that the art of painting "is related to God Himself", since "Painting is the grand-daughter of Nature." Traditionally, several of the fine arts like classical music and *Bharata-natyam* (classical dance)have been associated with temple worship to emphasise the holy connection between art and divinity. The Hindu Goddess of learning, Saraswathi, is depicted as holding a *veena* in her hands to symbolise again the link between music and God. "Beauty, you are my way to the divine", said the Mother of the Aurobindo Ashram in Pondicherry. Pursuit of the beautiful should indeed become the daily prayers of mankind; for, as Sri Sathya Sai Baba says, "God is Beauty and Beauty is God."

The power of music, as a prayer, has been experienced by artists. I recollect an experience narrated to me years ago, by Mr. Chowdiah a famed violinist. He referred to a happening during a train journey from Madras to Delhi. The journey had been undertaken during summer and in spite of fans whirling inside the compartment, they all found the heat unbearable.

One of the persons jocularly suggested to Mr. Chowdiah that he should try to make the rains fall, by playing on the violin. Mr. Chowdiah said he would indeed send a prayer to the Rain God, through an appropriate *raga* on his violin. One of them pulled down the shutters in the compartment and Mr. Chowdiah started playing. The train raced along and as the tempo of the music rose, everyone forgot the heat. More than an hour elapsed when one of them shouted all of a sudden in excitement: "Look! the rains have started falling!" Mr. Chowdiah* was so lost in the music that they had to physically shake him for a few minutes, before he could be made to realise that the rains had come down in response to the soulful appeal of the music.

Although Mr. Chowdiah is no more, I still remember his conviction about how art can reflect the music of the soul. He had experimented on notes that had soothing power on patients in hospitals. Scientists today are studying the effects of music on the growth of plants, the healing of diseases and a myriad other things. Such scientific studies have shown that processes like the beating of the heart, breathing in and breathing out of air and several other movements (all of which together constitute the *biological clock* of the human body) are influenced by music. It has also been shown that differences in the biological clock of the young and old are responsible for differences in their musical tastes.

Though science has a long way to go before it can prove the spiritual strength of

---

* I have also heard that Mr. Chowdiah once gave a recital before Sri Sathya Sai Baba. At the end of it, Sri Sai Baba materialised a medal. As those around were looking at the medal, Sri Baba asked for it, saying that he had forgotten to inscribe something on it. He held it in his hand for just a few seconds and when he gave it back, people read on it the inscription: Presented to Vidwan T. Chowdiah by Bhagavan Sri Sathya Sai Baba.

great art and the miraculous power of devotional songs, scientists have always been inspired by art and beauty. Prof. G. H. Hardy, in his book "A Mathematician's Apology", observes how "a mathematician like a painter or a poet, is a maker of patterns. The mathematician's patterns, like the painter's or the poet's must be beautiful; the ideas like the colours or the words must fit together in a harmonious way."

Throughout their careers, many famous scientists have been engaged in the quest for beauty. To Albert Einstein, music was a lifelong passion and the direct expression of the cosmic harmony which exists in nature and the universe, which was his idea of God. More specifically, music to him was "a method of allowing the sub-conscious to solve particularly tricky problems."

There is a school of thought which holds that art should be pursued only for art's sake. But then, would not the pursuit of art as an end in itself make one blind to its main purpose? Is the purpose of art only to entertain? Mere entertainment tends to pall after a while and produce a vacuity in hearts. The real purpose of art is to bring out the best in man which is the divine principle. To realise this, artists have to be essentially humble and pure at heart. They have to pursue art in the same dedicated manner in which saints pray to God. Only then will their works of beauty reflect the splendour of divinity and have the power to kindle the spirit of those who see their artistic creations.

It is often said that Art is *self-expression.* To really understand this, one should analyse what is this self that expresses itself. Is it erudition, worldly knowledge, intellect, power or position? Or is it the mere external vision of earthly grandeur?

Sri Sathya Sai Baba often says : "You are not one, but three...

The one you think you are,
The one others think you are, and,
The one you really are..."

The one you really are is your *self*. By *self* is meant the soul *(dehi)* inside the body *(deha)*. Thus, Art should become the expression of the inner *self* or spirit - a fact further emphasised by Sri Sathya Sai Baba when he states : "Art must come from the heart." Real art is that art which brings out the *Atma tattwa* or the essence, nay the music of the soul.

The aspirations of artists will get fulfilment only when they are true to their own selves. Artists may take a long time to know what the true *self* is, but they will unconsciously realize it, when they take up art to please God *(Bhagavath preetiarthum).* As true art is a manifestation of the divine, artists should consecrate their talents to God. Then, they will realise the God within them and be in tune with "the one you really are."

Artists of the dim and distant past reached the greatest climax of self-expression when they drew and painted figures of different Gods and Goddesses. They used colour and light evocatively to bring out the glow of the spirit and the forms they drew were the result of their perception, after intense meditation, or the visions they had of forms of the divine. We owe to a Ravi Varma the figures of several Indian Gods and Goddesses and to many great artists the portraits of several *avatars.* Only artists with intense devotion to God took up such hallowed work. They prayed as they worked, that the forms created be suffused with the divine spirit.

Dr. Svetoslav Roerich* touched on this aspect, when I told him that I was doing a collage painting† of Sri Sathya Sai Baba. "You have to do his full figure and the most important thing is to portray the soul - to bring out all that soul in his face and form,

---

* Internationally renowned artist.

† This painting has been printed on the back cover of this book.

which is the real job in the painting... Only if you do that will it be Sai Bāba, not otherwise!"

Though art is a gift of God, real self-expression is not easy. It may take the entire life span of an artist even to arrive at the threshold of the ultimate truth. The first step is the realization that art provides an excellent means for artists to discover their real identity and see the hidden beauty or truth in all things. As Swami Vivekananda said: "Without a faculty for feeling the beauty and grandeur of art, no man can be truly religious."

The beautiful sights of Nature and the magnificent works of God produce wondrous images in the mind and take it towards perfection, leading to the quest for more and more of beauty in daily life. The quest for the Beautiful leads ultimately to the realization that all things in the world are beautiful and that there is nothing ugly in the universe if one only knows how to look at all things. In this manner, Art can be defined as a way of looking at things to achieve absolute beauty. Plato echoed this thought, when he said, "From beautiful images, we shall go to beautiful thoughts, from beautiful thoughts to a beautiful life and from a beautiful life to absolute Beauty.'

Art should never become a matter of outward imitation. It should not be mere reproduction or reflection of an external form but rather the reverberation of the inner beauty of an object, person or situation, as echoed by the soul of the artist. The great painter Rembrandt alluded to this inner pulsation within the realized artist, when he said that a painting will exhale joy, if he, as the artist, "laughs in his soul while painting."

Artists often wonder why sometimes their creative efforts are exceedingly good and even outstanding, while on some other occasions, the results are just ordinary or even lifeless. The real reason is to be found in the mood and mind of the artists at work. When creative effort is the result of "inner" inspiration, then the artist goes about his job in a state of "intoxication" and complete absorption. He gets lost in his effort and is so much in tune with the job, that he forgets the world outside and is in a state of *yoga* or union with his work. Then hunger and thirst, the passage of time and the world outside do not bother him, in the least. Body consciousness being absent, the artist becomes part of the canvas he paints, the song he sings, the sculpture he sculpts and the poem he composes. In such cases, the artist after the completion of the job cannot believe that the work has been done by him, since the finished products are often what are called masterpieces. The state of such absorption in work experienced by artists is the natural state of great saints, who always do different jobs in a state of *yoga*.

Thus, the concentration in artistic work by inspired artists is a kind of *yoga* or union with the ultimate reality and as a result, all their work become manifestations of the divine.

I heard an interesting story* of the discovery of the *atma tattwa* (soul) through art. In Vijayanagar, there was a king who was a great lover of art. He was fond of music and had in his palace a rare and antique veena which was known as the *asaadhya* (extraordinary or impossible) *veena*, an instrument the sound of which is closest to the human voice. The king was very keen to hear the music of this veena, but whosoever tried to play on it failed. Even great experts, in spite of their knowledge found themselves unable to produce even a single note on the veena.

One day, the king heard that the great anchorite, Priyamvada was passing through Vijayanagar. As Priyamvada was a great veena artist, the king wanted to fulfil his wish.

---

* Recounted by Swami Ishwarananda Giri.

So the king invited Priyamvada to the palace to play on the *asaadhya veena*.

Priyamvada accepted the king's invitation and arrived at the palace. The king welcomed him and ordered that the veena be placed before Priyamvada.

The very sight of the veena thrilled Priyamvada beyond measure. He instinctively knew it was a unique instrument that had come to the palace by long *parampara* (ancestry). No wonder, Priyamvada's hairs stood on end, as he placed the veena on his lap. A thousand truths about the instrument dawned on his mind.

The instrument had been fashioned in Kashmir and Vajra Keerti of Kashmir had spent his whole life carving it, with love and care. It was his dedicated work that had given the veena such majesty of form.

Vajra Keerti had chosen the wood of the great *Kireeta vriksha* tree, for making the unique instrument. The *Kireeta vriksha* was no ordinary tree. It was so huge and gigantic that its branches rested on the clouds of the sky and its roots penetrated the very depths of the earth or the nether world. The king of the serpents, Vasuki, used to rest on some of the roots of the tree and inhale the fragrance of the flowers through the roots. The trunk of the tree was so mighty that the lions of the forest used to scratch their backs against it. The wood of the tree had imbibed the music of ever so many types and kinds of birds that rested on its branches. It had also been seasoned by several winters, autumns, summers and springs and had absorbed ever so many delightful sounds of nature.

The veena maestro-cum-saint had his eyes full. He said softly, "All that I am recalling now is just a part of your majestic form or the make-up of your physical frame, Oh mighty veena !... And if that be so, how great and magnificent must be the divine and resonant resident within ! If only that divinity could be revealed to us !"

"Oh! *Asaadya veena*, I offer my humble prayers to you and request you to reverberate your *naada* (or notes)."

In this manner, Priyamvada's voice caressed, coaxed and cajoled continuously, as he sent prayer after prayer to the very soul of the veena: "Unless you allow the *naada* to come out, unless you decide to grace us with the divine melody enshrined within you, Oh veena ! I cannot play on it... I can be successful only if you yourself burst forth into song!"

Priyamvada's fervent appeal literally touched the heart strings of the veena, for the veena instantly burst into song. Melody, after melody, *raga* after *raga* poured forth from it, as the veena player played on it.

The King and all those assembled were in speechless wonder, as the vibrant music threw them into a state of stupor and unalloyed joy. It was a veritable flood of music, with the floodgates of the closed instrument — silent for centuries — opening out suddenly, to pour forth the quintessence of all the melody in the universe.

The strangest thing was that to each person in the assembly the music reverberated differently. To the King, the veena notes were like the music of the majestic march of his victorious army. To the scholars, it was like the resounding chant of purifying hymns. Some very rich merchants heard in the music, pleasing sounds of the counting of money, the tinkling of coins and the jingling of gold. Some others heard the gentle cooing of birds and the sweet gurgling of the waters of the ocean. In fact, every one in the assembly heard mellifluous music related to situations dear to their own hearts. Indeed it was a state of bliss and *poornathwa* (or completeness) that the *asaadhya veena* had produced; for, it was the universal soul element in it that had pulsated and expressed thousands of decades of latent beauty, sweetness, love and melody, revealing the wondrous majesty of the truly eternal and divine.

The story of the *Asaadya Veena* illustrates the right attitude to music and the fine arts. Art may be used to entertain and make people happy; it could be pursued either as a profession or a pastime, but its main role is to help artists to discover their own *selves* and also help society to join in this discovery. The real influence of the arts should be more than *just physical;* enjoyment of music, painting and dance should be more than just sensuous or sensational. Only then can art make the latent soul in every one patent and demonstrate that the only real link between man and man is the link of the *Atma* or Divinity.

> *"Man is both animal and angel. He has in him the wolf, the monkey, the bullock, the jackal, the snake, the peacock and the bear. He has beneath all these the spark of divinity. It is the role of art to bring out this divinity. All dance, drama and the fine arts should cater to the spiritual urge, foster the spirit and take people nearer the divine goal."*
>
> —*SRI SATHYA SAI BABA*

SCIENCE AND SPIRITUALITY

"Science is like the C that is incomplete, whereas spirituality is like the O that is complete or full."

—SRI SATHYA SAI BABA

The Latin term *scientia* means knowledge and science is a quest for truth, through data obtained by experimentation and analysis. The results of scientific experiments are published as research papers to enable verification of the findings by other scientists. Thus, science believes in observation, reasoning and verifiable results. The world of science being vast, a scientist has perforce to specialise in just a few aspects of one subject. That is why a specialist in a branch of science is said to be a person who knows *more and more* about *less and less* !

The Latin term *spiritus* means breath and spirituality deals with the vital force of the spirit (or the soul). Spirituality is also a quest but the world of the spirit does not deal so much with theory or experiment, as with direct experience. Ancient *rishis* and saints in India reported their direct experience for the benefit of all mankind. The saints of yore also explained how any person following the spiritual discipline can achieve the same type of spiritual experience.

Such experience in the spiritual realm can be described as awareness of the spirit, or experience of the *atman* or soul. In essence, SPIRITUALITY is the SCIENCE OF EXPERIENCE — an experience which can be verified by other spiritual people — also through their personal experience. Experience thus becomes the source and core of spiritual knowledge. Mystics are people who obtain knowledge through such supreme, spiritual experiences.

Mystics belonging to different religions have taught the truth of how to realize the one God. Swami Vivekananda said: "As mathematics in every part of the world does not differ, so the mystics do not differ... Their experience is the same and this becomes law." Thus, the truth of spirituality as stated by a mystic becomes verifiable in the personal experience of a like person. The spirit of enquiry is therefore as much a part of spirituality as of science, though the method of enquiry may differ. So, there is no conflict between science and spirituality.* Since religion is only a

---

* See next page

means to make people spiritual, there is no conflict between science and religion too, as stressed by Einstein when he said: "Science without religion is lame, religion without science is blind."

Sri Sathya Sai Baba and other spiritual leaders do *not* say, "Have nothing to do with science!" They too use the cars, the aeroplanes, the fans, the microphones and various other scientific appliances. While they welcome science as a most important part of worldly knowledge, they also emphasize the limitations of science. To give an example, scientists have found it difficult to study at the same time both the position and momentum of any particle or object.† With all its resounding successes, science is confined solely to the objective universe, where the unknown is ever so much greater than the known. Every time science had added a little to the known, it has also added a great deal more to the unknown. Knowledge has grown but ignorance has grown faster. "Science can

---

* If by training, scientists do not believe that something is a fact unless verified by scientific experiments, spiritualists also do not believe in anything that is not verified by their experience. Ramakrishna and Ramana Maharshi conducted many objective observations in the spiritual field. Thus, as a boy, Ramana Maharshi was a conscious witness of the death of his own body from which he concluded that it is only the body that is subject to the cycle of birth and death.

† This is known as the Heisenberg principle of uncertainty!

only explain *how* things happen and not *why* things happen," says Sri Baba.

I have given Sri Baba's elucidation of the differences between science and spirituality in the form of a Table, from which it will be clear that where science ends, spirituality begins; or rather, where physics stops, metaphysics starts. The main point is that science has never promoted the moral development of human beings, since scientists try to only understand the universe and not the creator of the universe. They forget that God created both the universe and man and that God therefore is the author of all that science endeavours to study.

SCIENCE	SPIRITUALITY
1. Science studies the outer life. It deals with the (visible) material plane or the realm of matter.	1. Spirituality studies the the inner life. It deals with the (invisible) spiritual plane or the realm of the spirit.
2. Science seeks knowledge by a slow and painful process of reasoning from cause to effect.	2. Spirituality knows things direct and is much quicker.
3. Science deals with the relative truth.	3. Spirituality deals with the ultimate Truth.
4. Science is based on experiments and con-	4. Spirituality is based on experience and

fines itself to enquiry that could be understood with the help of the human senses.	deals with that which transcends the senses.
5. Scientists are engrossed with the laws and forces of nature or *Prakriti*.	5. Spirituality deals with self *(Atman)* or *Purusha* — the root cause of all things.
6. Results of scientific work have no finality about them, and so, scientific truths keep changing. For instance, at one time scientists declared that the atom cannot be divided. Much later, they declared that the atom can be divided into protons, electrons and neutrons.	6. Spiritual truths are eternal and never change. Thus, the *Atman* (soul), unlike the atom, can never be split.
7. Science helps in the discovery of the external world.	7. Spirituality helps in the discovery of the self.
8. Science is an intellectual discipline which helps to understand the created material world.	8. Spirituality is a moral discipline leading to a glimpse of the creator.
9. Science gives pleasure, physical comfort and increases human muscle power.	9. Spirituality confers peace of mind and real happiness or bliss. Spirituality always

In this way, while science does good, *it has* also been responsible for harm and destruction.	does good and can never do harm.
10. Science helps man to become a master of material knowledge.	10. Spirituality helps man to become a master of himself (*i.e.* his mind and senses).

Scientists sometimes decry the faith of people in spiritual matters. Faith is trust or belief in something or continuing confidence in something like the faith in God. Faith is caused by the hope that springs eternal in the human breast. Faith is the result of an inner prompting; otherwise, how would one be able to explain one's faith in oneself?

Nevertheless, it has become fashionable for scientists to talk about "blind faith" and "superstition"* on the part of those who accept things that do not yield to scientific

* Superstition means excessive reverence or fear based on ignorance. It is derived from the Latin word 'superstitia' meaning excessive belief in religious opinions. It is therefore wrong to call the spiritual people superstitious, as their reverence and belief are based on their supreme experience. If the origin of superstitions is studied, it will be seen that several of them were based on some reason. Thus, when it was said that one should not marry or start a new job on a Friday, it was because Christ was crucified on a Friday and so it is a day for endings and not for beginnings.
While superstition means being steeped in irrational fear, fearlessness is one of the pre-requisites of spirituality.

rhyme or reason. "Blind faith" is said to be that which placates reason, but is it necessary to qualify the word *faith* with the term *blind?* Faith has no scientific basis and so in its very nature is blind. Even rationalists display such faith in rationalism. And scientists who blindly have faith in science can neither explain scientifically their faith in science nor assess the quality or the quantity of the faith they repose in science !

Faith is connected with one's instincts or *intuition*, and as Sri Sathya Sai Baba says, "Even to accomplish small things in the world *viswaasam* or faith is a must... Thus when a person builds a house, he does so because of the faith that he will not only live to see its completion but also live in it. If faith is required for success even in small things in the illusory world in which we live, it is easy to imagine the deep faith one should repose in God, who has granted man the gift of life. Therefore, it is said, that where *vishwasum* or faith is absent, there can be no *swaashum* or breath !"

Faith cannot be explained by words or concepts. Its quality is such that it is said to move mountains. Without faith, mankind certainly cannot be on the move ! Faith in prayers has promoted worship of God, not only to ask for things, but just to be with God for at least a few precious moments. Daily communion with God through prayers gives inner peace and abundant strength to live a better worldly life of truer values. The Bible refers to three dozen cases of cure, through prayers — cure of conditions like leprosy, blindness, etc. It is said, that when Humayun remained critically ill in spite of all the medication prescribed by reputed hakims, his father Babur prayed to God to cure his son and take away his life instead. Soon Humayun began to get well and Babur fell seriouly ill! This could be dismissed as a case of coincidence, but the coincidence resulted from faith in prayers to God !

Faith is as much an integral part of man's make-up as the human will, which is not listed as one of the organs of the body in Gray's Anatomy — the well-known text book of medical students. Neither faith nor the human will can be dissected, bisected, vivisected and studied. Yet, they are vital assets to human beings. It is therefore said that while the atheist earlier was the one who had no faith in God, the atheist of today is the one who does not have faith in himself.

If through faith in God and prayers, people are able to find solace, cheer, comfort and guidance in personal problems and difficulties; if through faith and prayers, people are enabled to derive courage and make the best of what life has given them, what right have a few ignorant people to dub and decry the faith of many as "blind faith" or "superstition?" More so, when detractors are in no position to provide any other alternative beyond stultifying arguments, for the immensity of inner strength and peace people derive through faith in things that have meaning for them. Instances of achievements that have accrued as a result of the faith of people are innumerable. These can fill volumes and provide thousands of valuable case studies for those who may wish to probe into the reality of faith.

Lord Krishna in the *Bhagavad Gita* says: *Śraddhavān labhate jñānam* which means that a person with faith can gain real knowledge. Lord Krishna also says, *Aśraddhā paramam pāpam* or that lack of faith is the greatest sin. However, faith does not mean something to rest on and everything proceeds on the basis of faith, at least as the starting point. Thus, mathematicians work with an imaginary number called "i" as the square root of minus one.

Science has made impressive strides and taken man to the moon. Scientific advances have also created ever so many material amenities and comforts to the extent of making the common man worship science as a great power. Science has made notable advances in education, agriculture, medicine and other fields but science has also helped in the production of dangerous armaments like the atom bomb. While science has improved the circumstances of man and made human life more comfortable, it has not contributed to the happiness of man nor improved man himself. This is because science has severe limitations like relying on only those facts that one is able to measure or observe. Statements of scientists often give the impression that what is beyond scientific understanding is unreal and does not exist!

Science at its present state of development is incapable of total comprehension of truth which is possible only through spirituality. The numerous materialisations and miracles* of Sri Sathya Sai Baba stress this aspect admirably. An argument has however been advanced by some scientists that creation of "something out of nothing" is impossible, since this defies all known laws of science. The argument stems from non-appreciation of the

* Sri Sathya Sai Baba's miracles comprise: production of gifts by waves of the hand; healing or curing the incurable; multiplying food; being present in more than one place at the same time; granting visions; revival of dead persons; production of Shiva lingas from the stomach; appearance of nectar or holy ash *(vibhuti)* on photographs, etc.

spiritual realities, or the lack of knowledge of higher spiritual truths.

First, it is difficult to define scientifically "something" and "nothing." To give an example, two atoms of Hydrogen and one atom of Oxygen create water. Here Hydrogen and Oxygen may be considered "nothing" because they are not visible to the eye. But this "nothing" becomes "something", or water, when combined! Had this been done over three hundred years ago, it would have been hailed as a miracle but scientists know that this is no miracle!

Again, let us take the example of burning one gramme of camphor. The camphor which is "something" when burnt soon becomes "nothing". What has happened to the "something"? It is easy using Einstein's theory to equate one gramme of camphor to energy units; any chemist can prove by analysis that the energy units of camphor have gone into heat, light and other elemental energies. So, while it is scientific to burn camphor and dissipate it into elemental energy, it is spiritual or divine to combine the elemental energies and create camphor.

Thus, science though in a position to convert matter into energy has the biggest limitation of the inability to re-convert this energy into the original matter. But with metaphysical or spiritual power one can convert energy particles in the atmosphere into any form of the desired matter. This will stress why so called miracles are taken as natural occurrences by great saints who know that mass and energy are equivalent descriptions of the same reality. As Paramahamsa Yogananda observes, "The so called miraculous powers of a great master are a natural accompaniment to his exact understanding of subtle laws that operate in the inner cosmos of consciousness." In the lives of many great seers of India of the past, miracles were so common and such natural occurrences, that these were neither specially noted nor even discussed.

It is preposterous therefore to compare the miracles that flow from a great Master to the performances of mere magicians. The very concept of miracles as magic or sleight of hand is narrow and wrong, because no physical contact is involved in certain kinds of materializations like the appearance of nectar or *vibuthi* from framed photographs.*

---

* In a letter to "The Indian Express", Mr. Surendra Nayak of Manipal wrote, "I have seen with my own eyes the appearance of *vibuthi* (holy ash) of thickness from a micron to a centimetre on the picture of Sri Sathya Sai Baba, Sri Rama and Sri Krishna in private homes in Manipal, Udupi and Barkur situated nearly 300 miles from Puttaparthi. Does this phenomenon explain the principle of the conservation of energy or the law of action at a distance, which one finds in the theory of electrostatics, I am willing to accompany any rationalist to these places of worship."

Alternatively, to dub miracles as supernatural is only to reiterate the limitations of the sensory organs. It should stand to reason that what is *supernatural* for ordinary humans can be quite *natural* for *super* beings.

A bag of tricks is sustenance or a means of making money for a magician. Further, a magician never gives away the rabbits or other objects conjured by his magic, whereas great Masters like Sri Baba continually give away the things they materialise! That the public do not equate a great Master with a magician becomes evident by even a cursory glance at the crowds the Master draws in comparison! For which magician can provide tremendous peace of mind and have such a benign influence on thousands of people? The *siddha purusha* or Master can not only convert energy particles in the ethereal atmosphere into any material form, but can produce immediate results even through a powerful thought or *sankalpa*.

For spiritual Masters, whose twin concerns are goodness and godliness, miracles are only the means to the end of divinising life. Sri Sathya Sai Baba often says, "I give you what you want so that you may want what I want to give." Several thousands of people have developed faith in God after seeing his miracles. And this indeed is the role of miracles.

Nevertheless, the authenticity of saints and Godmen has been challenged occasionally by some, who have taken on themselves the role of conscious saviours of the "gullible" masses from the hypnotic hold of the mystics! While even such a holy field may harbour a few charlatans; quacks and impostors are not uncommon in the scientific field too. Viewed from this light, the tendency to accept all scientific statements that appear in print as gospel truth is unfortunate and needs to be discouraged. When anything is presented with the label of science, no one questions it. For the common people are not aware that sometimes, some scientists can and do make premature claims. The vested interest in announcing a scientific result or break-through is not inconsiderable, since the direct and indirect gains (like awards or honour) of a scientific claim could be computed into millions of rupees, even before it is falsified, through further experimentation !

Sometimes, even the names of scientific experiments are totally wrong; an instance is provided by the misnomer of the "test tube baby". It may be argued that no pronouncement of science is accepted without experimental proof and this acts as a built-in mechanism to correct mistakes. However, several case studies like the one on *Thalidomide* give the lie to this general statement.

Thalidomide was recommended as a tranquilliser for pregnant mothers round the world, after scientific experiments. Yet, its use resulted in the birth of several hundreds of maimed and deformed babies! Only afterwards was it realized that the scientific experiments had not been exhaustive. Although Thalidomide had been tested on experimental rats, it had not been tried on pregnant rats, and this omission had caused the disaster. Cases of scientists cooking up results and rushing to unwarranted conclusions are not uncommon. The eminent food scientist, Dr. V. Subrahmanyan often used to bemoan the fact that one scientist hardly respects another! Sir C. V. Raman once mentioned in his inimitable way about happenings in a few "temples of science" and concluded on the note : "Whether we have made advances in nuclear science or not, the internal jealousies, rivalries and dishonesty of scientists have attained nuclear proportions."

In fact, it is for the control of such human passions that spiritual leaders have been addressing themselves. The tragedy is that while devotees of spiritual leaders have never talked about the phoney "goings-on" in the world of science, some scientists have continuously made loud and irrational attacks on Godmen, creating an impression that all is wrong with the world of the mystics, and that scientists, by implication, are the real saints!

If only scientists would realise that modern discoveries are just unravelling the fringes of ancient insights, the world would be poised for better advancement on all fronts. The truths stated by seers of yore are being grasped by science rather slowly. Elementary facts about the inner consciousness are being appreciated in the scientific world, thanks to recent studies on *Psi* (psychic phenomena) and parapsychology. Newer knowledge of ESP (extra sensory perception) has shown how people can and do communicate through *telepathy* (i.e. through means other than the five senses), how people are able to see hidden objects through *clairvoyance;* how they are able to sense and know in advance about various happenings through *precognition* and how one could move objects without touching them through *psychokinesis.* So, science has just arrived at the turning point, or at the cross roads.

It is unfair therefore on the part of any scientist to brand believers in a particular mystic as gullible and say that even educated people are being trapped and misled. People believe in their gurus to obtain peace of mind and realize God. It is not for any one to bruise the sensibilities and beliefs of such individuals. Attempts to arouse animosity against great spiritual leaders in the name of science amount to needless witch-hunting of those peacefully engaged on a job of uplifting humanity. Even the so-called illiterate majority of the Indian people are by no means gullible and have instinctive and mature understanding of matters relating to the human spirit. It is unfortunate that some westernised scientists and scholars regard themselves as authorities on subjects in which they are the least qualified to express any view! On the other hand, the greatest of scientists like Einstein, Heisenberg and others have accepted the limitations of science and all their investigations into the mysteries of nature have been pursued in a spirit of great humility. They have often expressed a lurking consciousness of something beyond Nature, which transcends and controls it.

It would therefore be incorrect for some scientists to pronounce judgements on things which they are unable to understand or unravel. Present day science has to advance considerably before it can understand the truths of the spiritual world.

As already mentioned, spirituality is based on the scientific concept of the *experience* of truth, *as an experiment*. This was emphasised by Adi Shankara when he said: "If it does not stand to reason, it is no religion and it must be rejected." The real purpose of spirituality is to enable man to conquer jealousy, greed, hatred, anger and other baser instincts and attain excellence in personal and social morality.

Mere progress in science without morality will be disastrous; for the achievements of scientific and technological development will merely turn into a sword of Damocles suspended over the world. If science is to serve society and not become a liability, scientists have to be socially conscious and spiritually aware. For, a doctorate in science cannot make a scientist unselfish or build moral strength in him. This fact should not be treated lightly, since in industrially advanced countries, the armaments industry employs 50 per cent of all scientists and technologists. The Nobel Laureate, Dr. L. Pauling warned that a single 20 megaton bomb exploded over New York can kill ten million people. 500 such bombs (10,000 megatons) will be enough to exterminate the entire population of the U.S.A. ! After the U.S. dropped the atom bomb on Hiroshima on August 6, 1945, the great Einstein is reported to have told the Education Editor of the *New York Times* that had he known beforehand that his theory of relativity would result in the atom bomb, he would have happily become a plumber!

It is obvious that the skills of science and technology need to be balanced with ethics and spirituality. For only spirituality can confer wisdom on individuals and make them do good for society. To give an instance, while science and technology can provide television sets, wisdom and values alone will determine the type of programmes fed into the television. To quote Sri Sathya Sai Baba, "A knife may be developed by technology but only the wisdom of the individual will decide whether the knife is used either for cutting vegetables or for cutting the throat of another person."

"Modern physics revolves around the certainty of uncertainty."

—Sir C. V. Raman

SRI SATHYA SAI BABA'S HUMOUR

"My way of joking is to tell the truth. It's the funniest joke in the world."

— *BERNARD SHAW*

It has been said that it is easy to be wicked and witty, but difficult to be witty and wise. Sri Sathya Sai Baba's sense of humour has universal appeal, since it is a model of wit and instruction.

According to Sri Baba, humour should serve a purpose. Jokes should not be used without either relevance or reverence in talks and articles just to create effects! The seriousness or tone of a message is bound to suffer, when jokes are used out of context. Young people normally tend to treat everything as a joke and scoff at things. They should be trained not to treat all things in a light-hearted manner. If communicators do not integrate humour with themes, then the minds of youth get side-tracked and they miss the main points.

During an address, at a meeting, Sri Baba discussed the question of how a little knowledge or half-knowledge is dangerous. "It is easy to teach the ignorant or the wise but the half-wise and the half-ignorant are difficult material," said Sri Baba. He then recounted, in the lighter vein, the story of a soldier who did not know English and was tutored by his immediate boss about how to answer questions that were likely to be asked by the General when he inspected the soldiers' camp.

The tutor taught the soldier answers to three questions, in a sequence. He told him: The General will first ask you, "How long have you been in the Army?" and you must answer: Two years. For the next question "What is your age?", your answer must be *22 years* and for the third question "Do you like the army or the country?" your answer must be: Both! The soldier learnt all the answers in that order.

During his inspection, the General asked the three questions, but unfortunately for the soldier not in the same order!

The General first asked the question, "What is your age?" and the soldier replied, "2 years."

For the next question "How long have you been in the Army?", pat came the answer: "22 years."

Angry at the answers, the General shouted, "Are you a fool or am I a fool?"

"Both!" answered the soldier promptly.

* * * * *

Once when Sri Sathya Sai Baba was with his students, some one arrived and greeted him. Returning the greeting, Sri Baba smiled and told the students : Look!... Here comes a big doctor from Delhi... but he comes to me as a patient !" On another occasion, when the subject of modern eves relegating the care of their children to *ayahs* came up, Sri Baba remarked : "In such cases, the children will cry when the *ayahs* die and not when their mothers die!"

At a discussion, Sri Baba asked the question, "Do you know why a Committee does not function?" He also provided the answer, "The very name COMMITTEE suggests only one thing : COME TO TEA !"

Talking about experts, Sri Baba once defined a botanist as one who knows all about all plants, but not the value of the *Tulsi** plant !

* * * * *

One evening at Brindavan, I happened to be with other devotees and the hostel stu-

* A fragrant plant with the botanical name of *Ocimum sanctum* worshipped by many.

dents—all of whom had gathered for *bhajans*. Before the commencement of the *bhajans* Sri Sathya Sai Baba spoke on the concepts of devotion and love. Towards the end, he paused for a moment and smiled as he said, "I will now tell you about the worldly love of a married man for his wife"... He then continued, "On the day a man gets married, he is full of love and concern for his wife. Such a newly wedded man went out with his wife for a walk when he espied, from a distance, a thorn in the middle of the road. Immediately he sprang up shouting, 'My dear! there is a thorn there !... You must not step on it,' and made sure that she passed that spot without her feet touching the thorn !

A year later, the same man went out for a walk with his wife, when he saw a similar thorn but he stopped with admonishing her not to step on it !

Six months later, the couple were going out on a walk, when the man saw a thorn. This time, he did not even warn his wife to be careful but after it had pricked her, helped in removing it! A year later, when they were going out for a walk and a thorn pricked her leg, he shouted at her: "Why couldn't you have been more careful?... Well, you will have to suffer now !"

* * * * *

Discussing the question of controlling desires and developing detachment, Sri Sathya Sai Baba once narrated the story of a *sadhu* in Hrishikesh. The *sadhu* was in the habit of begging for food and then rushing with the food thus obtained to a nearby rocky terrain to sit on a special stone ledge and partake of the food.

It so happened that on one occasion he was delayed and so went to his favourite spot rather late. To his dismay, he found that another *sadhu,* who had got ahead of him, had squatted on his favourite stone and was enjoying his food.

Immediately the *sadhu* shouted, "That is my place and you should not have sat on it!"

Everyone laughed as Sri Baba concluded the story saying that even *sadhus* after giving up everything, sometimes get attached to a mere stone !

* * * * *

Sri Baba's talks illustrate how humour should be used to convey different messages effectively. Once he gave an ethical talk on the role of students and teachers and stressed how disciples should not only carry out the Guru's orders or commands, but do so with full understanding of the idea or the purpose for which these commands had been given by the guru. He then narrated the story of a guru and his *shishya* (disciple) who travelled from one village to another in a bullock cart.

The guru had with him his *kamandala*, (vessel with spout, to store water), holy books, his articles of dress and other items. As the bullock cart wended its way, the guru told the *shishya*, "Look, I am feeling very tired... So I would like to rest for a while, but you please stay awake and keep careful watch particularly of things that may fall out of the cart during the journey."

After a while, the *kamandala* fell down from the cart. The disciple kept looking at it carefully and did not make any attempt to get down and pick it up. The guru got up from his sleep after an hour and asked the *shishya* whether everything was safe inside the cart.

"Yes guru!... only the *kamandala* fell out, but as instructed I watched it very carefully from the cart, as long as I was able to!"

The guru asked him, "Why did you not pick it up and put it into the cart?"

The *shishya* said, "But you instructed me only to carefully watch and not pick it up..."

Thereupon the guru said, "That is not correct!... When I asked you to keep watch over things that may fall down, I meant that whatever falls down has to be thrown back into the cart!"

Again, after a while, the guru felt like having a short nap. So he went to sleep, this time after instructing the *shishya* to put back into the cart whatever fell to the ground. Soon, the bulls of the cart deposited some dung; Immediately, the *shishya* sprang into action; he collected the dung and threw it inside the cart and as he did so, it landed on the face of the guru!

The guru got up enraged but the disciple pleaded, "Guru, you asked me to throw into the cart whatever fell down and when the dung fell, I immediately collected it and threw it into the cart."

The guru was unable to do anything about it and so listed out all the things in the cart and said, "You must put back only the things listed here, if and when they fall down and nothing else!" (The list contained items like his papers, stick, articles of dress, etc.)

After a time, the bullock cart went up a small steep hill, near which there was a canal. During this upward movement the master who was asleep, slid down the cart and fell into the canal.

The disciple saw this but consulted his list and found that the master had not been specifically mentioned in it! So he ordered the bullock-cart to go ahead. The master who woke up after the fall into the canal, shouted and at last the disciple stopped the cart and came running to him.

"I fell into the canal but you did not bother to pull me out!" wailed the guru.

Thereupon the disciple said, "But Guru, you had not included yourself in the list of items to be restored to the cart when they fall down."

Sri Baba concluded saying that commands were given with specific objectives for ensuring results; so, while obeying orders, one should use intelligence and try to understand the goal or purpose in view.

* * * * *

Sri Sathya Sai Baba once narrated an interesting story to illustrate how hard it is to utter the name of God at the time of death, unless one has practised it for several years!

Once there was a prosperous shop-keeper, who decided to die with the name of God on his lips. For this, he thought of a good idea. He gave the name of different Gods to his six sons. He knew that he would certainly call all of them or at least one of them at the time he breathed his last.

He was immersed in commerce throughout his life. When that fateful moment came, he called his sons' names, one by one. First two of them came, next two others and immediately after them the fifth one and so he had called the names of God already five times. When he finally called for the sixth son, he had in this way mentioned the name of God six times in all !

All the sons stood around him, when suddenly the man looked up and as he was about to die gasped : "I say, I see all of you have come away, neglecting the shop ! Who will look after the business?" Suddenly he stopped breathing and thus he could only think of his commerce at the last moment and he died without the name of God on his lips!

* * * * *

Delivering a discourse on 18-8-1977 in Bangalore, Sri Sathya Sai Baba said : "When some one tries to deceive others, the idea often boomerangs!" To illustrate this, he narrated the tale of a school boy who was weak in arithmetic. On the day of the examination, the boy prayed to Sai Baba and took a vow that if all the questions were easy and he did all the sums correctly he would make an offering of 5 kgs of a sweet rice dish.

It so happened that the question paper was very easy and the boy answered all the questions correctly and that too, within two hours, although the allotted time was three hours. Since he had an extra hour on hand, the boy took a few sheets of paper and worked out the cost of the items to make the offering to Sai Baba as per his vow.

The boy added the cost of the rice, sugar, ghee, cashewnut, cardamom and dried grapes required for the sweet dish. The total worked out to fifteen rupees, but alas! he had only ten rupees in his pocket! He tried cancelling one or two items like the cashewnut and dried grapes and reducing the quantity of ghee—still, the cost was more than what he could afford. Finally, he told himself that Sai Baba did not really need the sweet dish and perhaps he would be satisfied with some fruits. He found however that fruits too were quite costly and argued to himself that flowers therefore would be a better offering. He also remembered the *Bhagavad Gita* which said that the Lord would be pleased with any offering: be it *patram* (leaf), *puṣpam* (flower), *phalam* (fruit) or *toyam* (water).

So, finally the boy decided that water from the well in his house would do for the grace Sai Baba had showered on him at the examination hall that day. He felt happy that thereby he could also save the ten rupees for seeing a film he had wanted to, for a long time. He calculated how much this would cost and found to his joy that he would also be able to take one of his friends with him to see the film. Just at the moment the bell rang and the invigilator asked the boys to hand over the answer papers.

The boy had been fully lost in his thoughts and mechanically handed over the sheets in which he had made all his calculations about the sweet dish, film, etc. Only when he went home and looked into the papers he had brought with him did the boy realise, to his chagrin, that he had brought away the real answer papers !

In the general laughter that ensued, Sri Sathya Sai Baba added, "What you plan to do to another person always recoils on you ! God is neither angry nor revengeful but is just the eternal witness. Only your own evil thoughts and deeds punish you, whilst you get the rewards for good thoughts and actions. That is the truth."

* * * * *

On one occasion, a devotee talked about a problem at a leprosy welfare rehabilitation centre, where the inmates refused to move out and live on their own, even after they had been fully cured and rehabilitated. This led to the narration of a story by Sri Baba about a guest who continued to stay on with a couple, who were his relatives. Months rolled by, and the guest did not show any signs of departing. The couple, in sheer desperation, tried throwing subtle hints. Once they asked: "Won't your family miss you? It has been months since you have seen your wife and children."

Yes! yes! I have also been thinking about them," said the guest in an undaunted voice. He then added, "I will write to them today to come over here. Please give me a post card," he demanded with nonchalance.

The couple were startled! Not only was he not leaving, but he was also trying to foist his family on them! What was worse, he was wanting them to supply even the post card for writing the letter!

The couple became frantic and finally chalked out a plan. The husband was to act as though he was very angry with his wife and ill-treat her. As a result she would not cook any food and the guest would not be fed. This way they felt sure their guest would pack up and leave.

The couple put on a convincing show and the guest, not getting his meals, packed his suitcase and left. The couple were so overjoyed at their success that they sat talking about it.

"How nicely we acted!... Surely my slaps couldn't have pained you, as I used my hands rather gently," said the husband.

"That was a good piece of acting and we have been successful in making our guest leave," said the wife, heaving a sigh of relief.

Just then there was a loud knock at the door. It was their departed guest, with suit-case in hand!

"You were both praising your acting? How about my acting? I also acted well and left the place as you wanted after packing up my things!... But then I have come back. Please don't start fighting again, for all of us need to have food," he said, and occupied his usual room.

The couple were too stunned even to react!

* * * * *

In the course of an informal talk at the residence of Sri Y. N. Gangadhara Shetty, Sri Baba talked about *mantras* and said *mantras* are for giving solace or protection and could be anything, so long as they served the purpose. He then narrated a story about a *mantra* given by Lord Krishna to Yudhishtira.

When the Pandavas had to spend the last year of their banishment *incognito* Yudhishtira was in great distress, because each one of them had to fulfil the condition of not being recognised by the others. He had to avoid even Draupadi and his brothers. He, therefore, sought Krishna's help, saying "Draupadi, a princess, has to undergo so much suffering!... I am unable to bear even the thought of it!... Oh Krishna ! please bless me with a *mantra* that will help me to bear such unbearable difficulties."

Krishna picked up a leaf and wrote something on it, folded it and gave it to Yudhishtira. He said, "When you are in abject misery or in a state of unbearable trouble you open out the leaf and read the *mantra* contained in it. If you repeat the *mantra* with sincerity, you will not find any trouble unbearable !"

When Yudhishtira had unbearable problems he took out the leaf and repeated to himself the *mantra* contained in it - *viz :* "*Barinchiraani Kashtamulu eppatiki undavu*" (unbearable troubles will never be there). Dazed, he repeated the sentence again and again : "*Barinchiraani Kashtamulu eppatiki undavu*" (Unbearable troubles will never be there !). Soon he found himself believing in the statement and getting solace!

Amid laughter, Srì Baba asked "Is that a *mantra?* But Yudhishtira did find relief, fór, his faith in the *mantra* touched his heart and gave him solace ! The purposes of a *mantra* is to think of a higher power to help you, and not just mumble some words, anyhow and in any way you want !" said Baba. He mentioned how these days pundits recite *mantras* improperly. Giving an instance he said, "The word *Om* has to be pre-fixed before the main *Namavali* (or Name of God) like *Om! Kṛṣṇāya Namaḥ* but now-a-days, the *Om* is chanted at the tail end instead of being used as an auspicious beginning and priests recite, *Kṛṣṇāya Namaḥ Om! Keśavāya Namah Om! Mukundāya Namaḥ Om!*" imitated Sri Baba, in a sing song fashion, making everyone go into peals of laughter !

Sri Baba discussing the *bhajans* at Whitefield said that after Swami's visit some people get up and go away, without realising the significance of group worship. He then related how at a *katha kalakshepam** the the *bhagavathar*** noticed only one person sitting and listening till the very end. So, at the conclusion of the session, the *bhagavathar* thanked him for his interest, when the latter said, "Please don't thank me! I had hired out the mike for this occasion and so had to stay on till the very end, to take it back!"

---

* traditional exposition of stories with songs.

** the narrator who is usually also a musician.

Recalling once his early boyhood days, Sri Baba said that in those days, one of the main vehicles of transport was the tonga—the carriage drawn by a horse. Some of the tonga horses were peculiar since they were only in the habit of walking backwards! The tonga-wallas had a hard time trying to make the horses move forward and reach their destination. So, Sri Baba humorously advised one of them to tie the horse to the tonga in such a way that the horse faced the cart and the tail was in front! In that event, the normal backward movement of the horse would really take the tonga forward!

* * * * *

Commenting on Sri Baba's humour, a devotee said, "His humour is lively, immediate and forthright—he enjoys the essence of it, leaving it to others to experience it in peals of prolonged laughter." One might add that Sri Sathya Sai Baba's humour is not humour for humour's sake; it is humour that instructs and enlivens; it is humour that never hurts but blesses all; it is humour that provides both light and delight.

SRI SATHYA SAI BABA : THE IDEAL MAN

"Generations to come, it may be, will scarce believe that such a man ever walked the earth."

—Albert Einstein on Mahatma Gandhi

Who is an ideal man?

An ideal man is one who is fully human and realises the sanctity of the human birth. "*Jantunaam narajanmam durlabham* (to be born as a human being is not easy)... Out of the 84 lakhs of species of *jivas*, or living organisms, man is the most highly evolved and is at the crown of creation," says Sri Sathya Sai Baba.

So, an ideal man is one who not only understands the glory of being born a man, but also reflects that glory in his daily life and living. The actions of the ideal man are ruled by *satya* (truth), *dharma* (righteousness), *shanti* (peace), *prema* (love) and *ahimsa* (non-violence). He is one who does his duty fearlessly, with devotion and discipline, but without expectation of reward.

The ideal man always loves and lives for all other men and never for himself. Above all, he is one whose thoughts, words and deeds are in total harmony. Truly, an ideal man is one who is the ideal for all men.

Those who are near and know about Sri Baba's life realise that his life is one of perfection. What first impressed me was the fact that Sri Baba is a perfect speaker and a delightful *bhajan* singer.

As Sri Sathya Sai Baba stands on the rostrum before a gathering, which on occasions is more than a hundred thousand strong, his flowing orange robe and crown of black hair arrest attention, in spite of his frail and small figure. The moment he starts speaking, his voice, rich, resonant and stirring, fills the atmosphere with a pleasing cadence. His speech is effortless and eloquent and he uses many parables and analogies. His dramatic personality, signs and exhortation evoke ready response in listeners. His message is communicated through his magical voice—a voice that lingers in the minds of people, reverberates in their hearts and moves millions round the globe.

To listen to Sri Sathya Sai Baba is not only a thrilling experience but also an object lesson in the art of public speaking. A friend of mine, a well known writer, after listening to Sri Baba for the first time confessed: "He is a supreme artist... He builds his arguments with lightning speed and **each** step is like a step in higher Mathematics. If you miss one step, you miss the whole! There is nothing that is extra or irrelevant in what he says, for it is all so compact."

When Sri Baba speaks, he has perfect and full mastery over the attention and heart of his audience. His talks are interesting to all the age groups in the gathering. My eleven-year-old son is not only able to prepare summaries of Sri Baba's talks but also point out a minor omission in a summary done by me! Sri Baba's talk truly cuts across all generation gaps. Some highly intellectual people may feel that some points are over-simplified by Sri Baba, but this is exactly what makes the talk appeal to a mixed group of people of different ages and stages of spiritual growth.

Sri Baba's talks are never pedantic and his appeal goes direct to the heart, because of the pure stream of love that accompanies it. When he speaks about truth and love, one gets the feeling that Sri Baba is the personification of what he speaks and that he knows truth and love with his total being. I have heard many others speak on such subjects and even though they made a good impact, somehow the feeling lurked in me that they and the things about which they talk are far apart!

When Sri Baba speaks, he is full of humility and his love for the audience expresses itself in the way he addresses them as *Divyatma Swaroopas** or *prema swaroopas.*** He begins his discourse with a poem, which he composes on the spot and which contains the essence of the talk to follow. He uses simple, daily situations to explain the most profound of truths. His brevity, clarity, fluency and faultless dictiton add to the universal appeal of his message.

The core of his teachings deals with the unity of God, the unity of mankind and the unity of all religions. His message is informal and has relevance to daily living. It enchants and moves the audience to heights of ecstasy. They absorb or drink in every word that comes from his lips, as if they are tasting "manna" from heaven. Such happiness suffusing an entire audience is rare and such spontaneous discipline is hardly ever seen at such large meetings.

I have listened with rapt attention to several discourses of Sri Baba and what struck me was the manner in which he promoted on each occasion the idea that all men are equal because of the same divine principle being present in all.

---

* Forms of the resplendent atma; ** embodiments of love

His analogies are simple and direct as for instance: "The heart of man is like a lock and his mind is like the key. If you push the lock to one side, the heart is turned Godwards and leads you to detachment, but if the same lock is turned to the other side towards the world, it leads to desire and attachment." His message becomes unforgettable because of his unique presentation. Stressing the importance of time Sri Baba says, "Does your watch indicate only the time?... No!... The five letters in the word have a timeless message", he says and asks you to:

W Watch your *W*ords
A Watch your *A*ctions
T Watch your *T*houghts
C Watch your *C*haracter
H Watch your *H*eart

Emphasising the importance of exercising care in speech, Sri Baba says, "Your speech indicates your character, reveals your personality, educates others and communicates experience and information. So be vigilant about words. If you slip while walking, the injury can be repaired. But if you slip while talking, the injury is irreparable."

Sri Baba often uses humour in his talks to explain a point. Thus, while giving a discourse on the *Bhagawad Gita*, Sri Baba said, "The verse in the Gita relating to a yogi keeping vigil while others are in slumber and sleeping while the rest of the world is busy in activity has been misinterpreted by some modern expounders of the Gita. If merely keeping awake at night and sleeping during the day was the goal, then all watchmen and station masters on night duty would indeed be yogis!" After the general laughter provoked by this remark subsided, Sri Baba explained, "the real meaning is that an enlightened person is fully awake to his own divinity and asleep to the trials of the external world, while ordinary persons are in ignorant slumber of divinity and struggle under the tribulations of the world."

Sri Sathya Sai Baba is an ideal and adorable singer — adorable, because his voice is so mellifluous, and ideal because the songs he sings move the hearts of listeners. He is very particular about *taal* (keeping time) and revels in its nuances. When his students sing, he plays the cymbals with uncanny charm and on occasions, like a music conductor, he lifts his forefinger and brings it down with a professional flourish! The way he moves his head and responds whole-heartedly to melody that stems from devotion is fascinating to watch. Mr. Kasturi reports how Sri Baba, during a tour of Rishikesh, sang a song

"Raghuvara Sugunaalaya" in a cave, at the request of a *sanyasi* living there. According to a devotee from Andhra pradesh, there is a tape of Sri Baba singing Hindustani music and my wife has a photograph of Sri Baba playing on the veena.

Musicians of varied schools consider it a rare privilege to sing or play in Sri Baba's presence. He appreciates equally all the different styles and schools of music. Over the years, several top singers and classical musicians from the East and the West have given programmes, during various festivals at Puttaparthi. Famed playback singers have revelled in the chance to sing in the presence of Sri Baba. Amongst devotees, one often hears about a Lata Mangeshkar having been present at a Sai *bhajan* or a P. Susheela having presented a concert in Sri Baba's presence. *Sai bhajan* records by Ghantasala, Juthika Roy and others as well as a *Suprabhatham** disc by Susheela are favourites with Sai devotees. Nadaswaram *vidwans* like Karaikurchi and renowned musicians like M. S. Subbalakshmi, Ravi Shankar and jazz player, Maynard Ferguson, have visited Puttaparthi and Whitefield to give performances before Sri Baba.

---

* *Suprabhatam* is the early morning chant to awaken the Lord in one's heart.

These artists of purist schools have often been surprised by Sri Baba's knowledge of all aspects of music. Violin maestro P. Sethuramiah recounts how he once had the rare privilege of not only playing on the violin before Sri Baba, but also the unique luck of listening to an exclusive carnatic music concert by him! Sri Baba had just told them, "You all have been giving me joy with your music... Let me now entertain you."

Sri Baba then gave a three-hour-long carnatic music concert accompanied on the violin by Sri Sethuramiah and on the *mridangam* by another expert. The intimate gathering there was intoxicated by the melody of the music, as they heard "this Krishna sing, like the *gokula vasis* (inhabitants of Gokula) during Lord Krishna's time", according to the maestro, who wondered how he had been able to accompany such divine music. "Only Sri Baba must have guided my fingers over the violin strings. For, I was so charmed by Sri Baba's singing that I was not even playing concisously. It was so entrancing... the melody... the masterly rendering and the superb style of singing."

Apart from his talks and *bhajan* songs the sheer presence of Sri Sathya Sai Baba elevates and invigorates, for such is his eternally fresh look. His energy is colossal and inexhaustible. Innocence and purity shine in his face, bright and effulgent and his personality exudes sweetness and light. When he either says "*Bangaaru*" (the golden one) or pronounces a person's name, it is so magically mellifluous that the person concerned is charmed and delighted. Mr. V. K. Narasimhan once confessed to me: "Balu, every time Sri Baba calls me *Bangaaru*... I melt a little!"

"*Chitta shuddhi* (purity of the heart) is the way to the divine," says Sri Baba and we know it is true for he is the very personification of a pure and selfless heart. There are no desires in him and there is not an iota of selfishness in his make-up, for all his thoughts and actions are on behalf of others. He never refers to anything as "mine." Thus, when he talks of his colleges he says "mana" (our) colleges.

Those ignorant of Sri Baba's greatness and glory spread defamatory stories about him to malign his holy name. Some criticize him out of sheer jealousy. A few have denigrated him in black and white, mainly to promote another faith. Sri Baba has never been affected even a bit by all such unjustified blame and unwarranted mudslinging, even as the mountain of praise showered on him leaves him totally untouched.

"People are endowed with a variety of mental attitudes. Each one judges according to his own angle... As the proverb goes, it is only the fruit-laden tree that receives the stones from the passers-by... So why take these things to heart? Truth will certainly triumph some day; untruth can never win... After all, praise and blame of the populace do not touch the *atma*, the Reality. They can touch only the outer physical frame", says Sri Baba, who has forever the same inner tranquillity. He greets all with the same love and consideration, whether he is rich or poor; learned or illiterate, the Governor of a State or a peon in an office. Though he is the same, people who meet him feel differently after the meeting; very often, a rich man feels very poor and a poor person feels more happy than the richest of men!

Sri Baba is known for his attention to little things. He never spares himself in any effort and never neglects even the minutest of details. Trifles make perfection but perfection is no trifle, is what he continuously demonstrates in all that he does. He often stresses that all big things are made up of little things and the universe can be perfect only when even the minutest parts of which it is composed are all perfect. When he talks to anyone or listens to the problems of a person, he gives 100 per cent concentrated attention and shows intense concern for them, which is a quality of greatness.

I have seen Sri Baba arrange lunches at the Hostel in Brindavan, where he moves around and enquires about every one. He is the last to sit down for the meal and at the same time the first one to get up. Sri Baba tastes *saathwic* food, but eats very little. He is living proof of the fact that man does not live by bread alone. Even so, he wants others to eat their normal requirements of food, since they are all not like him. Normally, while the leaders enjoy all comforts, their followers toil! In the case of Sri Baba it is the very opposite and he is continually busy with several jobs of work. He even washes his clothes himself !

Sri Baba is for ever busy building schools, hostels, hospitals and *bhajan* centres. He does the designing and planning of the buildings and is an expert on the art of architecture. All the Sai buildings appeal not only because of their elegance, form, simplicity and colour but also because of the blend of beauty and utility and of structure and ornament. Structurally neat and beautiful, with lotus motifs and sculptural decorations, the Sai buildings are all unmistakably spiritual edifices.

Sri Baba directs all the work from the beginning to the very end. He continuously gives his time and attention to the welfare of the hostel students. He organises training camps for Principals of colleges and teachers of primary schools to orient their thinking spiritually. He sets up Summer Courses for students from all parts of India during the Summer holidays.

Sri Baba is gentle, kind, loving and compassionate. He has shown in ever so many ways his love for animals too. Sai Geetha, his elephant, often pines for him in his absence and when he is there insists on either being fed by him or getting a pat from him. Sri Baba has a collection of pet animals and birds in Brindavan. He has had several dogs, many of which he has given away to devotees. He has had even a parrot in his upstairs room, which makes one wonder ! For, Shirdi Sai had a parrot in a cage near him. It is said that a few days after the parrot flew away, Shirdi Baba too shuffled off his mortal coil.

Sri Baba, the ideal man, is extremely humble, in spite of the huge organisation behind him, his large following and his immense power over people, many of whom worship him. Once, he narrated the story of how the great Emperor Alexander learnt this simple virtue from a yogi.

The yogi was resting under a tree unmindful of Alexander who passed by him. Piqued, Alexander tapped the yogi with his legs and gave a gentle kick saying, "I am Emperor Alexander who conquered the world." Hearing this the yogi laughed non-chalantly. Asked to explain why he laughed, the yogi told Alexander, "You say you are a great Emperor but just now you were doing the work of a donkey!"

Some people wrongly think that Sri Baba is only a man of miracles,* who uses miracles for achieving popularity! Nothing can be farther from the truth. As an ideal man, Sri Baba never attaches any importance to any of the extra-ordinary, psychic phenomena connected with him. According to him, the paranormal phenomena of miracles are of no significance at all: "What is more important are ethics and spirituality."

Nevertheless, his materialisations on different occasions are merely expressions of his love. Thus, during his visit to the Mosque in Puttaparthi on Ramzan day (September 5, 1978) Sri Baba created seven silver lockets in

---

* "The universe itself is a miracle," says Sri Baba, whose miracles are certainly not his materialisations. For, he himself is the biggest Miracle! Actually Sri Baba is gradually stopping his materialisations. In the past on Mahashivarathri day, he used to bring out Shiva *lingas* from his mouth, but after 1977 he stopped this. Again, in 1979 he stopped the materialisations of *vibhuthi* (sacramental ash) from an empty vessel that used to be rotated by him, for the *abhisheka* (ablutionary pouring of *vibhuthi*)-of a silver statue of Shirdi Sai Baba.

the shape of the Arabic inscription "Allah" and gave it to the convener of the Mosque Committee for distribution to the members. The Muslims and other devotees of Baba in the village were overjoyed at this gesture of Sri Baba's love.

Sometimes Sri Baba materialises things to explain a point in a discussion. Once he was telling some devotees from abroad that spirituality should become a part of daily life like a double *rudraksha** and should never be compartmentalized. The devotees did not understand what was meant by *rudraksha* and asked for the English word for it. Suddenly Sri Baba waved his hand and materialised the double *rudraksha!*

Sri Baba is a true patriot who says "The *desha* (country) is like your *deha* (body). Every part of it and every aspect of it needs attention. This is the Bharatiya tradition which people in politics have forgotten." He never tires of pointing out how people of India that is Bharat, have moved away from Indian culture and are blindly led by Western influences. He feels that every person who goes abroad must have at least a six month's orientation course on Indian cul-

---

* The *rudraksha* is the fruit or berry of the plant *Elaeocarpus ganitrus* and the double rudraksha is a very rare specimen

ture and spirituality. Otherwise, Indians with poor or no knowledge of the ancient culture and traditions of India will cut sorry figures! "Such a thing has happened occasionally even in the past during the time of the German Sanskrit scholar Max Muller," says Sri Baba. "Max Muller liked India and its culture so much that his daily prayer was that he should be born in Bharat, at least in his next life. He used to consider all Indians lucky to have been born in such a sacred land."

"Max Muller was engaged on a job of translating the Vedas, when an Indian named Chaturveda** Shastri went to call on him. This Shastri was a complete ignoramus when it came to the vedas, Sanskrit and Indian culture. He was even contemptuous of Indian culture and aped the west in everything. At that very moment Max Muller was struggling to get the exact meaning of a Sanskrit word. He referred to dictionaries but was not happy with the definitions. When he read the name of Chaturveda Sastri on the visiting card, Max Muller was delighted. He thought : What a Godsend! Here I am struggling to get at the meaning of a vedic word and in comes a Shastri of all the four Vedas. Now I can get all my doubts cleared."

** Chaturveda means the four vedas and Shastri means a pundit.

After requesting the Sastri to be seated, Max Muller asked for the clarification he needed. Mr. Shastri impatiently brushed aside his question saying "Oh Vedas! Who is bothered about such things... It is all waste of time."

Max Muller was aghast at this reaction from an Indian, bearing such a distinguished (through highly inappropriate!) name. "After that, Max Muller would have stopped praying for a rebirth in India", said Sri Baba, who feels that several Indians today are Chaturveda Shastris in their attitude and ignorance! They do not care to realise and learn the glory of the Indian heritage.

Sri Baba talks repeatedly about the culture and traditions of Bharat and demonstrates his first allegiance to the country of his birth and his mother-tongue Telugu, even though his love embraces the whole gamut of humanity and he communicates with people in the language of the soul and often understands any tongue. "There is only one language and that is the language of the heart," he says.

Sri Baba's life is exemplary in several ways. In Brindavan, one evening, some people prostrated and fell on Sri Baba's feet. A person next to Sri Baba said, "*Issh!...* Please don't!" Sri Baba motioned silence and asked the person not to worry. Later, I learnt that someone had dropped a heavy object on his leg and this had fractured his toe. A doctor in the group advised: "Swami, a cold compress should be applied immediately."

Another with an anxious countenance said, "Swami!... Please cure yourself."

Sri Baba's answer was characteristic, "When such a thing happens to my devotees, do I always cure it immediately? No!... Such things will keep happening to the human body, and in course of time, all will be well."

I learnt about yet another similar incident. Sri Baba had agreed to attend a wedding in the family of a devotee, who came with a car to take him. It was late in the evening and after Sri Baba got in, the driver slammed the door in a hurried fashion. Little did the driver realise that in the process, he had badly jammed the toe of Sri Baba's left foot. Later, Sri Baba had quitely re-opened the door, and withdrawn the toe and closed the door. The hurt toe had got swollen, but the host was unaware of it, since Sri Baba's long gown covered his feet.

Sri Baba spent considerable time at the wedding, addressed the people there, in his usual manner and walked about normally. However, after he returned, he did not stir out of his room for one full day, since he had high temperature and severe pain. When a close devotee asked Sri Baba about the incident he said that had he mentioned it earlier the driver would have been reprimanded, the master would have felt bad and unhappiness would have been experienced by all the people engaged in the marriage festivities !

These two instances show Sri Baba's consideration for others and also demonstrate how one must take pain and bodily suffering in one's stride. Pleasure is an interval between two pains and pleasure is produced when pain fructifies, says Sri Baba. Sometimes Sri Baba also takes upon himself ailments of devotees (who in his judgement cannot bear them) and suffers considerably. This is to demonstrate that nothing can be done about past *karma* or actions. "Every action has reaction, resound and reflection", says Sri Baba, and stresses therefore the need for "good conduct always"... His constant advice is "See Good, Be Good, Do Good."

Those near him know how right thoughts, right words and right action come naturally to Sri Baba like breathing and how boundless love flows spontaneously and unceasingly from his heart towards all. Sri Baba demonstrates in his life and daily living how love should be the governing principle of all human endeavour. While normally in life it is ofter a case of "Do as I tell you but not as

I do!" in the case of Sri Baba it is simply a case of "Do as I do."

Millions of people see Baba as a Father figure and worship him. However, Sri Baba says that considering him divine is without value if no attempt is made by people to see the God resident within every being! "Love God and you see God in every creature", says Sri Baba who sees only the soul or divinity in all and addresses people as *pavitratma swaroopas** If only mankind begins to see the divine spark within every human breast, the equality of all men would become a reality and the world would be populated with only ideal men and women.

"My life is my Message... Love is my instrument."

—SRI SATHYA SAI BABA

* forms of the sacred *atma* (soul)

SAI BABA[†]: THE DIVINE MAN

"Experience is the only authority for recognising divinity."

—SRI SATHYA SAI BABA

"Who is Sri Sathya Sai Baba?"

"Sri Sathya Sai Baba is God."

"How do you say this?"

"Sri Baba says this, but he also says that every one is God... The only difference, according to Sri Baba, is that while he is aware that he is God, others do not know their true nature... So, as he is prepared to acknowledge you as God, the least you can do is to reciprocate it and accept Sri Baba as God.*

When it is a question of the divine, there appear to be several persons on planet earth who have dedicated their lives to the denial of God. It is indeed funny that people should keep saying God does not exist. "They first

† The name SAI BABA means Divine Mother and Father. *Sa* means Divine *ai* or *ayi* means *mother* and Baba means *father*.

* From a conversation between the author and another person on Sri Baba, the divine man.

refer to God and then say God does not exist! If so, who is this God? How come that the name God has been given to someone non-existent? For, are not names usually given only for things that exist?" asks Sri Baba.

Divinity or God is described as *anoraṇīyān* and *mahatomahīyān* *i.e.*, as the tiniest of of the tiny as well as the largest of the infinitely large. Since God cannot be seen in both these forms, we cannot get *pratyaksha pramana* (or direct evidence) of divinity. However, indirect inference can be drawn as Cicero did when he said, "The celestial order and the beauty of the universe compel me to admit that there is some excellent and eternal Being, who deserves the respect and homage of men."

The concept of God plays an important role in ensuring the well-being of people. How can anyone take objection to the belief that God is the supreme one, who is for ever watching the actions of all men? If nothing else, the concept of God can be thought of as a down-to-earth, psychological one to help in the maintenance of equanimity, order and peace in life.

In 1955, a secular body like the U.S. Congress ordered that the motto "In God We Trust" be placed on all U.S. paper and metal money. A year later, the same body designated "In God We Trust" as the official motto of the Unites States. Like India, the United States has a secular Government; the inference that can be drawn is that as a nation, the USA - though considered the home of materialism and the Almighty dollar - acknowledges the Supreme Being or God even on every dollar bill.

God cannot be recognised by those who believe in the dictum that you must "believe only what you see." The reality of the divine can be experienced by all those who develop their spiritual perception and yearn for things of eternal value.

However, to experience divinity one need not go anywhere. As the *Bhagavad Gita* stresses, divinity lurks in every one and it is up to human beings to realize it. "You are divine, however often you may slide from humanity *to animality or even lower", says Sri Baba.*

Indeed, it is to help people to go Godwards and realize their latent divinity that Sri Sathya Sai Baba has come as an *avatar* (or divinity in human form).

An *avatar*, who is also referred to as Bhagavan, represents the descent of the divine for the express purpose of helping in the ascent of human beings. A doubt may however arise as to how the divinity of the avatar can be identified. The yardstick is to apply the tests of *omniscience, omnipresence, omnipotence* and (to borrow a word from Dr. Gokak) *omnifelicity.* That Sri Sathya Sai Baba answers to all these tests becomes more than evident from the countless experiences of people round the globe.

The scriptures stress six great qualities that emphasize the glory of God - qualities which can never be found to the same extent in men. These comprise: infinite motherly love; ability to grant freedom from fear, or fearlessness, to supplicants; removal of the affliction of the disressed; abundant generosity; drying up of sins and the ability to grant higher states.

Devotees have found in Sri Baba all these qualities in addition to compassion, forbearance and humility - all *atmic* attributes. The manner in which the reality of his divinity became manifest to ever so many persons round the world, will fill hundreds of volumes. Nevertheless, there is an illusory factor about Sri Baba, the divine man. In spite of everything, the very humanness of his physical form and behaviour sometimes blinds people to the reality of his divinity ! Even so, the *avatar* takes human form and behaves in a human way so that humanity may without fear feel kinship with divinity.

Several features about Sri Baba place him on a level much higher than ordinary human beings. As Doctor Bhagavantham* says, the realization that Sri Baba is unlike all other human beings and is superior to them, is the first step in the spiritual progress of an individual.

It is strange but true that people who have had the good luck to get near Sri Baba feel a strange euphoria and are never able to forget him; further, the remembrance is always pleasant, wholesome and joyful. Chosen people who come out of his interview room, emerge beaming and in absolute bliss.

The most miraculous thing about Sri Baba is that when he looks at or talks to a hundred persons, each one gets the confirmed feeling that "Baba cares for me most!" The omnifelicity, or general happiness, he is able to give a large community, while establishing at the same time a personal equation with every individual there, is something inexplicable.

Anbay Shivam is a well known Tamil maxim. This means that Love is God. The abundance of love that flows from Sri Baba

---

* reputed scientist, former Director of the Indian Institute of Science, former Defence adviser to the Govt. of India and a former Vice-Chancellor, who often translates Sri Baba's speeches from Telugu to English.

has to be experienced rather than explained and is the biggest of his miracles. To quote Dr. Baranowski, "No miracle is as great as the miracle of one man giving so much love to so many people." The Mahabharatha depicts how Dharmaja, the eldest of the Pandava brothers, not only understands love as a divine quality but also teaches Draupadi that love is the spontaneous nature of those who are ever in the awareness of the *Atma* or God. Many are able to experience not only the love but also the gentle peace that flows out from Sri Baba the peace that passeth all understanding. I have always felt both love and fear in Sri Baba's presence and others known to me share this experience.

Some have the strange experience of tears flowing out of their eyes in Sri Baba's company but these are not tears of sorrow but tears of joy! Invariably everyone experiences wonderful felicity when they have the physical proximity of Sri Baba. Some old persons who live and work for his mission remain remarkably young like the 90-year-old Shri Karunyananda and the 83-year-old Shri N. Kasturi, since their "finite energy gets charged by the infinite source of all energy."

Those fortunate to get personal contact have had the unique experience of Sri Baba divining their innermost thoughts. He knows fully the past, present and future of all persons and the reason for this knowledge, according to Sri Baba, is that he eternally resides in all hearts and minds and so nothing is hidden from him! Several thousands of devotees in different parts of the world have testified to the help they have received instantly when they have either prayed to him or cried out *Sai Ram!* in times of danger.

A retired officer belonging to the Indian Forest Service mentioned to me a true happening: "It was 7 p.m. on January 28, 1980. I was driving my car and my wife was with me. I had to pass through a narrow road, when my car got sandwiched between a scooter and a cyclist on the opposite side. The cyclist passed on his cycle to another person with him and started accusing me aloud of having hit him. He opened the door of my car and caught hold of my shirt color. He abused me in the filthiest of language I have ever heard, and threatened to break every bone in my body.

"I was at my wits' end, not knowing how to defend myself, when suddenly he looked at me fixedly and said: Since you are an old man I will allow you to go scot free; otherwise I would have broken all the bones in your body.

"It took me some time to understand why the attitude of that person changed so suddenly. All the while, my wife had been praying to Sri Baba and the change in his attitude was nothing else but the answer to her prayers.

"The very next day without my speaking anything, Sri Baba said: 'So, you escaped being beaten up by that cyclist! Swami knows!"

Several other devotees have averred how wherever they go, they sense Sri Baba's personal presence protecting and guiding them. They receive many signals and signs which let them know that Sri Baba is always there.

My first early morning darshan of Sri Baba during the Deepavali festival of 1978, remains a momentous memory. He was on the balcony of his Brindavan residence in Bangalore. A great white halo surrounded him, making him look divinely splendid; after a while, as he walked away, I saw the halo follow him too!

The sight was unforgettable and inspired me to do a painting. Later, when I got the opportunity to show a photograph of the painting of Sri Baba with the halo, I asked him: "Swami, how does the halo come?"

Sri Baba's gentle and nonchalant reply was: "*Lopala untay baita vosthundhi.*" (If something is inside, it comes out!)

Scientific study of Sri Baba's aura, by means of biomagnetic field radiation photography, has provided further clue to his divinity. To quote the expert from the Arizona University of the U.S.A., Dr. F. Baranowski, "As I saw him on Sunday on the balcony giving darshan, the aura Sri Baba projected was not that of a man. The white band was more than twice the size of any man's the blue was practically limitless and then there were gold and silver bands beyond even those, far beyond this building, right up to the horizon. There is no scientific explanation for this phenomenon."

Later, I had an opportunity to meet Dr. Baranowski. He told me that while some people have the natural ability to see auras, others could train themselves to observe them. Thereafter, on many occasions. I strained myself to locate the aura around Sri Baba but in vain. So, I gave up the attempt as beyond me and felt inwardly happy for having been able to see the halo at least once, during my first early morning darshan of Sri Baba on *deepavali* day.

It was a Thursday morning in June 1980. I was a little late reaching Whitefield. Sri Baba was already there at the *bhajan* shed, sitting on his chair.

I rushed and stood at the Information Booth, near the gate. I could only get a back view of Sri Baba's crown of hair and his right hand. Devotees were singing *bhajans* which had reached a high crescendo, the entire assembly being lost in the rapture of it.

All of a sudden I got excited, since I noticed a large band of white, rather like a white cloud of smoke around the hair! Was I day dreaming? I rubbed my eyes hard, but there it was - the halo, distinctive and distinguishable. And lo! It started moving up from the fringes of the hair.

As I tried to fix my gaze on this white band of aura, I noticed Sri Baba's right hand move vigorously and rotate in response to the tempo of the *bhajan* music. His hand moved and gyrated like the arm of a machine rotating at fixed speed in the same orbit and my excitement grew as I noticed that with each rotation of the hand more and more of the aura appeared, like spurts of smoke issuing out of a steam engine. The mist like white aura moved over the devotees. A continuous stream of aura generated by the motion of the hand flowed and spread over the entire assembly. Was that the method by which grace is distributed equally to all people by the divine Master, at a time when all forget themselves in singing the glory of God? The scene was thrilling, glorious and enrapturing. I experienced a very wholesome feeling and throughout the day, I was in a state of dazed delight.

The healing miracles of Sri Baba also provide proof of his divinity. He selects only some cases for healing. He has fully cured several cases of illness and diseases which reputed physicians and experts had been unable to heal. He has also healed people from a distance; but his cure takes effect only when there is the response of full faith from the concerned patients.

Mr. D. Srinivasan of Delhi narrated to me a few instances: "I had been a personal witness to the experience of a very aged person from Saudi Arabia... This happened in 1974... This old gentleman had been suffering from serious disease of the stomach for several years and he was unconsolable and beyond the affectionate attention of his two wives. During this time he had the vision of a person, with a very weird hair-do and strange male attire, beckoning him. After persistent enquiries for months, he could identify the person who came in his vision as Sri Sathya Sai Baba and so made the journey from Saudi Arabia.

"Swami was already aware that he was coming on a particular day and prepared us fully to receive him and forbade us from telling the same to the Arab. We received him right from Dharmavaram Station. For two days, Swami did not say anything. But on the third day, Swami sent the message that he would call the family of the Arab on the afternoon of that day. The Arab neither knew Hindi nor English. He was ushered in at the appointed time.

"What a thrilling experience I had, when I saw the family came out, after half an hour, visibly charged and if I may use the expression, rejuvenated. By the language of signs, the old gentleman conveyed to us how indescribable his joy was, how free he felt from the oppressive disease and how he could not even imagine that he ever had any disease at all! While none of us tried to probe into the language that was spoken, we knew that it was only the language of love and divinity that had pervaded the occasion.

"The second instance was during the birthday of Sri Baba in November 1970. I saw a person with all the four limbs twisted in different directions, struggling even to sit on a wheel chair. He had been coming to Prasanthi Nilayam for several years. That year, for the first time, he was summoned for an interview by Swami. When he came out after the interview, I saw him walking, with able, straight limbs, the wheel chair thrown away and a radiant smile adorning his face !"

Mr. Srinivasan described yet another incident, during April 1975 at a house in Simla, during Swami's visit. The house was that of the lady Seva Dal convener of Simla.

"As soon as Swami arrived at the house, the lady and her husband did *namaskaar*, falling flat on the ground. Thereafter, her father, a Professor of History in the Himachal University, bent forward and touched Swami's feet. Swami too, quite unusually, bent a little forward and touched the back of the Professor. This by itself, would have passed off as a normal case of an elderly person paying obeisance to Swami. But the Professor confessed later to a miraculous experience. He said, 'I had been suffering from a congenital ailment of the spine and lower ribs, as a result of which I have never been able to bend even a little forward, but somehow when I saw Swami, I felt like making my obeisance and without any difficulty I was not only able to bend but even touch his feet. Also, as I straightened myself, I felt the touch of Swami on my back, when a mysterious thing happened. A pleasant stream of warm blood seemed to gush through my spine! For several years, I had felt that blood was not flowing in that region but Swami's touch did this for me. After that, I have never had the problem again!' "

Devotees have related hundreds of such happenings, but in every case, removal of afflicted conditions have resulted mainly due to absolute devotion and faith in Sri Baba on the part of the persons concerned. This is based on the scientific principle of the positive and the negative meeting to establish full circuit.

It is very hard, nay impossible, to understand fully Sri Baba, the divine man. However, those who have opened their hearts to him, given up their ego and surrendered fully, have experienced peace of mind and a sense of well-being, even though they have felt they may be unable to attain the supreme state in this life-time.

Sri Baba provides for his devotees the link with divinity and a taste of the *yugas* of yore, when divine men like Sri Rama and Sri Krishna lived and taught people through example how to destroy evil and introduce *dharma* in daily living Sri Baba's presence is solemn assurance for people that God is neither remote nor distant and certainly not the exclusive property of sages and saints. He spells hope for the common man through his life and mission that spirituality can become part of daily living and that the real destination of all men is divinity.

Āścaryavat paśyati kaścidenam
Āścaryavad vadati tathaiva cānyaḥ /
Āścaryavaccainam anyaḥ śṛṇoti
Śrutvāpyanam Veda na caiva kaścit //

—*Bhagavad Gita* (*Chapter 2, Verse 29*)

(Some look at Him with wonder
Some talk about Him with wonder
Some hear about Him with wonder
But none really know Him.)

SRI SATHYA SAI BABA'S MISSION

"I have come to transform people, persuade them to serve mankind and grant them God-realization."

—SRI SATHYA SAI BABA

"I think your mind has been conditioned or clogged by Sri Baba... How are you sure Sri Baba's influence is genuine and he is a power for good?"

The question was asked by a person who was unaware that Sri Baba's powers have been proved beyond doubt, for over four decades. His immense powers, which science† has not been able to fathom, are never openly displayed, but used in a subtle manner to give hope and happiness in a myriad ways to millions round the globe.

---

† In the book "Sai Baba, the Holy Man and the Psychiatrist," Dr. Samuel Sandweiss after his study of, and experiences with, Baba discovers that what passes as psychiatry is an incomplete science and "the reality of this holy man could not be satisfactorily contained or explained by the concepts and principles I have learned in my years of psychiatric experience."

Dr. Sandweiss, expressing the hope that psychiatry may one day awaken to the reality of Sri Sathya Sai Baba, calls "This still young science, *Sai-chiatry.*"

People who go to Baba are from all walks of life and all fields of human endeavour, Amongst them are several eminent men of letters, reputed scientists, judges, military generals, industrialists, pundits, princes, poets, journalists, editors, scholars, world-renowned artists, musicians and others - people who would never have gone to him, had they not realized his transcendental qualities and greatness. Some people go to Baba either because they have had miraculous or spiritual experiences, or because they yearn for *jnana* (knowledge that is wisdom). Some visit him in the hope of obtaining solutions for their problems and worries, which they communicate to him through letters, prayers or just plain thoughts.

His benign influence has helped many to give up indulgence in cultivated desires like drinking, smoking, consuming drugs, etc. Sometimes, wives whose husbands have been alcoholics have wondered how Sri Baba achieves in no time what they had been unable to, in a life-time of nagging and condemnation ! Through his presence and lessons, Sri Baba is able to offer to people the alternative of unalloyed happiness, compared to the little passing pleasures they might have experienced with alcohol, cigarette, drugs, etc. His technique is to gradually make people find happiness within (*i.e.*, with themselves) so that they will not seek diversions and hanker for transient worldly joys. People play cards in clubs and watch all types of films, since they have not discovered their true selves (or *atman*) and so feel empty or inadequate and become victims of insecurity, desires and worries. Sometimes, Sri Baba asks in jest, "You say you have worries! Can you tell me the shape of your worries?"

Sri Baba points out continuously that it is man's thoughts and desires which cause worries. He says man becomes restless and worried when his thoughts are negative and coloured by anger, envy, hatred, etc. Unable to throw out such thoughts, he tries to take to smoking, drinking and drugs and other wrong ways. Sri Baba points out that money, position and power are also like these intoxicants, but even worse in their corrupting influence. All these keep man away from his true happy self or *atma* (soul). Hence, one should seek the knowledge of the self to experience happiness the like of which no diversion like playing cards and seeing cinemas (to give just two examples) can ever give.

Purification of individuals is what leads to purification of society, says Sri Baba. That is why it is so important to change individuals and make them *Be good*, *See good* and *Do good.* If an individual is good, society (which consists of individuals) becomes good and thus the nation becomes good. Many good nations will make the world good. So to build a good world, the key is the individual person.

Sri Baba's ways of changing people are mysterious and subtle. He influences them not only in person but also through dreams, visions, speeches and writings. Apart from individual devotees, who number millions, a lot of Baba's attention is devoted to several hundreds of students studying in his educational institutions.

Once people come under his influence, others can see the real miracle of how Sri Baba changes them, over a period of time. It is always subtle, step by step, or very slow but sure. The inward change after a while begins to reflect in the outward personality of the individual. For some, this does not take more than a few months, while for others it takes even some years. For, Sri Baba transforms persons imperceptibly, without the individuals concerned cognising it. He comes down to the level of every person and makes them happy with his pure and deep love. One can never guess why he has called some one; "Unless I call a person, he or she cannot come to me" is his firm declaration. His mission is is to point to devotees the Godward path and help them to realise the divinity within. As such, he is ever active with his divine mission.

Sri Baba's ways are many and varied, like his many splendoured personality. He not only distils for his devotees the essence of all the scriptures and the Vedas, but also enables them intuitively to feel what God or Divinity is. For, God is beyond the mind and the intellect and can be known only through intuition. One can experience divinity in the very person of Sri Baba. Also, abstract concepts about spirituality, religion and God become clearer, after experiencing Sri Baba. With such understanding comes about right perception leading to right intuition, or the intuition of the Divine experience. The God-awakening in individuals is done by him in his inimitable way, without the individual concerned being aware of it. That indeed is the essential, divine Baba.

By his love and serene simplicity, Sri Baba makes people shed their ego and sense of importance. They begin to feel humble, the moment they realize that one with abundant powers, one who knows so much about people and everything else, about the past and the future, never talks unnecessarily and never shows off. Inspite of all his undoubted position and glory, he remains a simple individual. He is such a mighty force, yet he moves about like any ordinary human being. His example in their midst is enough for people to realise how insignificant they are in comparison. It makes many people launch on self analysis and pinpoint their own faults, for Sri Sathya Sai Baba often says, "See only the good in others and the faults in yourself."

Also Sri Baba's limited talk is a pointer to many not to babble too much about their little knowledge. When he, who knows so much does not talk much, why should others express themselves unnecessarily on things about which they have comparatively very little or no knowledge.

Sri Baba often alerts people about the four sins which the tongue is prone to commit: *viz.*, speaking untruth, speaking ill of others, back-biting and talking too much. The way he says things make people ruminate over them. The way one ruminates about what Sri Baba says is a miracle. Why do people think so much about what he says? The answer is they cannot do otherwise, since he makes a direct appeal to their hearts. His soft, sweet voice, clear words, gentleness and gentlemanliness compel attention. The avalanche of his pure love makes one heed his loving command of not writing down or recording what he says, but "imprint things in your heart so that you can always take out copies of the same, whenever required."

Soon one discovers that what is recorded in the heart keeps playing at the back of the mind, ever so softly and gently making one aware of such truths like the inevitability of death, the temporary nature of the body, etc. The record plays so often automatically that it acts as a check on one's thoughts, words and deeds. One gradually begins to see the futility of such things like uttering falsehoods, causing harm to others, amassing wealth by wrong means and thus, the process of self-purification and harmonising thought, word and deed sets in. Further, the avataric Baba in human form, walking, talking, moving and proving an ideal example is what helps in the real spiritual progress of individuals. The progress starts with individual self correction and self purification - the surest path to reach divinity. "I have come to give you the key to the treasure of *ananda* or bliss; to tell you how to tap that spring; for you have forgotten the way to blessedness", says Sri Baba. "In order to transform oneself and see *Pashupati* or the Lord, immanent in all things, one must give up the *pashu* (or animal) qualities. One should clear one's heart and mind of all bad thoughts and ideas and fill them with sacred thoughts. Otherwise, man will continue to suffer in the changing world of diversity without understanding his goal and role as a human being."

"When we are born, we cry. When we die, they cry. In between, we cry, but have we ever cried that we have not established a righteous life? So why did we cry? Just to cry! We don't even know why we cry? That is the unfortunate position of man in the world today. If at all we cry, we must cry, seeking God's grace and cry that we should realize soon how sacred and divine life is," says Sri Baba, who has the rare gift of making people think about him often and even constantly in many cases. They are never able to forget his person, his gestures, his talk, his *bhajans*, etc. This attraction is one of his divine attributes. Since he personifies divinity, this power is nothing but the power to make people think always of God. It is indeed a difficult feat to divert people's ever-changing mind towards the one goal of Sri Baba or divinity.

Many who do not even consider themselves devotees often remark that Sri Baba is often in their thoughts. He fills their mind with joy and they want to think about him and make that joy recur as often as possible. That way they learn to attach themselves to Sri Baba, as personifying the Lord. Once they form such an attachment, they find that they do not care so much for other worldly pleasures. Gradually this gives them detachment from all worldly attachments; this detachment in turn strengthens their attachment to the Lord. This is yet another manner in which Sri Baba, with his great powers of attraction, provides practical help to individuals in making progress on the divine path.

Sri Baba is not only a spiritual teacher, giving divine discourses and teaching *vedanta* to his devotees; he is the Divine Man or *avatar* who is able to give an inkling of the nature of The Infinite, through the medium of his own person, besides affording special, intuitive experiences. It is this feature that singles out Sri Baba from other teachers and preachers who are able to teach abstract philosophy of the vedanta and the scriptures, in a lucid manner, but unable to provide any insight into the elusive, intuitive reality. The experience can be had only by devotees who are fully humble and receptive. For, only when the positive and negative charges meet can the spiritual circuit be complete or whole.

Being fully divine, Sri Baba is able to gauge the level of an individual's divinity, or the degree of brightness of the spiritual spark within. To make it into a bright flame that will lend resplendence, he makes people follow different paths, all leading to the same goal :

for some it is *bhajan,* for others it is *japam* or meditation and so on; for a few it could well be writing, teaching or lecturing on the divine. Each one could follow the line most suited to him or her—"the path after one's own heart is the best path to the divine.

Sri Baba also knows the dosage of spirituality each devotee can take in. He neither gives too much nor too little, thereby enabling the individual to make progress. At the same time, he sees it that every one continues with his daily duties in a disciplined manner. It is here that one sees the role of the avatar who is not only divine but also an ideal man of the world. All people who wish to give up everything and join his ashram are not encouraged to do so. Firmly and gently they are told to go back to their home, work and duties and they soon discover that in his own mysterious way Sri Baba is always with them in their hearts.

People who are in the Ashram and the college hostel boys do every job there as an offering to God, which is indeed the way man should learn to do his everyday duties. Every work when done as an offering to God, becomes pure, unsullied and the best; the results or rewards of those actions also become an end in themselves.

The mission and message of Sri Baba are carried to people through the medium of a monthly journal "Sanathana Sarathi", which circulates round the globe, besides a host of special books. There are also the activities of Sri Sathya Sai Seva Organizations, functioning all over India and abroad. These include several *Samithis, bhajan mandals, Seva Dals,* Study Circles, *Bal Vikas* Groups and *Mahila Vibhags* (Women's Wings) which deal with different strata of society and people of all ages and all religions. In addition, there are dispensaries and hospitals, besides educational institutions like technical and ordinary schools and colleges in different parts of the country. The old students of Sri Sathya Sai educational institutions have formed themselves into a unit called the Kingdom of Sathya Sai. Several specialised activities are also taken up from time to time like organising Summer Courses for college students on Indian Culture and Spirituality.

However, for Sri Baba, the organization is not as important as the people who work for it. He is never impressed by show or the external view of any operation, but rather by its quality and intensity of dedication. Whether a person is connected with his organization or not, Sri Baba's grace and love flow out equally to all. His pre-occupation is with his divine mission of making humans live and work in the world as ideal human beings and gradually taste the *ananda* or bliss of divinity.

"The main object of religion is not to get man into Heaven but to get Heaven into him."

—THOMAS HARDY

HOW DR. V. K. GOKAK CAME TO SAI BABA

"Discover the self (ananda) hidden within you to discover the Lord in everything."

—SRI SATHYA SAI BABA

Well known scholar, poet, philosopher, educationist and a highly respected literary figure, Dr. V. K. Gokak is the winner *inter alia* of several Sahitya Academy Awards, the Padmashri title and the D. Litt *(Honoris Causa)* from the Karnatak University of Dharwar. He has worked in various capacities as Principal of Colleges in Maharashtra, Gujarat and Mysore, as Director of the Central Institute of English, Hyderabad, as Vice-Chancellor of the Bangalore University and as Director of the Indian Institute of Advanced Study, Simla. He was Vice-President of the Commonwealth Conference on the teaching of English in Uganda in 1961. Currently he is Vice-Chairman of the Central Sahitya Academy and Chairman of the Jnanpith Awards Committee.

I asked Dr. Gokak how he came under the influence of Sri Sathya Sai Baba and he said,

"It is a long story... I am a staunch believer in Sri Aurobindo and the Mother... In August 1965, I was at the Sri Aurobindo Ashram in Pondicherry in connection with a seminar, for a week. During the final night of my stay in Pondicherry I had a very strange dream. In that dream I was assigned a piece of work I had never done in my waking hours. The task was to arrange flowers in a particular order (like lotus for the head, rose for the heart centre, etc.) on the *samadhi* of Sri Aurobindo, as is done every day."

"Why in a particular order? I interrupted.

"Floral symbolism is a science in Sri Aurobindo Ashram and each flower has a psychic or spiritual significance. For instance, the May Flower, which blossoms only in May, is the symbol of supramental realization", said Dr. Gokak, and continued, "I placed all the other flowers first and finally the rose on the heart centre. To my surprise, the rose started moving in a horizontal direction and finally fell down! I was astonished, having never seen such a happening before! I placed the same flower again but it moved across horizontally and fell down! Then I woke up and wondered about the strange dream. After a while, I went to sleep, but the same dream recurred—the moving rose falling down. Even though I woke up five or six times, I got the same dream soon after I fell asleep.

"The next morning, when I finally woke up, I felt greatly depressed .So I went to my esteemed friend (the late Shri Rishabchand, one of the respected devotees of Sri Aurobindo) and discussed with him the significance of the dream. I asked him why it was that, although I had been visiting the Sri Aurobindo Ashram for nearly sixteen years, (since 1949) I had not progressed much spiritually."

"Without a second thought, he said : *you have not loved enough !* I was puzzled about this statement, all the more, since the rose had refused to stay at the heart centre, or the centre of love ! I began to wonder : What is loving enough? and how can I love?... Even after I reached Hyderabad, the question haunted me, but soon, owing to the work at the Institute, it gradually faded away from my mind."

Had you not heard about Sri Sathya Sai Baba at that time?"

"Yes ! Some time in October or so of 1965, a boyhood friend of mine and a fellow literary figure in Kannada, Sri Chulki, who had been to Puttaparthi stayed with me in Hyderabad, on his return journey. He was full of enthusiasm for Puttaparthi and Sri

Sathya Sai Baba and it was he who made the first deep mention of Sri Baba. He told me that Sri Baba is seen *in all his glory particularly in the morning at 4.30 in the meditation hall. He is a glorious figure and you feel he is almost divine !*"

Sri Chulki told Dr. Gokak that though he had been impressed with Swami, he could not think of him as really God! Later, when Swami called Sri Chulki for an interview, (he had gone in connection with his son's illness) Swami had told him: *you still do not have full faith... Come after you are settled in your faith !* Dr. Gokak was puzzled at Sri Chulki saying that Sri Sathya Sai Baba is almost divine and Sri Baba getting hold precisely of that point ! Finding that a friend like Sri Chulki could be so impressed, Dr. Gokak felt his estimation of Sri Baba go up.

"During December 1965," continued Dr. Gokak, "I got three letters from friends close to me: Prof. Bendre, N. P. Bhat, (my son-in-law, who used to be a sceptic) and another person from N. India. The three letters came during the same week. You see, I had a daughter but we lost her... She suffered from mental depression and we were getting her treated in Hyderabad. The Mother gave her a talisman and advised us to get her photograph taken every three months and send it to her.

Mother used to see the photograph and give directions, which we followed. But we had to be at home all the time watching her and we were facing this problem. All the three letters were in this connection and said : "Why don't you go to Sri Sathya Sai Baba? The Mother is busy with the mission of creating a new world, but Sri Baba is the destroyer of evil and so he may cure this malady."

"When three trusted friends wrote like that, I was shaken in my mind... I thought over it and decided to write a letter to the Mother..."

"In my letter to the Mother I said that I was satisfied that whatever Mother was doing for me was more than enough. But since three friends had written asking me to see Sri Sathya Sai Baba and obtain his grace for my daughter, I would like to be told what to do. Actually I sent this letter to Mother through Mr. Pandit. He had read out the letter to Mother, who had simply said : *Let him do as he likes.*"

"I thought over this sentence and felt that if Mother had wanted me to see Sri Sathya Sai Baba, she would have certainly said,: *Go and see him.* Therefore, I concluded that the Mother did not think it necessary for me to see Sri Baba. Threupon I wrote a letter of apology to the Mother saying that the chapter was closed. After posting the letter, I forgot all about the subject."

In early March of 1966, Dr. Gokak read a news item in the *Deccan Chronicle* that Sri Sathya Sai Baba would be visiting Hyderabad and delivering some public discourses. For a moment, his mind went to the past, but he soon dropped the matter saying to himself: *So many great men come and go... How am I concerned?*

However, during the middle of March, Dr. Gokak received a letter from Mr. B. Ramakrishna Rao, (a retired Governor settled in Hyderabad), asking him whether he would speak under the chairmanship of Sri Sathya Sai Baba on any spiritual topic. Since this was a talk on a spiritual topic and he used to give such talks in Hyderabad, Dr. Gokak agreed.

"After having accepted to speak, I began to think about it," said Dr. Gokak, "I thought it would be extremely discourteous on my part to sit on the same platform with a great saint without paying my respects to him prior to the function. So I rang up Mr. Ramakrishna Rao and asked for an appointment with Sri Baba."

"I was given the time at 10.30 a.m. on a particular day. Then I had again other thoughts... Since I was going to Sri Baba any way, I felt that my wife and two daughters who were there could also go along with me so that all of us could bow down to the saint. I rang up Mr. Ramakrishna Rao again and after consulting Sri Baba he gave us the green signal."

"In the spacious garden of the residence of B. Ramakrishna Rao, there were more than five hundred people, standing in rows, but we were marched along and taken inside, right in front of Sri Baba's room. At exactly 10.30 a.m. the door opened and Sri Baba came out saying, yes!... yes!... Kannāda or Telugu?"

"Kannada" I said.

" 'I will be back after seeing the people,' said Sri Baba in Kannada as he walked out.

"We were curious and so peeped into the garden from the window... It was such a soul stirring sight. The first person Baba saw outside was a lady with a mentally disabled child. The pity that welled up in Baba's eyes and the way his face was suffused with sheer compassion was something unforgettable. The way he materialised *vibhuthi* for them was also an act of pure love. Again, as he patted a tottering, old man, it was such a spontaneous outburst of many-splendoured love.

"I used to see the Mother once a year. I could see Sri Aurobindo only once, on 24th

April 1949, for he passed away in December 1950. I shall never forget the solitary sun-glance that he threw at me. The Mother was the link between the devotees and him. And she was accessible. But a government servant at his job, I had no opportunity to go to Pondicherry frequently. My love threfore did not open out as it should have. It looks as though I was sent to Baba for being bathed in his love and for the opening of my own heart in his presence, for he would be in Bangalore for quite some weeks each year.

"Sri Baba came back and seeing a bare floor asked, *What about a carpet?*"

"Mr. Ramakrishna Rao ran inside and brought a carpet on his shoulder. All of us spread it out and after asking us to sit, Sri Baba sat with us in our midst, even though a chair was placed there for him."

"Mr. Ramakrishna Rao tried to introduce me but Swami said, *No need for introduction!* and thereafter Mr. Rao left the place."

"Swami spoke to my wife and then to my ailing daughter who was sitting next to her. I tried to say something about her. But Swami stopped me and said 'Yes, yes! We know. You have taken her photograph two days ago with a view to sending it to our friend (That is how Swami referred to the

Mother). It is no disease. It is just mental weakness.' And then he turned to her and asked her : 'Will you take *prasad?*' She said, 'yes!' Swami produced graciously some *vibhuti* with a wave of his hand and gave it to her."

"As Swami talked and I listened to him, the feeling that suddenly came to me was that the patriarch of our family, sage Kapila of 5000 years ago, had come and sat right in the midst of his great, great grand children. This was my first vivid feeling—a feeling of closeness as with the patriarch of my family! The next impression was an over-powering intuition that we were sitting in the presence of Lord Shiva, in all his grandeur and dignity. He had several arrows concealed in his hair and whenever evil reared its head he took out an arrow from his hair on the right side, fixed it to his bow and destroyed that evil."

"As Sri Baba talked, my wife closed her eyes and went into meditation. She saw Baba inwardly and on his head two flowers—the May Flower, which in Sri Aurobindo Ashram, is held to be the symbol of the supramental attainment of Sri Aurobindo; and the lily which is white, white light standing for the Mother's power. Thus *Purusha* and *Shakti* were symbolically concentrated in Swami—that was her vivid, intuitive grasp."

"I was very deeply moved by what happened to my wife and myself. We bought a photo of Swami and went home feeling extremely happy. I also wrote a poem called *Darshan** projecting the experiences of the day."

"The next day I went to the meeting to speak under Sri Baba's chairmanship. There was a huge crowd of over 30,000 persons, and when I was called upon to speak, I first read out the poem and offered it at Sri Baba's feet. As I touched his feet I looked up and noticed a very strange thing. His whole face was flushed and he panted for breath! I kept this to myself and wondered whether I had done or said anything wrong!**

"The next day we all went to Sri Baba's public meeting, to see him and to be seen by him and to listen to him. We were greatly inspired by his speech, which had a great impact on the audience."

"The next opportunity I had of meeting Sri Baba, for nearly two hours, was at a

---

* See Appendix for the poem.

** Late in 1967, after I came to know Sri Baba intimately, I asked him why he panted for breath and had a flushed face, when I offered my poem at his feet. "Look! he said... It was not just a poem. It was the truth! You described me as I am! And if one heart sees me as I am, then my heart is also moved. What you saw was my response to your perception which you conveyed in the poem."

dinner, at the residence of Mr. Appa, in Ramachandrapura, 18 miles off Hyderabad. There, before and after the dinner, Sri Baba talked to me about his boyhood days, quite innocently and happily. I was charmed because it was as though he was speaking about some one else! He conveys a sense of impersonality even when he speaks about himself. This meeting with Swami was some time in May 1966, after which I lost touch with him. I had Swami's photo and I had great affection and respect for him. It stood at that, and my old Sri Aurobindo devotion continued as ever before."

"Five months later, I moved over to Bangalore to take charge as Vice-Chancellor of the Bangalore University. I reported for duty on 14th October 1966. About three weeks later, some members of the Sri Sathya Sai Samithi in Vijayapura, who had read my poem on Swami in *Sanathana Sarathi* approached me to speak about Swami at a meeting to celebrate his birthday. I was busy finding my bearings in the university. So I said that they might proceed with the birthday celebrations. I would come later and speak on Baba. They agreed and left. But what was my surprise when they came again and said: "Sir, please come when it is convenient to you. We shall celebrate the birthday on that day!"

"I opened my eyes wide. Did they really mean it? If they did, they must have gone to Baba and taken his advice, for none but he could have spoken like that about his birthday! Without probing further into it, for they came from Vijayapura, which is only 70 to 80 miles from Puttaparti, I gave them the earliest date I could. This led to another development, for Shri Kaṣturi came from the Ashram to this meeting. At that meeting, Shri Kasturi asked me whether I would speak about Swami at the first All India Sathya Sai Conference which was being arranged in Madras on 23rd April. I agreed though this posed a problem since I was not in the habit of applying for leave for my own delight. As Vice-Chancellor, I had also no vacation at all! But soon, I found that the date of the conference fell in ideally with my plans.

"24th April was one of the darshan days in Pondicherry and I had mentally decided to go to Pondicherry and take Mother's blessings, since I had not offered my homage to her after joining as Vice-Chancellor. Madras being on the way, I did not have to take any special leave. When I wrote to the Mother, she asked me to go over for an interview at 10.30 a.m. on the 23rd. The Sathya Sai Conference was on the afternoon of that day. So, bowing down to the Mother in the morning at Pondicherry, I rushed to Madras and three hours later, bowed to Swami. The strange coincidence of meeting the two of them and bowing down to them the same day meant to me, as it did in my wife's vision, further verification of the fact that the Mother and Sri Baba represented the same infinitude of spirit. I played with this logic but did not come to any definite conclusion, because I still had my mental reservations. However, Swami was as gracious and loving as ever and appreciated my speech. I was greatly enthused by this further contact."

"The contact did not stop there. It continued in Bangalore. Dr. P. S. Rao who used to visit me told me soon after my arrival from Madras and Pondicherry : *Swami is in Bangalore.*

Where does he stay? I asked.

In Whitefield, he replied.

Where is Whitefield? I asked.

If you like, I will take you there, said Dr. Rao.

"So I went with Dr. Rao. I learnt it was Swami's practice to spend a few weeks in Whitefield during the summer."

There were two lines of devotees flanking the road inside the compound and I too stood there, at a convenient point, waiting for

Swami. As Swami went round, he said: 'O, Gokak! Go in. I would like to speak to you.' And I went in and sat in the famous interview room in Brindavan. As Swami came in, I bowed down to him and thanked him for the opportunity he gave me to spend a few hours with him in Madras and address the Sathya Sai conference. However I was shocked at Swami's reaction: *No! We are not satisfied!*"

"I felt perplexed and wondered whether I had committed some error unconsciously. But Swami quieted my doubts: There is the vast sea. A stick floats on it, without knowing that it is the very immensity of the sea on which it floats. A swimmer swimming in it and breasting the waves knows that it is the vast sea in which he is swimming. Now, how many are there who know that the sea is the sea?"

"I was very happy for I felt that Swami had indirectly recognised me as an authentic seeker of spirit. I was delighted at the gracious manner in which he spoke about a humble aspirant."

"Thereafter, I paid regular visits, since I found it nectarously sweet to listen to Swami. I used to address him as 'Sir', but he never seemed to mind it. I think I did this for more than eight months and Swami tolerated it without the least discomfort. At least, on an afternoon, when I should have joined a few invitees to tea with Swami, I was held up at the railway gate and was late by a few minutes. Apologizing, I said: "I am sorry I am late, Sir!" Swami knew that this was a chastened moment when a correction would be easily taken. "It is all right. Don't worry," he said and then added gently: "One should say *Swami*... One should not say, Sir! I was profusely apologetic and I never said 'Sir' again, except when I knew Swami was in a mood for taking in the exotic and the unusual."

"On one occasion, he talked about poetry, giving a new type of exposition that was truly marvellous. But even with all this, I hovered on the edge. My soul had accepted Baba as a Master. But a gulf had to be bridged, since my intellect remained unresponsive, in spite of positive experience (mine and my wife's) that Baba, Sri Aurobindo and the Mother were one. My wife had accepted this position much earlier than I."

"In 1968, I was elected the first President of the Karnataka State Sathya Sai Samithi. A memorable feature of that occasion was a short, ten-minute speech Swami made. It was memorable because I have never listened at any time to such a precise and concise assessment of all that I stood for. Yet another thing that Swami said, touched me: When we saw Gokak in Hyderabad, a *sankalpa* (will) crossed our mind-why should he not be in Bangalore? And, after about six months, we read in the papers that he was appointed Vice-Chancellor of the Bangalore University and we were very happy about it. This was an eye-opener to me, for it was abundantly clear now that Swami was responsible for the chain of events that led to my appointment in Bangalore.

"In the middle of 1968, my wife had a very peculiar experience. We had gone with friends to Whitefield and sat waiting in the verandah for Swami, who was upstairs. Swami took some time in coming and my wife closed her eyes in meditation, as was her habit. She saw a remarkable thing in her meditation. She saw the Mother of Pondicherry leave Swami's room and start coming down the very staircase by which we were expecting Swami to come. She came down the steps slowly, but very gracefully, walked into the verandah and stood before my wife. Expectantly and in ecstasy she opened her eyes,—to see Swami stand before her smiling! This psychic experience proved to be one more link in the chain and an unbreakable one at that... Even so, my professionally trained intellect didn't treat this as sufficient evidence to equate Swami either with Sri Aurobindo or the Mother."

"A turning point in my attitude occurred, as a result of the question my youngest daughter once asked Swami rather innocently: *When will you come to our house for dinner, Baba?"*

"Swami's answer was spontaneous: Whenever your father wants me to come !"

"I felt greatly disturbed by this reply and said: 'I have invited you, Swami, but such crowds are coming to see you and you are so busy. I thought it would be selfish to trouble you and monopolise you... But nothing will give us greater joy.'

"Swami just laughed."

"Why did Swami say so?... was the question that gnawed into my heart as I returned home that evening. I wanted to decipher any subtle meaning that I might have missed in Swami's words."

"As soon as I reached home, I walked into the worship room, without meaning it, and without any apparent reason... Suddenly it struck me that the reason was the absence of Swami's photograph with those photographs of Mother and Sri Aurobindo on the shrine! Though there was a photograph of Swami in the room, it was at quite a respectable distance, away from the shrine and only nailed on the wall!... Further, the thought struck me that the distance I had maintained in my own mind between Swami and my Masters was reflected in the placement of the photographs."

"I was discriminating! So I lifted the photograph of Swami off the wall immediately, bowed down to it and placed it on the shrine, side by side with those of Sri Aurobindo and the Mother."

"We went to see Swami the next day and before we could broach the subject, Swami said: Day after tomorrow is *Guruvar* (Thursday). I will come to your house for dinner, day after tomorrow."

"You can imagine how supremely happy we must have been then!"

"I invited some fifty friends so that they could have the opportunity to see and hear Swami.The main question that worried me was the mode of welcoming Swami on his first visit to our home. We finally decided to welcome him as our Master with a specialised Marathi song, which had the lines:

Shirdi Mazay pandaripura
Sai Baba maazee aayee*..."

"The next problem was that we did not know the full song!... But how could I get a

---

* Shirdi is my Pandaripur (place of far-famed pilgrimage) Sai Baba is my mother.

Marathi song of a special kind in Bangalore in the course of a day? However, the next day when I went to office, the very first visitor who called, happened to be the Secretary of the Shirdi Baba Bhajan Mandal! Quite excited, I asked him about the song. Surprisingly he knew the song well and he wrote it down for me. With such help from all sources, Swami's visit to our home became a very memorable occasion.

"I gradually learnt from Swami many lessons, the main one being the lesson of love. The answer was mostly provided in the infinite love that flowed ceaselessly from him—a purifying love which besides me, numerous people have experienced. Indeed disciples can hardly find a more loving or humane Master than Swami."

"The conviction and understanding of Sri Baba as an *avatar* gradually grew on me, after I accepted him as my master," continued Dr. Gokak. "When I was asked to attend the World Conference in Bombay in 1968, I knew I had to speak about Swami's avatarhood and mission. So I asked Swami one day about the characteristics of an *avatar*. He explained the sixteen *kalas* or phases by which an *avatar* can be distinguished. Human being and animals have five of these, viz sight, hearing, smell, taste and touch. Another four kalas which the *avatar* shares only with human beings are the mind, heart, intelligence and intuition.

"The remaining seven phases belong exclusively to the *avatar : Grace* or reward for effort; *anugraha* or special grace (whether the recipient merits it or not); the *power to create* a new order of life in society, new states of consciousness in individuals or new objects; the *power to support and sustain* that which is inherently good (but may be defenceless); the *power to destroy* evil; and a form and name which, whenever remembered rightly, result in the immediate spiritual presence (sometimes even physical) of the *avatar* and or a solution for problems.

In spite of Sri Baba's exposition of an avatar's characteristics, a doubt still lurked in Dr. Gokak's mind. To him, Shri Aurobindo was an *avatar* - and he had accepted him as such through conviction and understanding over a period of twenty years. Dr. Gokak wondered if it was possible for quite a few avatars to be present on the earth at the same time. So, he made bold to place his problem before Sri Baba.

Sri Baba's answer was spontaneous : "I am *Lokanath* and Sri Aurobindo *Vyaktinath*."

"These two words conveyed a world of meaning to me," said Dr. Gokak, who felt convinced about the great intellect of Sri Baba He explained that Sri Baba is the Lord of the collectivity and Sri Aurobindo the Lord of the individual. How beautifully and yet how accurately Sri Baba had pinpointed the distinction! thought Dr. Gokak, whose doubts were cleared. He now knew that *avatars* could be of distinct categories and contemporaneous. After the clarification, Swami was firmly planted in Dr. Gokak's heart as an *avatar* come to the world with an epoch-making mission.

In October 1969 he completed his term at the Bangalore University. He was reappointed for another three years, but Dr. Gokak did not feel inclined to accept the appointment. Thereafter he was offered the post of the Director of the Indian Institute of Advanced Study in Simla, where he worked for a year. "After that I decided to send in my resignation, as the period of my contract was over, but I wished for Swami's guidance in this regard... I was overjoyed when the green signal for my decision was provided by Swami in an interesting way. There was the emission of a jet of nectar from the heart region of a photo of mine taken with Swami on the occasion of my sixtieth birthday."

"After I sent my resignation, I wired to Swami stating that I wished to settle down in the Ashram. Swami replied, 'You are welcome!' That decided it and in August 1971, I straight went to Puttaparthi. I had a wonderful stay for over a month. Thereafter I went to Brindavan, in Whitefield, where I lived for five years, under Swami's benign care."

"During this period Swami was so solicitous about even minor details and looked after us (my wife and myself) with such meticulous care that I was overwhelmed. I had never before experienced such affection anywhere. At the time I joined him I experienced a certain blankness and alienation from the world. But thanks to Swami, I rapidly came into my own."

"Soon I took up with Swami as the guide and patron, the job of putting into an academic framework a general idea given by Swami for running Summer Courses on Indian Culture and Spirituality for students during their holidays, I also started working on my epic *Bharata Sindhu Rashmi* (Bharat, river and Ray) and a research project on spiritual education for the U.G.C."

"Five years raced through and I felt myself gradually corrected and bettered by the tests and challenges I was subjected to, by the divine Master. It is not easy to live with Swami, for he is such a powerful force and one has always to be on one's toes! It is not even correct behaviour that will sustain one; it is only a pure heart that can stand his proximity", explained Dr. Gokak.

"The ways of an *avatar* are strange. To give an instance, on his fiftieth birthday celebrations at Puttaparthi, I went up the stage to garland Swami. I had hardly garlanded him when he stunned me by saying 'Wish you a happy birthday, Gokak!' An occasion like that where lakhs of people had gathered to wish Swami many happy returns had been chosen by him to tell me that a new chapter should begin in my life in every way! This is how an avatar works", said Dr. Gokak.

"Why did you not continue to stay with Swami in Whitefield?" I asked.

"I have a house in Bangalore which I had rented out but when it became vacant, I did not wish to give it on rent again. So I decided to move over and stay in Bangalore and continue to visit Swami from there," said Dr. Gokak.

"When Swami returned to Bangalore, after his 50th birthday celebrations, I asked for his permission to leave."

Swami said, "Do you want to go? Then, I will keep coming to you."

I was so touched that I caught hold of his hand and said with emotion, "yes! Swami!... you must come!'

"Don't you miss Swami's physical nearness after coming over to Bangalore?" I asked.

"No... not at all! I don't need him like that, since my love for him is deep and nothing can ever shake it... whenever possible or essential, I go to him and this has been quite satisfying", he said.

Dr. Gokak is often at Whitefield to give lectures at Summer Courses and at other Sathya Sai meetings. He is also asked to address gatherings where Swami is scheduled to give discourses, to introduce or explain essential aspects.

At 70, Dr. Gokak is busy from dawn to dusk, attending to various literary activities along with creative writing. He does everything with a mind that is fully at peace and with love for the Lord. Reminiscing, Dr. Gokak said, "Once when Swami asked me what I wanted most, I told him : *I want to realise my soul*. That has always been my desire and Swami has said 'yes' to it. I don't crave for union with the oversoul to start with. I first wish to realise my soul."

Thus, Swami has indeed been a God-send in Dr. Gokak's life. He has made him learn about pure love, experience it and move on the path to self-realization.

EXPERIENCES OF SOME DEVOTEES

"Your own experience is the best guarantee of truth for you."

—SRI SATHYA SAI BABA

(i) Shirdi Sai and Sathya Sai are the same

"I came across a photograph of Shirdi Sai Baba which seemed to communicate the message: *Think of Me* and I shall bear your burdens. That was in 1951; from then onwards, I have been praying to Shirdi Baba. I feel, everything in my life, good and bad, is because of him, for I take everything as His will", said Mr. Nagarajan, a leading distributor of pharmaceutical products for S. India and partner of Ganapathy & Co., Madras. Mr. Nagarajan confessed that he had never been a very godly or religious person, but "Shirdi Baba completely captured my heart."

He recalled how as a young lad, he had a strange spiritual experience. He was sleeping on the terrace of his house, when just before dawn he had a vision of Goddess Laxmi, who vanished after handing over something in his hand. When he woke up and opened his hand he found an almond *(badam)* fruit. Members of his family did not give much credence to this and felt that the fruit might have been dropped into his hand by some bird! Nevertheless, to Mr. Nagarajan the vision was real and even thrilling! After that experience, he found that Goddess Laxmi was continually kind to him, keeping him in happy affluence. Thus, the vision made him aware of divinity though he did not take to a religious way of life. It was this awareness that made Mr. Nagarajan receptive to the influence of Sri Shirdi Baba in 1954, when "Shirdi Baba began to directly invade my life."

Mr. Nagarajan had a small Ford Prefect car in which he moved about. Once he sojourned in Vellore at the Masilamani Mudaliar *Chatram* (Choultry) in the heart of the city. It was around 5 p.m. and he was working at his table in his room upstairs when all of a sudden he sensed the presence of some one behind him. He turned round only to see a tall figure in new clothes, exactly like Shirdi Sai Baba. "*Paisa Do!* (Give me money!) was the instant command of the person. In great fright, Mr. Nagarajan took out some coins and gave it to him.

"*Allah accha kartaa Hai*" (Allah will do good!) he said as he walked out. On a sudden impulse, Mr. Nagarapan followed him to find out from whence he had come. But even as he neared the steps from his upstairs room, he did not see any one going down!

Where had that old man disappeared? he wondered. Surely the old man could not have walked down all those steps that fast and gone away!

Mr. Nagarajan came down and saw the watchman of the *chatram* (choultry) sitting near the only entrance to the steps. On seeing him, the watchman asked, "Sir! do you need some coffee? If so, I shall fetch it for you. Actually I have been sitting here waiting for your order."

Mr. Nagarajan did not reply him but asked, "Watchman! Didn't you see an old man come down the steps?"

"No Sir !...

I have been here since this afternoon... No one either went up the stairs or came down !" said the watchman.

"The incident both thrilled me and shook me! I felt that it was only Shirdi Sai Baba who had paid me a visit and actually taken the coins from me on that day which happened to be a Thursday. I felt truly blessed," said Mr. Nagarajan, who continued to offer prayers to Shirdi Baba.

In 1957, while at the Hotel Embassy in Bangalore Mr. Nagarajan had a unique vision. It was early in the morning and the vision that appeared was the full size statue of Shirdi Sai Baba seated in a hall with an umbrella over the head. The statue was so lifelike that it made a lasting impression on him. When in 1963, Mr. Nagarajan visited Shirdi for the first time, he saw there the same statue and the hall he had seen earlier in the vision!

Mr. Nagarajan went to Whitefield for the first time in 1963, along with his friend Ratnam. Even though the *darshan* was over, Sri Sathya Sai Baba sent for them and materialised *vibuthi* for them. In the presence of Sri Sathya Sai Baba, Mr. Nagarajan experienced the same happiness he always got while thinking of Shirdi Sai Baba.

After that, Mr. Nagarajan went to Bombay along with Mr. Ratnam. He felt like visiting Shirdi and "so I rang up Indian Air-Aurangabad. The person at the Indian Airlines who answered me on the phone spoke cordially. He said that he would reserve the seats and arrange, through Penn Travels, a taxi from Aurangabad to Shirdi. He also promised to reserve tickets for the return flights to Bombay and Madras and arrange accommodation at the airport, so that the very next day we could catch the flight to Madras. He was very helpful and so I asked him his name. He spoke in Tamil and said "My name is Anderson." The next day I went to the office of the Indian airlines and collected the tickets. Before leaving, I enquired about Mr. Anderson when they told me that there was no one there by that name! Nevertheless, all the reservations and arrangements had been done so perfectly that our trip was comfortable and enjoyable. I had no doubt in my mind that Shirdi Sai had played the role of Anderson !"

Mr. Nagarajan continued both his visits to Sri Sathya Sai Baba and his prayers to Shirdi Sai Baba. However, he was often assailed by doubts about the two Sais being the same and wondered whether he should keep going to Sri Sathya Sai when his heart was with Shirdi Sai !

In 1966, Mr. Nagarajan felt the urge to attend *Maha Shivaratri** festival at Puttaparthi and witness the *Lingodhbava* (materialization of lingam).** His mind again got engrossed in comparing and contrasting the two

---

* The great 'Shivaratri dedicated to God Shiva. The moon and the mind, over which it presides, have each 16 phases. On Shivarathri fifteen of these disappear and there is just a small streak of the moon in the sky.

** The lingam is an ellipsoid symbolising Shiva-shakti.

Sais; to go or not to go was the question that agitated him.

Late that afternoon, after lunch Mr. Nagarajan closed his eyes for forty winks, when he got a vision of Shirdi Baba who said, "Why are you still doubting? If you go to Puttaparthi, you are going only to see me" Happily reassured by this, he went to Puttaparthi.

Mr. Nagarajan recounted another incident that happened in 1966. He had been to a home in Fraser Town, Bangalore, to see for the first time encrustations of *vibuthi* (holy ash) on Sathya Sai photographs. He was thrilled by this manifestation of the divine. The next day early in the morning since it was a Thursday, he decided to visit that house once again and break a coconut in worship. But he dozed off wondering which market would be open that early in the morning. He soon woke up with a start, hearing a big thud. To his utter amazement he noticed that a big coconut had fallen down from the tree in his compound. "Call it coincidence or anything you like !... But to me it was thrilling, as a kind of grace shown by the merciful Lord, who answers even the smallest sincere desires of devotees."

After a few days when Mr. Nagarajan visited that house again, he had another strange encounter. Outside the house, he saw an old man just like Shirdi Baba, walking with a tin pot in his hand. Wondering how similar to Shirdi Sai was the figure and clothes of the old man, Mr. Nagarajan parked his car and got down to have a closer look. But the old man had disappeared mysteriously ! He was nowhere to be found, though Mr. Nagarajan searched in the neighbourhood frantically!

Just prior to the marriage of his son Ramani, Mr. Nagarajan had a vision of Shirdi Sai Baba at the mosque, who said, "Give me two coins"* The vision was there for a few seconds and left a lasting impact on Mr. Nagarajan's mind. The vision persisted during his daily prayers and sometimes a surprising thing happened : the Shirdi Sai vision and that of Sri Sathya Sai, exuding love and compassion, appeared together !

Mr. Nagarajan said that ever since Sri Sathya Sai Baba came into his life, he has felt the subtle influence of the Baba in the solution of many problems. Thus, when he was undecided about the question of the marriage of his son, Sri Sathya Sai Baba came near him at the Poornachandra auditorium in Puttaparthi, in spite of the overwhelming crowds that had

* The two coins symbolically represent faith and patience since holy men do not bother about money.

assembled for the birthday celebrations, and said, "Settle that Lloyd's Road girl for your son!" With a difficult decision thus made for him, Mr. Nagarajan's mind became free and filled with happiness.

He left Puttaparthi for Bangalore and on the next day early in the morning, he had a vision of Kanchi Kamakoti Swamiji enquiring about his son's wedding. Within a few minutes after that Shirdi Baba appeared. Thereafter he could feel the presence of Sri Sathya Sai Baba. "So you see!" said Mr. Nagarajan" once you are near Sri Sathya Sai Baba, all others are also with you."

He drove straight to his home in Madras and after reaching there took a bath. He then went to the *puja* room and stayed there for a long time lost in prayers. When he opened his eyes, he noticed with great joy *theertha* (holy water) flowing out from the toes of Shrdi Sai Baba in the photograph!

Asked about the first interview given to him by Sri Sathya Sai Baba, Mr. Nagarajan described it in a moving tone. The very first question that Sri Baba had asked him affectionately was: "Do you know me?" When he had replied "No! Swami " Sri Baba told him, "Oh! you been thinking of me for a long time!... Rama, Shiva... Sai...all are the same.

Forms are different but the divine principle is the same."

Sri Baba asked Mr. Nagarajan to make progress spiritually and promised to guide him.

"Sri Sathya Sai Baba has been very kind to me and my family. My children have immense faith in him and he takes care of us in many ways: He corrects me and guides me with infinite patience and compassion," said Mr. Nagarajan, and narrated yet another touching episode.

He had been obliged to do official entertaining with alcoholic drinks one evening. The next day when he went to Brindavan, Sri Baba did not grant him *namaskar* saying, Why do you want to do *namaskaar*... you only want parties!"

Mr. Nagarajan returned to his home in Madras sad and dejected. He went straight to the *puja* room and implored, "How can I avoid such cocktail parties? I am a business man! A few tears rolled down from his eyes, as he thought of how he had been unable to prostrate to Sri Baba.

Suddenly Sri Sathya Sai Baba's photo registered a reaction! Tears flowed out from the eyes of the picture, as though to acknowledge the devotee's penitence ! "Then I really felt grieved that I had caused such grief to the compassionate Sai... Such is our Baba who has said : 'You shed one tear and I shall shed a hundred tears for you," said Mr. Nagarajan with folded hands and a far-away look, his thoughts and mind immersed in those nectarine-sweet experiences.

Mr. Nagarajan had a few heart-attacks, including a paralytic stroke but he survived the attacks. "It was only because of the grace of Sai that I am alive, normal and working. Shirdi Baba gave me a vision during the first paralytic attack and told me I would be alright, even though the doctors did not hold out any hopes. When I had a second heart attack, Sri Sathya Sai appeared in my dream to assure me that he would look after me. So, I know that I owe this life entirely to Sai's grace and I will always bow to the two Sais in gratitude, for they are both the same," concluded Mr. Nagarajan.

(ii) Why fear when I am here?

"I have been a devotee of Shirdi Baba for many years. When I was living in East Africa, I always prayed to Shirdi Baba and asked for his help in solving problems. I used to feel close to Shirdi Baba and I made it a habit to mentally converse with him about everything that troubled me", said Sheroo Pithawala with intense emotion. "I had not seen Sri Sathya Sai Baba then. I had only seen a small photograph of his, in a friend's home. I was not particularly impressed and so never even gave a second thought to Sri Baba. I continued to pray to Shirdi Baba and derived much solace from such prayer."

"In 1970, my husband and I decided to return to India for good. We packed our belongings in crates and got ready to sail for India. At that time we received several letters from our friends who had gone to India ahead of us. They said they were harassed by the customs in India and told us not to bring with us anything."

"This upset me and I began praying to Shirdi Baba to give me guidance... Should I sell away all things and after going to India buy whatever was needed anew. I did not want to face trouble with customs or pay exorbitant duty!... When I was in such a mental condition there was another letter advising us not to bring our car since the Indian customs would not clear it at all."

"That night I did not get a wink of sleep. I was terribly upset and worried... I prayed and implored Shirdi Baba again and again to guide me. I wanted to take our car and other possessions to India since I had been using them. 'I don't want trouble with customs...

Baba!... Please advise me!' I said to myself as I finally slipped into sleep."

"That night I had a vision. Yes! near my bed stood Sri Sathya Sai Baba, showing his right palm... He said "Why fear when I am here?' and then disappeared."

"I got up, bewildered and dazed... I recognised him as Sri Sathya Sai Baba, because I had seen his photograph and remembered that round afro hair and orange robe. But why did he come? Was I dreaming? Even if it were a dream, why him? For I had not even sub-consciously thought of him! I had only prayed to Shirdi Baba, but this Sathya Sai Baba had appeared to tell me 'Why fear when I am here?"

"The more I thought about it, the whole matter became more puzzling. Finally I dismissed it all as nothing more than a bizarre dream. I brushed aside the subject and went to sleep again."

"But... the vision appeared again! It was Sri Sathya Sai Baba telling me very clearly 'Why fear when I am here?' "

It soon dawned on Sheroo Pithawala that her prayers to Shirdi Baba were being answered by Sri Sathya Sai Baba! She decided to test the assurance given in that manner by Shirdi Baba. So she took her car and all other possessions with her to India. She had absolutely no trouble at the Bombay Customs! "It was not only smooth sailing on the sea, but also with the Customs and we got everything cleared within an hour!"

Sheroo Pithwala thanked her Shirdi Baba for coming to her rescue. Within a few days of her arrival in Bombay, she learnt that there was a Sathya Sai centre called Dharmakshetra at Andheri. Somehow, she strongly felt like visiting the centre, and as she walked in, she saw a photograph of Sri Baba which resembled exactly the vision of Sri Baba that had appeared to her twice. The full length photograph showed Sri Sathya Sai Baba, with the right palm raised and there was the legend at the bottom : "Why fear when I am here?"

Tears rolled down Sheroo's eyes, as she realized that the two Babas were the same and when she had prayed to one, the other had rushed to her rescue !

Sheroo decided then and there to make Bangalore her home and asked her husband, who was in the printing line in Africa to set up his printing press here. Actually Sheroo had not given any thought to the question of where she should settle down in India, but Sri Sathya Sai Baba had decided it for her.

She is happy she chose Bangalore, as this has enabled her to have *darshans* of Sri Baba in Whitefield. Her devotion for Sri Baba has increased over the years.

Sheroo has been fortunate to have Sri Baba's grace and blessings and tide over serious illnesses. "Baba cures people only when they have full faith and complete surrender", says Sheroo with conviction born out of her own experience.

(iii) **Swami knows everything**

Colonel C. B. Sridharan worked for the Indian Army, in the Corps of Engineers (Madras Sappers) for nearly thirty years. Before his retirement, he was decorated with the *Athi Vishista Seva Medal* (AVSM) for long and distinguished service in the Army. The Sridharans who have been devotees for several years narrated a few of their experiences which have proved to them beyond doubt the omnipresence of Sri Sathya Sai Baba.

Mrs. Prabha Sridharan said, "One day, in 1969, Swami called me along with some others to the interview room and asked: ***Why did you fight with Sridharan yesterday?...***

"Taken aback, I said in a low voice : ***No...*** *Swami ! I did not quarrel!*

"Thereupon Swami narrated in detail the entire happening of that afternoon at our lunch table and repeated verbatim all that I had said! He also mentioned that though my son was not present at that time, my mother was very much there! Finally Swami advised me! *Do not behave like that any more... As a wife, your dharma is to look after your husband's comforts...* Tell Sridharan also not to get so angry...

"I was speechless!... I just cried. That's all I could do!"

* * * * *

Colonel Sridharan recounted another instance: "In early '69 Swamy gave my younger son, Harsha, a ring in silver with Swami's image on it in gold. Swami put it on the third finger of Harsha's right hand and told him never to take it out.

"A few months later, all of us went to Bombay in connection with the passing out parade of my son Arjun from the National Defence Academy. During our stay in Bombay, Harsha noticed that the skin under the ring had turned white. So he removed the ring for about half an hour to air the finger. We thought nothing about this, until we returned to Bangalore, when Swami, on seeing Harsha asked in Tamil: *Don't you remember what I told you when I gave you the ring?*

Why did you remove it for some time, while you were in Bombay?

"Harsha, who had never expected Swami to know about it fell at his feet and said he would not do so again! This demonstrated to us Swami's knowledge of even trivial happenings!"

* * * * *

Another incident was also recounted by Colonel Sridharan. "In September 1978, our (then one-year-and-eight-month-old) grand daughter slipped and fell down from a window of their flat in Bombay. She fell from a height of about ten feet, landing on her head, on a huge stone. She suffered a big cut, running from the eye brow across the forehead. She was rushed to the hospital and the cut was stitched under anaesthesia. After a few days, she was discharged from the hospital.

"We learn about this only later, when we went to Bombay and saw the girl with the plaster across the forehead and up to the skull.

"After our return to Bangalore, Swami asked me all of a sudden: *Wasn't Arjun's daughter hurt in the head?*

"I was so surprised since I had not mentioned anything about this to Swami!... But Swami knows everything.

(iv) "Swami Will Catch You"

"I had just joined the Seva Dal, when I first went to Puttaparthi. I did not have any idea of the kind of work I might be expected to do. As soon as I reached Parthi and joined the Bangalore Seva Dal group, I was given the tough job of transporting huge granite stones, since a lot of construction work was in progress in connection with Baba's 50th Birthday," said Dr. A. V. Krishnamurti,* who had never done any physically hard work till that day and found it extremely painful to lift the heavy stones. "My hands started burning and I found it difficult to carry on. I slowly slipped away from that job and moved on, only to be caught by another group who were passing baskets of sand in a relay from one to another, to reach an area that needed levelling with sand." As a Seva Dal worker, Dr. Krishnamurti could not refuse any duties that were given! Resigning himself to the situation, he joined the line of workers and passed on basket after basket of sand. All the hard work made him very hungry; but when he went to the canteen, there was such a long queue that he was unable to get any food within the time allotted for lunch. So he went back to his job.

---

* Professor, Department of Aeronautical Engineering, Indian Institute of Science, Bangalore. (also Visiting Professor, ITI Bombay, 72 - 73); Convener, Sri Sathya Sai Seva Dal, Bangalore.

Around 4.30 in the evening, Swami gave *darshan* from the first floor of Prasanthi Nilayam. Dr. Krishnamurti was then at a place from where he was able to see rows and rows of men and women passing on baskets of sand rather quickly and with effortless ease. He also saw various other groups, silently concentrating on various tasks. Suddenly he recalled the Ramayana and felt that everyone including monkeys and squirrels, must have worked for Sri Rama in that manner ! He experienced a strange calm as he went back to the heavy manual work. At one stage however, when he found it impossible to lift the basket, a miracle happened. The heavy basket became light as a feather ! He was able to throw it to the next person like a bunch of flowers ! He never felt the weight of the sand and exclaimed aloud, "What wonder! This is now like a flower basket!"

Dr. Krishnamurti continued to be dazed by that strange experience even while he had his dinner at night. Sleeping however posed a problem, because he had not come prepared with any night wear to sleep out in the open and that was exactly what he was forced to do! He had to sleep under a small tree on a night that was extremely cold. He had no warm covering: he tossed and turned, thoroughly exhausted both mentally and physically. After a few exhausting hours he said to himself, "What is all this for!... O Lord!... Is this *sadhana?* Why am I here when you are not even giving me a wink of sleep?"

Within minutes of his saying so, he fell asleep!

When Dr. Krishnamurti woke up it was about 6 a.m. He felt very fresh and experienced a beautifully rested feeling. He rubbed his eyes, looked at his watch and sat up, all of a sudden, with a start. For lo! his palms had become smooth as ever, *sans* cuts and scratches! His body showed no signs of exhaustion or pain; everything had miraculously disappeared and he felt as good as new! "Then I knew, it was the work of Bhagawan Baba and none else!"

Dr. Krishnamurti recalled yet another experience. His distant relative died suddenly and he had to take the body to their village. Four friends and the son of the dead person went with Dr. Krishnamurti.

After the body was handed over to the relatives, he paid half the fare to the taxi driver. (The rest was to be paid after they returned to 'Parthi'). During the return journey, Dr. Krishnamurti was accompanied by a friend and the taxi driver also had his friend. *En-route*, Dr. Krishnamurti and his friend dozed off in the running taxi, since the grim experience of travelling with a dead body for over 14 hours had been rather nerve-racking!

When they woke up, they found that the taxi had halted at a village. Dr. Krishnamurti felt like buying some fruits from the village fruit vendor. As he looked for his purse he got a shock! The purse was missing and he was unable to believe his eyes! His friend too searched for the purse but did not find it! How was he to pay for the taxi? The driver said, he knew nothing about the money and added, "Ask your friend!"

Dr. Krishnamurti got angry and said, "Only four of us are here and the money could not have gone anywhere!... Don't talk like that!... If you have the money give it to us... Otherwise Swami will catch you!"

The driver remained callous: "Where could I have taken it and hidden it Sir?" he asked and began to show all his belongings. He even pulled out the car seats and covers to prove his innocence.

A crowd began to collect, hearing the altercation between the driver and the occupants of taxi.

The driver got annoyed and said, "I want to leave now!" All of a sudden, an old man made his way through the crowd and signalled them to stop, showing a raised palm ! He looked sternly at the driver and asked him to open the bonnet. When the bonnet was opened, Dr. Krishnamurti's purse was there for all to see!... Right on the battery!... The driver thought, he had found a good place to hide the purse and get away with it !

The angry village crowd turned on the driver and wanted to take him to task. They did not want Dr. Krishnamurti to pay the driver anything but hand him over to the police. Dr. Krishnamurti did not want to do so. He paid the driver the exact charges and got out of the taxi, not wanting to use the vehicle any more ! He then looked out for the old man who had come in the nick of time to save the situation ! But the man could not be found! No one had noticed him go in all that confusion !

Later, after all the excitement had died down, it struck Dr. Krishnamurti during a calm moment that the man with the raised palm who had come to his rescue could have been none other than Swami ! Who else would have known the driver's hiding place and arrived in time to save an innocent devotee who had just remarked in justified anguish "Swami will catch you!"

"Ever since I have been more than convinced about Swami's omnipresence and his divine powers. He is none other than *Paramatma* and all of us should know how lucky we are that he is with us", says Dr. Krishnamurti.

(v) **Beyond reason**

November 1979: A rather unusual international conference was organised in Bangalore, under the auspices of the International Institute of Integral Human Sciences, founded by Dr. John Leslie Rossner, Anglican priest, parapsychologist and professor of comparative religion at the Concordia University Montreal, Canada, and his spouse, Prof. (Mrs) Marilyn Zwaig Rossner, a Canadian "sensitive" or psychic expert.

My wife and I had discussions with Dr. Rossner who said that "the conference sought to bring together the East and West in a holistic alliance... While the West has astronauts and cosmonauts probing outer space, the East and particularly India has *psychonauts* who go deep into *inner space*. We have 40 foreign delegates in the group attending this conference and all of them are experts in different disciplines... We have been priviledged to visit the Aurobindo Ashram, the Shivananda Ashram at Rishikesh, the Vivekananda Rock Memorial at Cape Comorin and the Ashram of Sri Sathya Sai Baba at Puttaparthi. We had a meaningful interview and highly stimulating discussions on God, spirituality and the integral human being, with Sri Sathya Sai Baba, who answered all our questions and cleared our doubts."

We talked to the Rossners about their experiences with Sri Sathya Sai Baba. Marilyn gave a beaming smile as she said, "When I saw Sai Baba, I noticed that the aura behind his head was white and gold, with streaks of mauve. He was all energy... one with the energy all around - one with the universal and cosmic energy. I would say that Sai Baba was bathed in an ocean of energy and his body merged with his energy.

"When Sai Baba talked, I saw pastel shades of colour emanating—shades of mauve, pink and blue. His words *Very happy to see you all!* were so full of love that I saw the colours form into a heart. His hand movements were spirals of energy. It was constantly in spirals. Suddenly there was a spark (like a spark of electricity) and there was a ring that he had made!'

"I saw the figure of Jesus Christ superimposed on him... When he lifted his hand in blessing, I saw Jesus Christ again on his hand When I saw him and the visions of Christ, on him, a voice said in my ear: Even if Jesus

Christ came as he was to this earth now, who will believe him?... No one!

"Sai Baba is an *Avatar.* He is all love. He is all energy. He is divine... He went to a member of our group straight and asked her 'How is your leg?... The pain?' That was astounding! He looked at the blisters on her leg and the lady confessed a little later that all the excruciating pain in her leg vanished totally!"

Marilyn is specialising in yoga as a tool for healing emotional disturbances of children. She is known not only for her psychic powers but also for a very popular T. V. programme conducted by her entitled: "Beyond Reason."

Marilyn's first contact with Sri Sathya Sai Baba was in 1978, when Sri Baba appeared as a vision in her living room, in answer to her general prayer "Oh! Help me... God!" Again in 1979, during a television show, she was once so very tired that her brain refused to work. So, she mentally called out for God's help to give the correct answers, when suddenly there was a materialisation. Everyone saw the resultant cloud of smoke but Marilyn saw something more: Sri Baba's solid form emerged and walked across the closed glass partition, to her side and whispered the right answers into her ears, as question after question was asked. She was excited as she did the show, repeating his answers. Marilyn was so much overwhelmed that she kept saying to herself "Thank you, God!"

Her husband, Dr. Rossner recounted several instances of *vibuthi* manifestations. Once when Marilyn did not feel well, he looked for Baba's *vibuthi*. All of a sudden, they noticed *vibuthi* on Marilyn's eye and cheeks. Rossner soon realised that the *vibuthi* came from his own hand and emanated from a finger... They were both astounded beyond words... On another occasion, during a bus journey, it was Marilyn who again needed the *vibuthi*. And it appeared, on Rossner's shirt, from nowhere!

Marilyn, who does much meditation and yoga says "Baba is extraordinary in many ways." She has seen energy emanating from Baba's picture in her shrine. Once Baba suddenly appeared for a student in her meditation class, even though that person had not even heard of Sai Baba! In her own deep meditation, whenever she had Baba's form in mind, "there is never any form lingering, after a while!... It is absolutely gone and this represents to me the totality of Sri Baba's divine nature or his complete oneness with the cosmos."

Dr. John Rossner mentioned an interesting phenomenon during their interview with

Sai Baba. The group of people with whom he had gone to visit Baba sang a hymn in praise of the Lord:

"Joyful, Joyful, we adore thee,
God of glory, Lord of love
Hearts unfold like flowers before thee
Praising thee, their sun above,
Melt the clouds of sin and sadness;
Drive the dark of doubt away;
Giver of immortal gladness.
Fill us with the light of day
All thy works with joy surround thee."

As Baba swayed to the music Dr. Rossner saw Baba encompassed by a big energy field... That field of energy was so huge and extensive that Baba's figure appeared a tiny fraction of it! That clearly proved to Rossner "that Baba is indeed no ordinary person." Dr. Rossner's faith in Sri Sathya Sai Baba is deep and abiding.

(vi) The Cosmic Christ

"He is the Cosmic Christ", said Ron Mason*, in a deep and measured tone, solemnly nodding his head.

---

* Ron's great grandfather was in the Cabinet of Mr. Gladstone, who was the Prime Minister of Great Britain when India was under British rule. His grandfather who was with Lord Dalhousie in India, wrote a book in 1960 on Zorastrianism. Ron's father was a classmate of King Edward VIII (when he

"Yes! He is none other," said his wife Peggy.* A former actress, Peggy Mason is a well known writer of novels and plays. For the last twelve years she has been writing on spiritual and metaphysical themes for renowned journals in the field like the hundred-year old magazine "Two Worlds." The Masons, a spiritual-minded couple in their seventies, were on a visit to India to see Sri Sathya Sai Baba.

"We were very doubtful about undertaking the trip. At our age, things are not easy!... We were worried about our health, the Indian climate and the food... but luckily, we have had a smooth and lovely trip without set-backs", said Ron. The Masons are a very sincere and God-fearing people always wishing good for others and wanting to live in love of the Lord. They have been on the quest for God for years on end.

When they were face to face with Sri Sai Baba, they felt that they were face to face with the ultimate Reality. "It is very difficult to explain this immense spiritual experience. Sri Sathya Sai Baba is the Truth. He is the one who sent Christ to us", says Ron, tears

---

was Prince of Wales) and from the age of 10, Ron had seen Prince Edward coming to his home.

Peggy's grandfather was a Governor of Bengal and members of their family have lived in India.

streaming down his eyes, and Peggy nods her head in complete agreement with him. Both brim with reverence and devotion for Sri Baba and are grateful for the grace and love showered by him on them. "He is so busy, yet he gave us so much of his time and attention," they said.

Peggy and Ron went to Brindavan, Whitefield, near Bangalore. They waited near the hostel, and when Sri Baba walked towards them it was the gratification of their prayers. They knelt down and kissed Sri Baba's hand.

Later, at an interview, Baba materialised a rosary of 108 crystal beads for Peggy and a Baba ring for Ron. They were overwhelmed with the gifts. It was as though an avalanche of love had swept over them, leaving them dazed, ecstatic and satisfied. "It was a rare treat of bliss, worth waiting for even a life time!"

How did they come to know about Sri Baba, and how were they able to establish such rapport with him?

It was Peggy who first had a Sai spiritual experience. She had cut out a photograph of Sri Baba from the magazine "Psychic News" and put it on a table, opposite her bed. She was unwell and experienced great pain in her left leg to the point of her being unable to walk beyond a few yards. The doctor advised a major operation, but even so did not guarantee a cure! On the other hand, he warned her that in the event of the operation not being successful she would lose her leg!

One night, as Peggy was contemplating on the Baba photograph, she received a shock. The photo suddenly jumped an inch or so, to one side and back again; at the same time a glimmer of light lit up the table and shone with a strange iridescence. Everything else in the room was normal as before.

Was it a special experience or a clairvoyant vision? Peggy was too dazed to decide. Thereafter, this happened on several nights "and still does, off and on." Subsequently she learnt from others how they too had similar experiences with Baba photographs.

The leg problem soon assumed acute and agonising proportions. So, Peggy prayed to Sri Baba saying: "Oh Baba! I wish you could do something about my leg!"

A day later, she got a copy of the book "Sai Baba and the psychiatrist" and she kept looking at Sri Baba's photo on the cover, when the phone rang. It was a man's voice: "I am ringing up on behalf of Swami Ganesha Ananda. She is very much interested in your writings and would like to meet you."

Three days later the lady who lived at Sevenoaks, fifteen miles away, came to meet Peggy Mason. She was a widely travelled Indian lady and said that she knew Sri Sathya Sai Baba and had seen him in Bangalore; but what was more, she was a healer who was "bursting to heal!" She gave Peggy healing quite briefly and with no fuss. But it was very effective! Peggy could scarcely believe it, when the leg pain disappeared in a few days and she felt well enough to dance all night at a ball!

Peggy instinctively knew that the Indian lady had been prompted and used by Sri Baba, to whom Peggy had appealed to cure her leg pain... Not that he needed to use any one, but at times this is the way he works, feels Peggy. Further strengthened in their faith, the Masons started reading continuously all about Sri Baba, studying his writings and published speeches and asking devotees about their experiences. This developed in them a yearning to see Sri Baba in person and "Now that we have seen him, we know that he is none other than the Lord in our hearts." They feel that he is the universal spirit, the cosmic love, and the creative force.

Meeting him and talking to him have convinced them that he is the Father that

Christ always talked about and ultimately realised, when he said "I and my Father are one."

As they took leave of Sri Baba, Ron asked, "Are you the cosmic Christ?"

Baba's answer was unhesitating and natural. "Yes!" he said ever so simply. "The way he said it; the way he looked straight into my eyes while saying it were enough to make us realise that he is the cosmic Christ. We are lucky to have him with us, lucky to have the privilege of his moving amidst us like any ordinary man, enabling us to talk to him and hear him speak, sing and laugh. We are indeed blessed", said Ron, in a voice that communicated a longing for communion with the eternal spirit.

(vii) **"Ram!" and "Hare Ram!"**

January 1980 : During a casual chat, I found a very keen Sai devotee in one of the senior retired Officers of the Coffee Board, Sri R. Narayana Iyengar (64). The questions I asked him and his replies are reproduced verbatim.

Q : When did you first come to know about Sri Sathya Sai Baba and when did you meet him?

A : I heard about Sri Sathya Sai Baba in 1949, but I had my first interview with him only on 1st November 1957. The interview was a short one and was given to me at the residence of a friend of mine, in Bangalore. Sri Baba had gone there for the house-warming ceremony. Sri Baba spoke to me only a few words. He said, "You have been wanting to meet me for the last so many years but only now has the time come for it!" He also asked me to go over to Puttaparthi in March 1958.

Q : Can you tell me something about the interview in March?

A : Baba granted me a short interview for 10 minutes. He told me all about my past, with great accuracy and several of them were facts I had not told anybody. He also mentioned about a case in which I was wrongly implicated. He said I had nothing to worry about, as I was innocent. Much later, I found that Baba's words came true, for no further reference was ever made about it.

Q : Now that you have been a devotee for over two decades, what difference has this made in your general conduct and behaviour?

A : I have become more God-minded and God-fearing. I have been able to conquer feelings of jealousy and hatred, to a very great extent. I have developed the tendency to help others. I have become more compassionate to those in distress and even in my official life I was very honest because I knew Baba was for ever watching me. I feel Sri Baba has been continuously guiding me... He has made me experience a lot of peace in daily living.

Q : Can you explain how exactly Sri Baba has been guiding you?

A : Baba has been guiding me by appearing, at regular intervals in my dreams. Of course, like all human beings I had my problems from time to time. So I used to write to Sri Baba about them. The surprising thing was that after I posted a letter, Baba would appear in my dream either the same night or 3 days after the posting of the letter. He would advise me in my dreams about the problems mentioned by me in letters.

Q : I do not understand clearly... Will you explain this with some specific instances?

A : Yes! Once I wrote to Baba listing out several problems. That very night Sri Baba appeared to me in my dream. I saw him holding my letter and he gave answers, following the same serial order in which I had mentioned my problems.

Q: But this becomes guidance for purely materialistic matters. Has not Baba been guiding you spiritually?

A: Yes! Of course! One night, in 1960, Sri Baba appeared in a dream. In a forest, he beckoned to me and placed me on his lap as though I were a child. He then initiated me into a *mantra* and asked me to repeat it often, to progress on the spiritual path.

Q: Can you mention any other significant instance of Sri Baba's guidance to you?

A: Of course... I would like to mention one instance relating to my mother. Baba appeared in my dream and told me 6 months in advance about her impending demise and asked me to take good care of her. Again he appeared a month before her demise and indicated the period of her end, and asked me to apply for leave and stay back in the house. As Baba had said, my mother's end came and I had the privilege of having her on my lap, during her last moments. The last words my mother uttered before her death were first the word "Ram!" and then the words "Hare Ram!" After her passing away, a strange fragrance resembling the fragrance of jos sticks, flooded the room. The fragrance persisted till the body was removed from the house and the surprising thing was we had not lit any jos sticks. This clearly indicated to me the presence of Sri Baba, and later when I met him, he confirmed that he was present during the last moments of my mother's life. He also said that she only uttered the word "Ram" but that he had made her utter the words "Hare Ram!"

I would also like to give another instance. In 1972, I was suffering from a severe carbuncle on the right side of my chest. The surgeon advised me to get it operated but there was much hesitation on my part, since I suffered from diabetes. So I felt I should go and take Baba's blessings before undergoing the operation.

I went to Puttaparthi and had Baba's darshan. I thought I would have an opportunity to talk to Baba but Baba blessed me from a distance and went away. I returned greatly disappointed at the thought I had been unable to talk to Baba about the operation.

However, on reaching Bangalore I realised why it had not been necessary for me to talk to Sri Baba. Indeed to my amazement I found that the carbuncle had disappeared leaving behind a red scar! The surgeon who was to have operated on me was mystified and asked me how this had happened. I just said: "*All because of Baba's grace*" and this only served to confound the surgeon all the more!

Q : What do you think is the main reason for Sri Baba showering his grace on you?

A : I really cannot answer this question. I have immense and total faith in Sri Baba, who has often said that only when devotees have full faith can they establish a link with him.

(viii) **Don't think!... Just be aware**

"Sai *bhajans* and a mango took me to Puttaparthi and to Bhagawan Sri Sathya Sai Baba..." said the 54-year-old Nassin Mishaan of Guatemala.

Asked to explain his statement, Mr. Mishaan said, "I was in New Delhi in 1974 when I attended a Sai *bhajan* session. At the end of the *bhajans*, I was presented a mango, that had been placed before the picture of Sri Sathya Sai Baba as an offering. I must frankly tell you that before I went to the Sai *bhajan* I was very low in spirits... But somehow after I ate the mango, I felt so happy inside that I thought I was in Heaven."

"Within a week after this happening, I went to Puttaparthi. You see, I was in quest of a Guru and I had been to several holy places in the world and in India. At the end of it all, I was in Puttaparthi..."

"After considerable waiting for several days, Swami gave an interview just on the day I was leaving... He told everything about my wife and myself and I cried out of happiness..."

"The next year I visited Puttaparthi, along with my daughter in England; but this time I came with a lady and her seven year old daughter, who had been born with a hole in the back. She suffered from malfuctioning of the kindneys and liver; her spine had been injured and she was in a wheel chair, unable to walk, since her legs were almost dead; the doctoros had given her only two months !"

The moment of our arrival in Puttaparthi was the usual time for *darshan;* Swami gave *vibuthi* to the girl and said, "I will take care." We stayed for a month and during this period Swami gave so much love that the girl became much better. He also gave her a bottle of medicine and materialised a medallion for her with Shirdi Baba on one side and Sathya Sai Baba on the other. We went back and many months elapsed. The doctors were surprised... Not only was the girl alive, but she had actually improved to a very great extent... And she was able to walk with the help of props. The funny part of it all is that the doctors really cannot believe it at all!..." said Mr. Mishaan.

"Can you tell me something about yourself before and after coming to Swami?"

"Yes, before coming to Swami, I was a businessman for sixteen hours in a day (Mr. Mishaan is a stock holder of several companies and has a textile plant and chewing gum factory in Guatemala). My ambition was only to make money... more and more money... But soon I realised that though I had everything, lots of money, home, cars, children... something was missing and that I was not at all happy deep inside. This was how I started my spiritual search. At first, I did not understand Swami and it took me long to be convinced about Swami's divinity..."

"How did you finally get convinced about Baba's divinity? I asked.

"Well! You see even before meeting Swami I had given up smoking and eating meat because I very much wanted to come to India. I decided also that I do not want anything... I just wanted to meditate. Here I made many attempts without success."

"But when I first met Swami I really started meditating and I felt some power within, guiding me particularly when I applied Swami's *vibuthi* on the forehead. I am able to meditate much better now and Swami seems to be telling me subconsciously, 'Don't think... just be aware!' He has been really guiding me in this form within me and I feel this is an indication of his divinity," said Mr. Mishaan.

"Again, I never knew what love really meant. I used to think it is giving somebody something, being nice or giving a kiss to somebody. Love is something only Swami can give you!... No one else! ...you realize what love is when Swami gives it to you and you experience it. Once you experience Swami's pure love, then you realize, who he is—not before," said Mr. Mishaan visibly moved.

"Swami has also made me feel the impermanence of things; that nothing belongs to us and that whatever is given is only given by the divine power and whatever happens is always for the best. I used to be indifferent to the poor previously but now I care for them also. This is what I have learnt from Swami, but very slowly."

"Have you also had any material benefits after meeting Swami?" I asked.

"Of course! After meeting Swami even the first time, my business improved hundred per cent... But then I am not at all interested in money or such success!"

"Have you any ambitions?" was my next question.

Mr. Mishaan halted for a minute and said, "My ambition is to make all my countrymen know about Swami, feel his love and follow his teachings."

Have any of your countrymen been to Sri Baba?" I asked.

"Yes, many have. I also came twice with two groups of people from Guatemala to Puttaparthi and several of them have been experiencing visions of Swami and a silent transformation is taking place in their lives."

"You say, you have felt the divinity of Swami. Tell me, whether you have always believed in God?" I asked.

"Well! well! Even though I was born a jew (you know jews are strict in religion), I have never believed in God. But now, I not only believe in God but feel the God inside me."

"Has Sri Baba appeared in your dreams?" I asked.

"Oh yes! Once he came in a dream and said, "you will experience *Sat* or existence... It is not enough if I say I exist, because we are all living like robots. We take everything for granted and once you do so, you live like a machine! you really live or exist only when you realize the inner God... God is not some one with a wip!... After meeting Swami, I know God is love. Once you know this, I am convinced you will be on the *dharmic* path," said Mr. Mishaan, a feeling of love suddenly flitting across his face.

(ix) **Who was that old man?**

Professor Indra Narain Bhatnagar, retired Principal of Ram Lal Anand College, University of Delhi, and his wife Dr. Gunwant Bhatnagar, a Licentiate of the Faculty of Surgery and Medicine, from the Medical School (now College) Amritsar, and formerly an Asst. Surgeon in the Punjab Medical Service, are devotees who live in Baba's Ashram.

The Professor explained how he had felt drawn to Sri Baba: "Sometime in 1968, I happened to read an article on Bhagawan Sri Sathya Sai Baba in the 'Illustrated Weekly of India'. It was an admirable summing up but a little too condensed for quick absorption. Just then, an old teacher (and later, the Chairman of the Governing Body of the Ram Lal Anand College), Prof. S. R. Grover, passed on to me four copies of the 'Sanathana Sarathi'. During that very period another devotee of Sri Baba lent a copy of the 'Sathya Sai Speaks (Vol. I)'. I must confess that when I had read all this material, I felt literally sensationalised!... I could have shouted for joy: 'the Lord has come in human form!' Sri Baba's announcements are so authentic that they convinced me from the very beginning that they were like the announcements made by Lord Krishna and Jesus Christ. On that basis alone I felt he is God, since only the divine can boldly do so!... And I started worshipping him."

"Sometime later, I paid a visit to Prasanthi Nilayam. A day before departure from Delhi, I had a dream in which I saw Baba walking on the balcony of a building from one side to the other. On arriving at Prasanthi Nilayam I was agreeably surprised to find the same building I had seen in the dream and Baba walking from one side to the other. The same day, while devotees were sitting in rows, he passed by me, smiled and raising his hand of blessing, said *achcha* (good)."

"In the evening of the next day, he called a large group of devotees from Delhi for a collective interview. At this meeting I beseeched him for a personal interview. He said in Hindi "*Interview maangta hai, Dilli main bahut achcha interview daegaa*" (you want an interview... I shall give you a very good interview in Delhi)."

"I must mention here that before I left Delhi for Puttaparthi, an old man had come to my office. I had received him and offered him tea. I do not remember how the subject cropped up but I told him, 'I am going to Puttaparthi to see Sri Sathya Sai Baba... Perhaps you have heard about him?'... He said, 'Yes, I have heard about him... They say he is a great magician'... I then told him 'I do not know that !... I think he is an *avatar!*' I also told him that I would be returning in ten days' time, whereupon the old man remarked, 'I am also here for ten day's.' The meeting then ended and I saw him off at the gate."

"Surprisingly when I returned from Puttaparthi, I found the same old man awaiting me at the gate. I escorted him in, offered him a seat and ordered tea for both of us. I don't know why, but I never felt like asking him who he was... Instead, I just said, 'I have been to Puttaparthi... I think Bhagawan Baba is an *avatar*'. At my remark the old man smiled, nodded his head and softly said 'yes' "

Then he started speaking about spirituality He briefly dealt with several subjects like (i) the elusive nature of the mind and the need to control it, (ii) the significance of the *principal mantra 'OM'* and (iii) the cultivation of values such as *yamas and niyamas*. Finally he dictated to me a *poem of prayer* which translated into English reads as follows:

"O magnanimous Father, Sri OM.
Sustainer of the Universe,

Pray confer on me the ability
To practice *sadhana*
So that I can find my way to Truth
Help me develop the qualities of *yama* and *niyama*
So that my spiritual advancement is facilitated.
May I practise love
And spurn deceit and cunning,
O ordainer of Law Divine!
Without your will,
Neither can a leaf stir
Nor a flower blossom.
Your will is marked by purity
Whereas I am afflicted by lust and other desires.
Therefore I pray for your benediction
So that I may rid myself of desires and become pure,
Hey Ram! May your will prevail !*

* The original poem in Hindi was as follows:

Ai Mahadaani Pita, Shri OM
Jag Ke Dhaata
Dekar Hame Abhyas Bal
Dikhawo path san marg ka
Ham Yam Niyam Dharm Kare
Sanmarg par chalte rahe
Path prem par age Badhe
Chal Aur Kapat ko tyag kar.
Teree Sattha ke Bina
He Prabhu mangal mool
Pata koyee na hil sake
Khile Na Koyee phool

"I listened to him half in wonder and half in rapture. He soon left me and I saw him up to the college gate. After a few moments, I turned back to see if he was still close by. But he was nowhere to be seen! How had he disappeared so soon? I felt puzzled!"

Mr. Bhatnagar later asked Sri Baba about this when to his great delight, Sri Baba smiled and said, "Yes!... I was that old man who after you had seen him off, vanished !"

Many happenings thereafter, convinced the Bhatnagars about the omnipresence, omniscience and omnipotence of Sri Baba. "At an interview given to us some time in 1971, my wife and I received an autograph from Bhagawan Baba on the title page of a book. I valued it immensely and resolved to get it framed as soon as we reached Delhi. But on reaching Delhi, I found no frame at home and before I could procure one from the market, some time elapsed. Soon inertia got the better part of my original enthusiasm and the matter almost slipped out of memory."

"One night Sri Baba appeared in my dream. He put his hand into a heap of old

Teree Iccha Ram Hai
Meree Iecha Kaam
Prabhuji ye vardaan do
Sada Rahoon Nishkaam
He Ram! Tere Ichchha Poorna Ho!

newspapers stored in the drawer of an inbuilt cupboard and took out a frame! He inserted the autographed page into it but finding the frame a little too big, rejected it. He put his hand once again into the drawer and brought out another frame containing a photograph which he quickly removed. In its place, the inserted the autographed page and the frame was the correct size. This operation finished, the dream ended."

"On getting up in the morning, I remembered the autographed page and as indicated in the dream, searched for a frame amidst the old sheets of paper in the cupboard. I was delighted when I actually found one! It was a little too big and so I searched again in the cupboard and brought out another frame containing a photograph. I removed the photograph and in its place inserted the autographed page which fitted into it extremely well! I must confess that I had totally forgotten that I had these two frames at home, but the omniscient Baba had not only pointed out that they were there, but had also rehearsed the details of a subsequent operation with absolute precision."

Narrating other experiences, Professor Bhatnagar said, "I was still in job... It was nearly ten years ago, when for no apparent reason I discovered that I had developed two spots in my left eye from which descended a few hairlike lines producing a complex structure. This structure blurred my vision a little. But what was worse was that when I sat to meditate, the spots loomed large seriously impairing my concentration. I mentioned this to my wife, but since there was no pain, somehow or other, we took no special care and postponed consulting an eye-specialist. In the meantime, an opportunity offered itself for us to pay a visit to Puttaparthi. Here then occurred what I believe to be one of my major experiences and an act of sheer divine grace.

"Bhagawan Baba during one of his evening *darshans* called me for an interview and pointing to my eye said "Your eye ! But I was lost in other thoughts and paid no attention. Towards the end of the interview he materialised *vibuthi* and gave it to me saying, 'Eat it'. I ate it straightaway. That evening, I remained absorbed in the contemplation of Sri Baba's loving treatment of devotees... The next day when I got up early in the morning and sat down to pray, I felt that the blurring impression of the left eye had gone. For, I could see with it as well as I did once. To make sure, I closed that eye several times but each time on opening it, I felt that a miraculous cure had been effected by Bhagawan...

The spots with their hair-like structure had simply disappeared!"

"As I got more and more engrossed in the thought of Bhagawan, I developed a personal technique of concentration", said Professor Bhatnagar. "For instance, while going to bed I would imagine that I was holding on to Sri Baba's foot and in order to concretise this thought, I would place one of my hands at the edge of the pillow. This went on for quite some time till one day, I was startled to find Sri Baba's actual foot in my hand! I repeat, it was Baba's actual foot!... a foot of flesh and blood... and my experience of grasping it lasted more than a few seconds!... Later, I had the good fortune of being called for an interview when Sri Baba gave a *padanamaskaar*,* he extended his foot towards me and allowed me to hold it in exactly the same way as I had done, during my extra-ordinary experience!"

Talking about other colourful experiences, Professor Bhatnagar said, "We were then in Whitefield residing in the hired premises of a bungalow. Perhaps change in the weather or the long strolls in Whitefield, while looking for a small cottage for permanent residence, led to my illness with temperature running to 103°F. I was under my wife s treatment but

---

* Prostration at the feet of a hallowed person.

the temperature persisted. In that situation, I was unable to avail myself of Bhagwan's *darshan,* so I urged my wife not to miss it. She used to go to Brindavan and sit under the tree. One day, Sri Baba came close to her and said '*Bahut phirta hai*' (He wanders a great deal). Obviously he referred to my wanderings in Whitefield! But my wife said, 'Baba, he is ill and down with temperature!' "

"Sri Baba laughed and commented '106°F?' but added, '*prasad daegaa*' (I shall give *prasad*). But she got no *prasad!* The next day too, she had a similar experience and while my fever remained unabated, Sri Baba's hilarity was the only *prasad* I got! But as evening set in, two students of the Sri Sathya Sai College came on bicycles and said 'Sir, Swami sends herewith some packets of *vibuthi as prasad!*"

"I was delighted. Instantly I consumed a packet and in keeping with the certainty of my belief, within minutes, the temperature came down to 97°F! The decline of the temperature would have been a small matter had it not been accompanied by a wonderful experience which both my wife and I shared with a feeling of thrill."

"I was in bed even though the temperature had come down and my wife was standing at the doorway. She shouted for joy, 'Come and see the pink colour around the compound!' I hastened to the door and watched a unique sight. The whole compound of 200 ft. by 100 ft. at that hour of 5.30 p.m. on that cloudy day had been covered by a pink hue. It looked as though a pink carpet had been spread on the ground. Also, the light shone like a bright lace on the flowers of a small sapling there, bringing to mind Wordsworth's description "*apparelled in celestial light.*" The Bhatnagars felt sure that besides sending the *vibuthi*, Sri Baba had also rolled out a pink carpet of grace for them!

Professor Bhatnagar recalled another allied experience in Delhi way back in the early seventies. "One morning when my wife got up for her usual meditation, she opened the door of the drawing room, when she called out to me 'Come and see how the drawing room is thick with jasmine perfume! I rushed there and had the unique experience of a wave of the fragrance hitting my nostrils. I opened another door of this 300 sq. ft. room and the same aroma wafted out. However, as this was our first experience we wished to test it. So, the next day, I kept a handful of jasmine flowers before a picture of Sri Baba but where was the perfume? It was as conspicuous by its absence as it was conspicuous by its presence the previous day!"

"Have you had any exciting dreams?" I asked and Professor Bhatnagar said, "I have had quite a few and here are a couple concerning the world of politics... Bhagawan Baba appeared first as *Nirakaar* and in a subsequent dream as he is, *Sakaar*. "He declared, 'Gandhi? He is liberated! The revelation haunted me... So during the course of a personal verification which Sri Baba kindly permitted, he mentioned 'Gandhi is liberated!... Don't you know the last words, he uttered : *He Ram!* During this talk, Sri Baba also highlighted the personality of the late Netaji Subhas Chandra Bose, whom he called a very good man."

"In another dream which I recollect I had in Canada, Sri Baba and I walked together... I asked him 'How about Madan Mohan Malaviya?' He did not say anything. Finally I asked 'How about Babu Rajendra Prasad'? He beamed. 'Rajendra Prasad?... He will come again and lakhs will follow him!"

Professor Bhatnagar mentioned yet another experience : "I was gloomy and sad, as I sat in the hall in Brindavan, unable to join the full throated chants of the devotees. A fit or blues had overtaken me! Bhagawan Baba watched me from his sofa chair ten feet away, more than once, as though to stir me out of my melancholy, but I remained burdened with grief. Then at night, as I lay in bed, I dreamt of Shirdi Baba, who passed by me saying '*Sai Sampad!*' (Sai's grace). He advanced a few feet and as he mounted an elevated platform his form changed into that of Lord Krishna. The sight of Krishna was very very beautiful. His complexion was light blue and he was clad in light green and pink. That charming smile, which we sometimes see in paintings, played around his lips. Then, from somewhere appeared water and he sprinkled a few drops of it on me, and I felt greatly relieved. In the morning, I found that I had regained peace and was free from the torment of distressing thoughts!... I realise Lord Sai is our saviour!... May we all earn his shelter!..." concluded Professor Bhatnagar.

(x) "The day is not far off when everyone will worship him."

Sri Karunyananda, who looks exceedingly youthful for his ninety years, is a respected figure, often seen in the company of Sri Sathya Sai Baba. Speaking to him is a nice experience; so full of devotion is he for Sri Baba that he marvels every other moment "at our immense good fortune to be with a *poorna avatar*."

I asked him about his spiritual odyssey and how he came to Sri Sathya Sai Baba. In a voice, at once full of kindness and enthusiasm, Sri Karunyananda explained that at first, Ramana Maharshi attracted him and he spent a few years at Tiruvannamalai. Later, for a while, he came under the influence of Malayala Swami of Gogarpam (near Tirupathi) after which he went to Rishikesh in 1927, where Swami Sivananda initiated him into *sanyasa* or the spiritual path. He did several years of spiritual *saadhana* in Rishikesh.

Sri Karunyananda said that Mahatma Gandhi's life and ideals of service made a great impression on him; Swami Vivekananda's book, "Viveka Suryodayam" also lighted up in him the spirit of service. So, when he went to Rajahmandry (in Andhra Pradesh), he started a service organization for lepers and other destitutes called "Gautami Jeeva Kaarunya Sangham." This Institution grew from service to service and from strength to strength and is well known in Andhra Pradesh for sincere and dedicated social service.

Sri Karunyananda confessed that he first heard of Sri Baba in 1936. When some people told him then that the Young Sai was divine he was highly sceptical to the point of advising them to disregard such tall claims! However, when he met Sri Baba in 1956 he felt attracted. Thereafter he kept visiting him though his mind was full of doubts. Is he really an *avatar?* was the question that often assailed him, for a period of nearly nine years! He constantly subjected Sri Baba to several tests: for instance, he used to keep the *vibhuti* materialised by Sri Baba in an air tight box: after a long time when he found that it had not disappeared, he felt convinced that "it was after all not a magical hoax, for had it been so, the *vibhuti* would have vanished!"

Sri Karunyananda recounted several instances that made him gradually realize the divine powers of Sri Baba.

Once, a few days before *Shivaratri*, Sri Karunyananda set out for Puttaparthi. Though he had five vehicles at his centre in Rajahmundry, he undertook the journey by bus along with his cook. After travelling a little distance beyond Chittoor, the bus broke down. All the passengers were asked to get down and wait. It took a very long time before the bus could be repaired and Sri Karunyananda was upset. Talking to some of the passengers he lamented the fact that Sri Baba should have thought of such a remote place for his stay, thus giving them all problems! Why could he have not chosen a more central place easily accessible to all?

Finally the bus was repaired and they reached Prasanti Nilayam *via* Bukkapatnam. Sri Karunyananda bathed, changed and went to see Sri Baba, who was then with several scholars and others. The very first question that Sri Baba asked him was "Karunyananda! How many cars have you got?"

Sri Karunyananda felt highly embarassed at Sri Baba's question about insignificant worldly possessions. But since the others prompted him to answer, he said, "I have a fiat car besides jeeps and vans."

Sri Baba asked, "Then where was the need for you to travel by bus? Why do so and lecture to others about Swami staying in a remote place and also feel bad about it?"

Sri Karunyananda was stunned: "Who could have told him?... No one!... since I had not told any one! This proved that sitting at Puttaparthi, Swami knew what had happened many miles away!"

In 1965, Sri Karunyananda had a "thrilling experience" which even today sends "shivers like electric current" passing through his body. He had accompanied Sri Baba to Bombay. At Dharmakshetra, Swami was upstairs and Sri Karunyananda was in a room downstairs. It was around eleven in the morning and many were going up to meet Sri Baba. So, Sri Karunyananda bolted the door of his room from inside, and sat down near a small window-like opening, from where he could see the people go up the stairs and come down, after meeting Sri Baba. Though he could see others he was hidden from their view, since he had nicely bolted the door. After a while, he experienced a tickling sensation all over his back. Startled, he turned back and was unable to believe his eyes!... For, there stood Sri Baba with a smile on his lips!

"What is this play? Are you going back to your Krishna *leela* days?" asked Sri Karunyananda.

Sri Baba said innocently, "What! I only came to call you for lunch!" Sri Karunyananda got up and went near the door. The bolt was there all right well secured! There was no one else inside who could have let Sri Baba in! Unable to contain himself, Sri Karunyananda exclaimed, "Swami! how did you come in?... I had bolted the only door to this room!"

Sri Baba asked, "If I want to come in, can that bolt be an obstruction?"

Sri Karunyananda's body shook at the tremendous revelation! As he trembled, Sri Baba went near him and patted him. Instantly he forgot all about the great revelation, became normal and went with Sri Baba for lunch. "You see! Again his doing!... Noticing that his physical appearance inside a room through a thick, well secured door, (through which even an ant could not have entered) had a nerve-shaking impact on me, he restored me to normalcy with just a pat !"

"That is Sri Baba!... His powers are so immense, his will so potent!... He is no ordinary mortal or super man. He is the Supreme Truth... But he will not reveal even a fraction of it! He covers up everything purposely with a veil of *maya*", explained Sri Karunyananda, sharing yet another intimate experience of his glimpse of the Divine.

Sri Karunyananda used to hesitate sleeping in the same room with Sri Baba because of his habit of snoring. Once, Sri Baba asked him not to worry about his snoring habit and sleep in the same room. "Sri Baba never sleeps... He lies down always on the left side—eyes almost closed but not fully. He knows everything that happens around and does not really sleep", said Sri Karunyananda.

That night, Sri Karunyananda had a unique vision. All of a sudden on the cot on which Sri Baba lay, he saw a boy—almost like a young Krishna without much hair on the head.

Sri Karunyananda sat up, rubbed his eyes and stared. Was he dreaming?... No! not at all! He was very much awake. He stared again. It was the young boy! Sri Karunyananda got up and peered closely. Then he only saw Sri Baba! What *leela* (play) of the Lord was this? Overwhelmed, he questioned Sri Baba about it but did not get any direct reply. "Must be your imagination!" he had thus teased Sri Karunyananda.

But it was not his imagination or a dream. "I was fully awake. I saw the vision of the boy and the boy change into Sri Baba! Oh! I have seen so many such *leelas* and experienced many divine revelations. Believe me! Sri Baba will not reveal himself but he is divine! Probably Sri Baba thinks that if he does so, there will be only more crowds... As it is, people come in such large numbers!"

In discussions, Sri Karunyananda described another important fact. He said the wooden pot used by Sri Baba for *vibhuti abisheka* (showering of the holy ash) on the silver statue of Shirdi Baba is a light-weight one. "But the minute Sri Baba puts his hand into it, it becomes so heavy like a mountain, that it is a struggle to hold it up and I have to often tell 'Swami! It is so heavy that I find it difficult to hold it!' The *shakti* (power) that enters the pot as a result of the mere touch of his hand is amazing", says Sri Karunyananda who also confessed that in the beginning, he used to think that Sri Baba must have closely packed the *vibhuti* inside the pot, which poured out when shaken! However, he now knows for sure, that Swami is all power and can create with his *sankalpa* anything he wants!

Sri Karunyananda also enlightened me about the *lingam* which Sri Baba used to materialise from his body on *Shivaratri*, day. Sri Karunyananda was near at hand once when a solid gold *lingam* was brought out by Sri Baba. The lingam was quite big and heavy and the corners of Sri Baba's mouth had been hurt a little as it emerged! What pain the passage of such a big and heavy substance must have caused Sri Baba as it came out through his throat, thought Sri Karunyananda.

Sri Baba quieted his doubts; "When I will its birth, it is born only as a very soft, pliable substance. It is soft as it emerges from the stomach and comes up the throat. It hardens only at the time it is ejected from the mouth." There are several explanations regarding the significance of the *lingodbhava* (emergence of the *lingam*) but Sri Karunyananda was concerned more about the physical pain for Sri Baba at that time.

"I am a *yogi*, a sanyasi and I know about *siddhis* (powers). I have myself got through yoga powers of curing, etc... But these do not last!... After a while, show or use of these powers becomes a burden in the path of spiritual progress... Sri Sathya Sai Baba's powers are completely different. They do not come under the *siddhi* category at all! He is *Bhagavantha* or God with the typical six attributes of *aishwarya* (wealth), *samadristi* (equal sight), *prataapa shakti* (immense strength), *keerti* (fame), *jnaanam* (wisdom) and *vairagyam* (detachment).

"From 1970 onwards, I have the firm conviction that Sri Baba is the supreme Lord in human form and none other! In the *Markandeya Purana* there is the mention that in the Kali yuga, there will appear a Bhagawan, who will be worshipped by people of all religions. That reference is only to Sri Baba," said Sri Karunyananda with tears in his eyes. "I will not be there to see it... But you and other young people will certainly see the day when the whole world will throng to worship him... That day is not far off!"

EPILOGUE : OH PUTTAPARTHI !

"Everyone says 'I want peace' but to get peace one should give up the ego or I and the want or desires. Take away 'I' and 'want' from the thought 'I want peace', then peace will remain with you."

—SRI SATHYA SAI BABA

The once unknown and unsung hamlet of Puttaparthi has become the pride of India and the glory of the world. Its glory stems not only from its being the place of Sri Baba's birth but also because it was chosen by him to become the centre of his divine mission.

Puttaparthi proclaims to humanity man's love of God and God's link with man. A highly sacred spot, it reverberates to the world, Sri Baba's message of spiritual socialism or the equality of all people based on the same divinity dwelling in every human breast. "No materialistic attempt will ever succeed in equalising either man's desires or society. Only the practice of *sathya* (truth), *dharma* (moral order), *prema* (love) and *ahimsa* (non-violence) combined with duty, discipline and devotion will change individuals. If individuals reform, society will reform. If society reforms, the world will reform", says Sri Baba. Thus, if the individual man is right, the world will become automatically right."*

Situated in a valley surrounded by small hills, Puttaparthi in general and Prasanti Nilayam in particular present a blend of the ancient and the modern; for here, the latest type of structures sport the most traditional sculptures and the bullock cart occupies pride of place on the road along with the Benz Car!

At a time when the nations of the world are hungering for peace, Puttaparthi offers hope: for such is the tranquility that abides here; such is the peace of mind one enjoys here—a state which money, high position, physical pleasures and comforts do not continuously confer. Otherwise, why would every one including the richest of people and those in the highest of positions flock to Puttaparthi?

---

* There is the story of a busy industrialist who returned home one evening, unduly fatigued because of over-work. He wanted to read quietly a newspaper but his young son would not let him. In disgust, the industrialist tore into a hundred bits a part of the paper which had a world map on one side and the picture of a man on the other. He then asked the son to put back the map together again! To his consternation, the son came back within fifteen minutes, completing the job. Since the boy was not particularly good in geography, the father wondered how the boy had managed it. "You see dad!" said the boy, "All I did was to put the man right and lo! the world became automatically right!"

The stream of true *prema* (love) that flows out from here helps to put out the fires of irreligion, ignorance, hatred, anger, jealousy, ego and attachment that rage in human hearts. The pure love of Sri Baba dissolves all strife and diversity and promotes unity it transforms all those it touches.

For the students in the schools and college in Puttaparthi, geography becomes the easiest subject to learn. They have only to ask the in-coming people where they come from and they will get to know the names of all the countries in the world! The students can also get to know the types of job specialization in different parts of the globe by asking the same people about their work! The older people at Prasanthi Ṅilayam too are students who seek the light of the divinity within; for this purpose, each one follows the *sadhana* of one's choice. Thus, at the Hospital here, higly qualified professionals utilize their training and skills, with selflessness and love, as their form of worship. In fact, all work in the ashram is done by devotees as a part of their devotion to God.

"Why does not Sri Baba have theological colleges?" is a question that is sometimes asked. This is because Sri Baba wants people to pursue their normal activities in the world and make spirituality a part of it. At his educational institutions, the rich cultural and spiritual heritage of the country form part of the curricula and soul power is infused into education.

"Does Sri Baba foster a cult for his devotees?" was a question put to me by a journalist. I explained that there is nothing secret about Sri Baba's mission or message. It is an open book... There is no compulsion of any sort for anyone to follow any ritual. There is the instance of how the *omkar, suprabhatam* and *nagar sankeertan* start early in the morning at Prasanthi Nilayam but no one is obliged to participate unless one wishes to. No one is asked to give up praying to the God of one's choice. Every one is encouraged to follow his or her respective faith. Sri Baba's catholicity is evident not only in the emblem he has adopted but also by such examples as his building a mosque for Muslims living in Puttaparthi and all religions figuring in his *bhajans*.

Sri Baba's emphasis is on self-discipline to achieve self-realization. He wants every individual to blossom into an embodiment of love. Some think of love as the opposite of hate! Nothing can be more untrue, since if one does not hate, one does not necessarily love. Love is positive and is never strained. No one can be forced either to show or receive love. Pure love is that which is given without being ɔked. It is self-generating, spontaneous and ɜelfless.

"God is love and love is God", says Sri Sathya Sai Baba, whose magnetic charm is sacred, because of the pure and selfless love that suffuses eveything he does. For the first time in my life, after observing Sri Sathya Sai Baba, I came to understand what pure love is—that is, love untainted by possessiveness greed, lust or selfishness. To have Sri Sathya Sai Baba's *darshan* is not only to see divine in human form but also to experience the purest of love in its boundlessness.

"How do you say that Sri Baba's love is the purest of love?" asked a friend. My answer was that his love is such that if there is a group of thousand devotees with him, every one in the group feels that 'Sri Baba loves me most!'

"Love is selflessness. Self is lovelessness. Love lives by giving and forgiving. Self lives by getting and forgetting", says Sri Baba, whose message is that human beings should live every moment of their lives in the love of the divine. When pure love is awakened in every breast, the whole world will get linked with one another's love and become boundless like the love of God. Spirituality is nothing more than the love for God and love for all the creations of God.

How can such spirituality be practised in daily life? Sri Sathya Sai Baba answers: "By slowly giving up all attachments and desires."

How can this be done?

"First you must understand the cause of all desires and attachments... The mind is the cause... Let us take the example of a piece of cloth... Now what does this cloth consist of? It consists of several threads of cotton woven together. If you remove thread after thread, what remains is no longer cloth. Like cloth, the mind is woven of threads of desires. Remove all desires and then the mind dies and you are free... When you make the *mind die* you scintillate like a *diamond!*" Sri Baba has also expressed this as a mathematical formula:

Life+desire=man
Life—desire=God

He further explains in his inimitable manner how attachments and desires bind a person. "When you are young, you are free and you move with two legs. When you get married you are no longer that free since you have to move with four legs. After you have a child you are further bound, since you have to move with six legs... So you grow gradually into a centipede and crawl. Thus, with more and more attachments you get restricted and burdened."

"My life is my message", says Sri Baba and his message is not only for India but for the whole world and all humanity. The embodiment of *vinaya* (humility) and sweet reasonableness, Sri Baba asks people to eschew the twin evils of *mamakaara* (attachment) and *ahamkaara* (ego) as these act as obstacles to the flow of love from one's heart and delays the journey of man towards God.

"How can any person, however big, ever have any ego, if he realizes his real position?" asks Sri Baba and by way of illustrations says, "The world is a tiny speck in the solar system. Again, a country becomes a smaller speck in the totality of the world. Further, in a country like India, a town becomes a still smaller speck. And even in a town like Puttaparthi with lakhs of people coming to Prasanthi Nilayam, one individual becomes a very very tiny speck! So, how can such a microscopic speck of one individual, whatever the qualifications by way of degrees, position or wealth, have any ego?"

As an apostle of pure love, Sri Baba is never affected either by praise or blame and wants everyone to develop equanimity of mind. He often relates the story of the Buddha, who went to a home with some followers asking for alms, when someone there heldforth against him and his teachings and abused him. The magnanimous Buddha did not say anything, nor did he allow his followers to intervene. He said ever so gently, "When some one indulges in abuse and you do not accept it, the abuse goes back to the one who uttered it !"

Sri Baba explains this further saying, "When you receive a registered letter and you refuse to receive it, the letter goes back to the sender!"

The proof of the pudding is always in the eating. Those who have gone with full faith to Sri Baba have experienced his purifying love and enjoy peace of mind, and in several cases, a state of beatitude. Those who seek guidance in a spirit of surrender to come to grips with the ultimate reality receive continuous help in the expansion of their spiritual awareness.

Sri Baba's very presence gives the greatest day to those around him and crowds continually pour in, attracted by his holy charisma. The most wondrous things have happened to several devotees because of their devotion to Sri Baba. Several people from different parts of the world and different walks of life have confessed how Sri Baba has amazed them with his appearance in their dreams, with his visions and with his knowledge of the most intimate details of their lives and work. Several others have attested to the meaning and purpose he has given to their lives.

Sri Baba's movement is aimed at promoting a world view of all religions and love of all religions since the basic truth of divinity propounded by all religions is the same. For, according to Sri Baba, "There is only one religion in the world, the religion of love" and this religion is the only hope for establishing *dharma* or the supremacy of the moral order throughout the globe.

The world will really live only when it lives by moral values and love; what will guarantee lasting peace to humanity is not the love of power but rather the power of love as exemplified by Sri Sathya Sai Baba. When love power rules the world, the Kingdom of love which is the Kingdom of God will be truly established on earth. This Kingdom with a difference will only have a capital and a presiding diety. Puttaparthi has already become the capital of such a kingdom without frontiers, of which Sri Baba is the presiding deity.

The Kingdom of Sathya Sai truly reigns from Puttaparthi. All glory to it!

DARSHAN

HAVE you seen Baba
Who sets cities aflame with longing
And drenches them with the delight of existence?
You've missed the very meaning of your life
If you haven't seen him and been spoken to by him.

Baba is a lawn of blue light
With a may-flower on top of his hair
And a golden lily on his cranium

He is the healer of a world in pain,
The blue-throated god
That drinks the poison of its suffering
To make it happy and whole.

He is the patriarch of each family
That gathers around his knee
And drinks the golden honey of his love.

He's the eternal child playing in his garden
Winning back the adults of an erring world
Through sheer simplicity and innocence of heart.

Baba's aura of hair
Sends forth incessant arrows
To destroy the evil in the world.

He defies the laws of physics and chemistry
That he might assert the higher Law of Spirit.
A lingam materialises
That a million souls may be born.
Matter and Spirit are Siamese twins
That have an identical body but a different
face.
Only the androgynous god -
Ardhanarishwara -
Purusha and Sakti in one -
Can solve the riddle of their birth and growth.

Have you seen Baba
Who sets cities aflame with longing
And drenches them with the delight of
existence?
You've missed the very meaning of your life
If you haven't seen him and been spoken to
by him.
